PORTALS

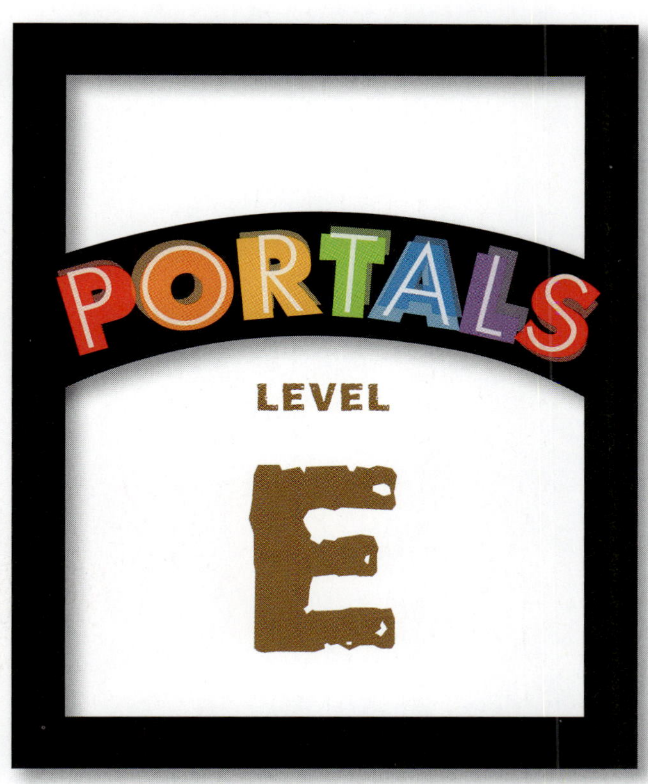
PORTALS
LEVEL
E

LEVEL

Developed and designed by CCI NY in conjunction with Houghton Mifflin Harcourt Publishing Company

Printed in the U.S.A.

ISBN: 978-0-547-07625-6

23456789-KDL- 17 16 15 14 13 12 11 10 09

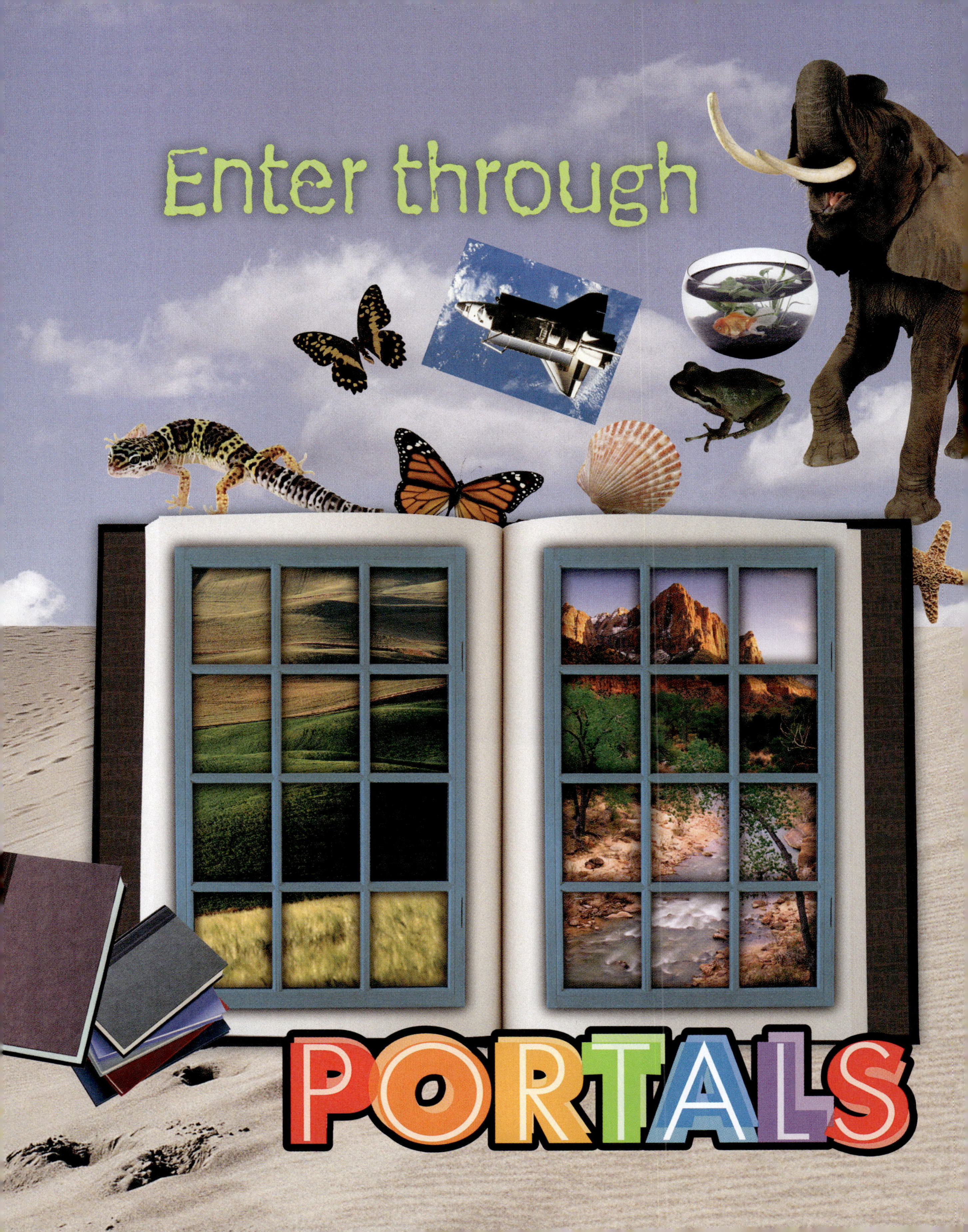
Enter through
PORTALS

to a world . . .
adventurous
thrilling
enlightening
stimulating

magnificent
mysterious
FIRST AID KIT
PARIS
uplifting
and WONDERFUL.

UNIT 1 — 2 ROAD TO CIVILIZATION

THE BIG QUESTION: What allowed civilizations to flourish thousands of years ago?

UNIT 2 — 36 ECO DISASTERS

THE BIG QUESTION: How are humans, plants, animals, and resources on Earth connected?

UNIT 3

70 IDENTITY

THE BIG QUESTION: How do people figure out who they really are?

UNIT 4

106 LOOK TO THE EAST

THE BIG QUESTION: What contributions has Asia made to the world?

140 Earth on the Move

THE BIG QUESTION: How does the moving Earth affect us?

174 Beyond Boundaries

THE BIG QUESTION: What lies beyond a boundary?

UNIT 7

THE BIRTH OF JUSTICE

UNIT 8

A JOB WELL DONE

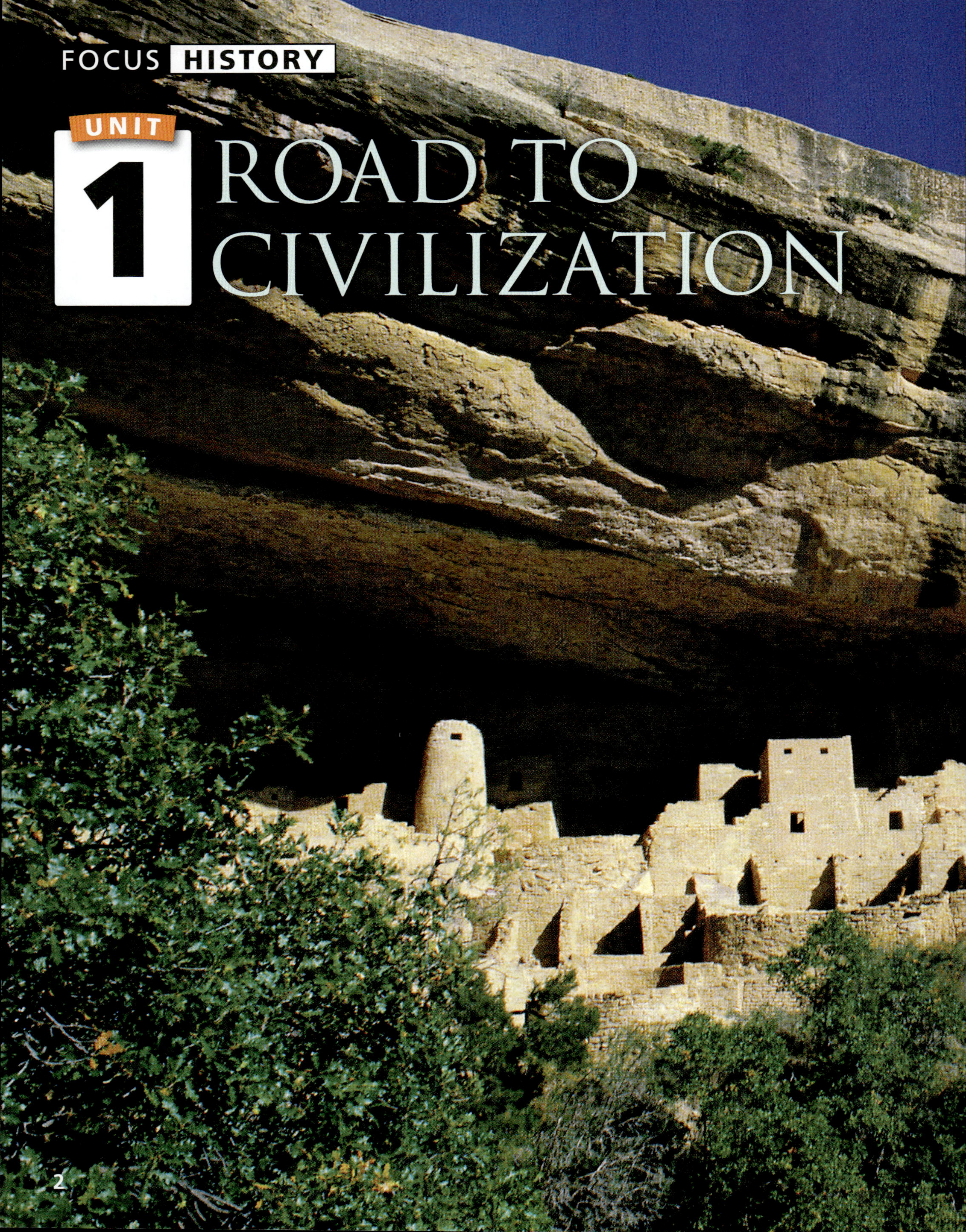
FOCUS HISTORY
UNIT 1
ROAD TO CIVILIZATION

THE BIG QUESTION:
WHAT ALLOWED CIVILIZATIONS TO FLOURISH THOUSANDS OF YEARS AGO?

READINGS

CIVILIZATIONS FLOURISH

When were the world's first cities built?

The world's first cities were built in...

- ☐ the 1400s.
- ☐ the 1800s.
- ☐ 2000 B.C.E.
- ☐ earlier than 2000 B.C.E.

Why did many cities grow up near bodies of water?

Cities grew up near bodies of water because...

- ☐ water was needed for farming.
- ☐ water was needed for drinking.
- ☐ boats could be used to transport goods.
- ☐ people could fish for food.

What are scientists who study ancient cultures called?

Scientists who study ancient cultures are called...

- ☐ biologists.
- ☐ astronomers.
- ☐ archaeologists.
- ☐ geologists.

How do scientists learn about ancient people?

Scientist learn about ancient people by...

- ☐ studying the tools that they used.
- ☐ studying the art they created.
- ☐ studying the ruins of the cities where they lived.
- ☐ studying ancient writing.

Why is it important to study past civilizations?

It's important to study past civilizations because...

- ☐ we can learn where we came from.
- ☐ we can learn what made civilizations successful.
- ☐ we can learn why civilizations failed.
- ☐ we can learn how each civilization's progress led to where we are today.

History Words

attest
capital
cylinder
edible
preserve
remains
site
strategy
symbol
vein

attest

Attest means to bear witness, or to declare to be correct or true.

"I attest that the package contains no liquids."

capital

A **capital** is the city or town that is the seat of government.

"Washington, D.C. is the capital of the United States."

remains

Remains refers to all that is left after other objects are used up, destroyed, or taken away.

"When we arrived, we saw the remains of the ancient village."

site

Site refers to the position or location of a town or building.

"The site of the ancient city was on a river bank."

cylinder

A **cylinder** is a barrel-shaped curved solid.

"Writing was etched into the surface of the clay cylinder."

edible

Edible means fit to be eaten as food.

"The guide book said the wild red berries were edible."

preserve

Preserve means to keep up or maintain.

"We will preserve the ancient ruins."

strategy

A **strategy** is a plan or method used to attain a specific goal.

"John had a good strategy when it came to studying for a test."

symbol

A **symbol** is something used for, or representing, something else.

"The bald eagle is a symbol of our nation."

vein

A **vein** is a long strip of igneous rock or mineral that fills a crevice in another rock.

"She could see a vein of gold in the rock."

READ TOGETHER

FIRST CITIES

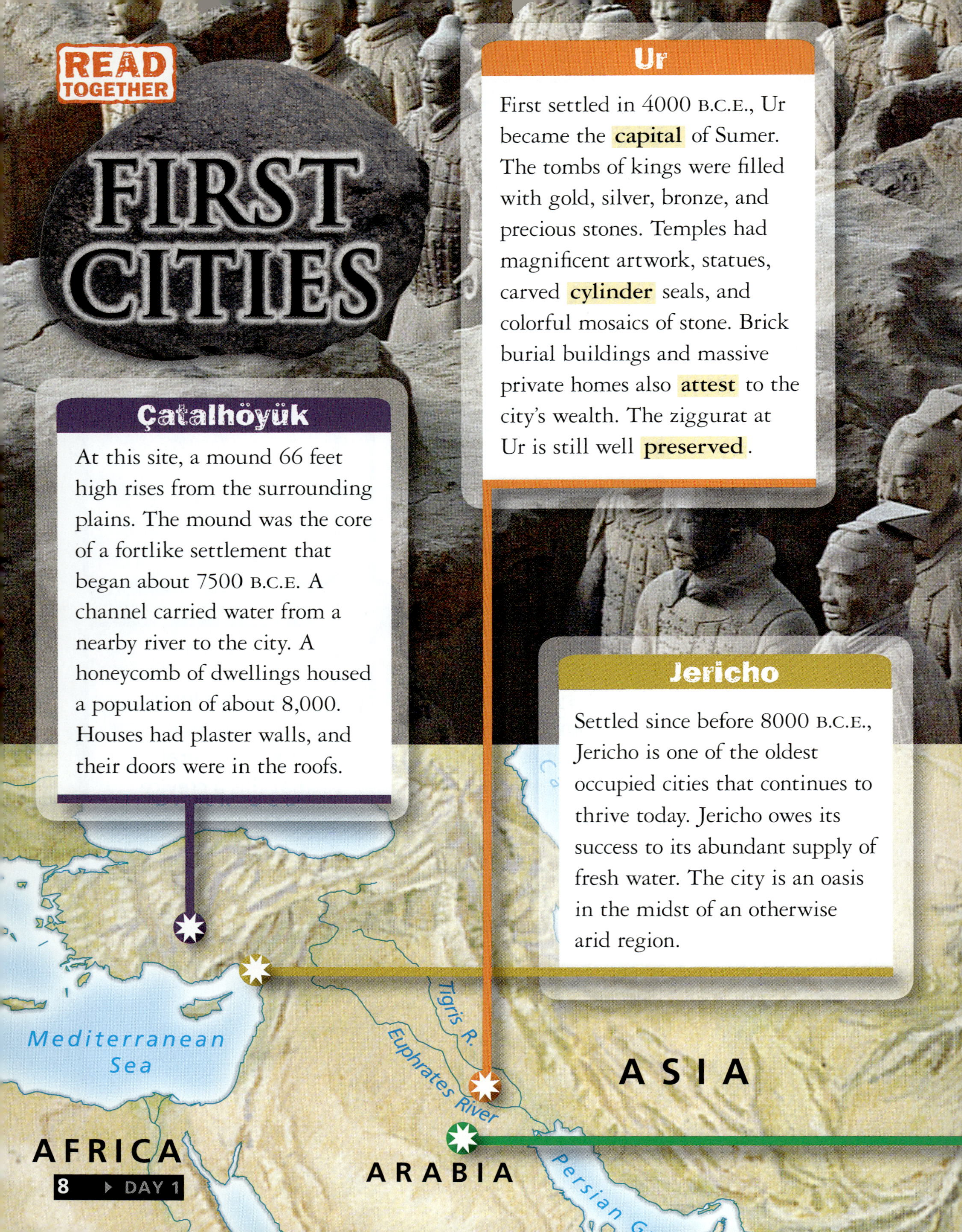

Ur

First settled in 4000 B.C.E., Ur became the **capital** of Sumer. The tombs of kings were filled with gold, silver, bronze, and precious stones. Temples had magnificent artwork, statues, carved **cylinder** seals, and colorful mosaics of stone. Brick burial buildings and massive private homes also **attest** to the city's wealth. The ziggurat at Ur is still well **preserved**.

Çatalhöyük

At this site, a mound 66 feet high rises from the surrounding plains. The mound was the core of a fortlike settlement that began about 7500 B.C.E. A channel carried water from a nearby river to the city. A honeycomb of dwellings housed a population of about 8,000. Houses had plaster walls, and their doors were in the roofs.

Jericho

Settled since before 8000 B.C.E., Jericho is one of the oldest occupied cities that continues to thrive today. Jericho owes its success to its abundant supply of fresh water. The city is an oasis in the midst of an otherwise arid region.

Eridu

Around 5000 B.C.E., people began building mud brick houses at this site. Eridu was associated with the Sumerian God, Enki, "lord of the sweet waters that flow under the earth." Eighteen temples have been discovered under a gigantic unfinished structure called a ziggurat, a type of pyramid found in Mesopotamia.

Mehrgarh

Dating from 7000 B.C.E., Mehrgarh is one of the world's oldest cities. It was occupied for nearly 6,000 years. Some of the earliest evidence of farming and goat herding are found here. Mehrgarh also boasted the first dentists. The city had grain storage areas and complex burial chambers.

Xian

The earliest East Asian city, Xian, was the starting point of the Silk Road, the great trading route. Xian served as the capital of twelve dynasties that ruled China for over 3,000 years. The tomb of the emperor Shih Huang-ti is near Xian. Buried with him was an army of 6,000 life-size clay soldiers.

Comprehension

TARGET SKILL **Sequence of Events** A passage or selection often tells about a series of events. These events happen in **order** or **sequence**, beginning with what happens first, next, and continuing until the series of events ends. A string of related events such as this is called a **sequence of events**. **Time words** and **verb tense** can help a reader identify the sequence of events.

The following paragraph is taken from Selection I, titled "People of the Stone Age," on page 7. It contains words and phrases that help you understand the sequence of events.

Verb tenses—present and past—give clues to when events happen.

The paintings do reveal something very important about Paleolithic people. They understood that they could use a symbol to stand for a real thing. They knew that a flat mark on a cave wall could show a living horse. This symbolic thinking was a huge leap forward for humankind. It was the beginning of art. It was also the beginning of using symbols to stand for ideas. One day this ability to make pictures would lead to language.

Time words and phrases are clues to sequence.

Verb tense signals future event.

First: They understood the use of symbols.

Second: Their thinking was the beginning of using symbols for ideas.

Next: This ability to make pictures would lead to language.

Last: Today, the paintings reveal something important about Paleolithic people.

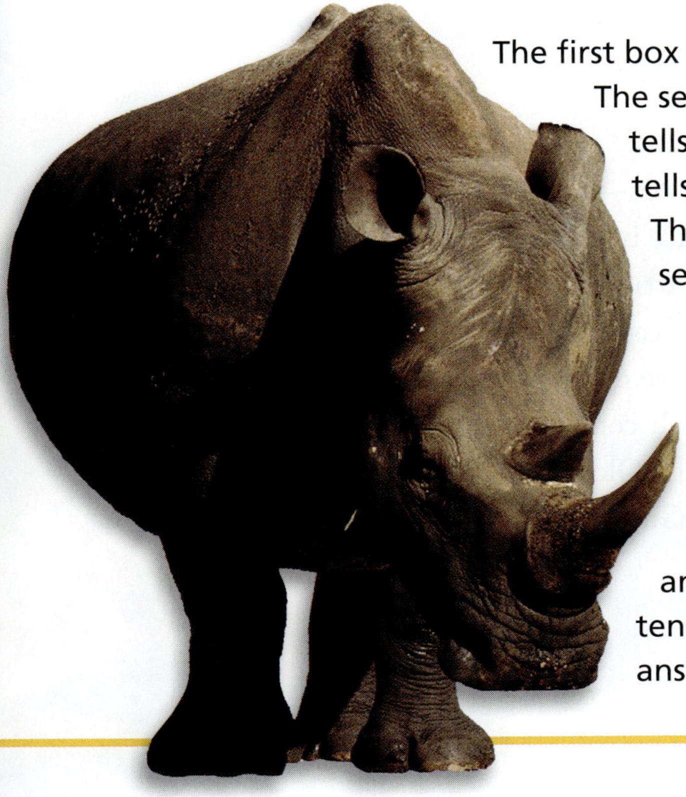

The first box tells the first event in the sequence. The second box continues the sequence and tells what happens next. The third box tells the event that happens after that. The fourth box tells the last event in the sequence.

TARGET STRATEGY **Question** Ask yourself questions about the events as you read. Think about when an event happens, before or after another event. Look for clues—verb tenses and time words—that will help you answer your questions.

PEOPLE of the STONE AGE

FOCUS: What was life like for Paleolithic people?

How old do you think this picture is?

Would you believe that it is at least 12,000 years old—maybe even more? Look at the shape of the animal. Notice how it seems to be running. Whoever drew this was an artist. Animals like this have been found on the walls of caves in France, Spain, Turkey, and elsewhere. Scientists have dated the art to anywhere from 15,000 to 35,000 years ago. It comes from a time known as the Paleolithic period, or the Old Stone Age. The Greek word *paleo* means "old," and the Greek word *lith* means "stone."

Life Thousands of Years Ago

Archaeologists are scientists who study the **remains** of earlier cultures. They examine things such as graves, artwork, and tools to understand the people who left them behind. Archaeologists have learned that the people who lived before 10,000 B.C. had a very hard life.

Here are some things Paleolithic people did without.

- Cloth
- Crops such as wheat or corn
- **Domesticated** animals such as sheep, cattle, or chickens
- Houses
- Towns or cities
- Roads
- Metal tools
- Wheels

Here are some things Paleolithic people had.

- Clothing of animal skins
- Bone needles for stitching the skins together
- Stone tools such as knives, spears, harpoons, and hammers
- Materials for drawing pictures
- Fire

We know that Paleolithic people had fire because archaeologists have found burned animal bones at **sites** dating from those times. The ability to control fire was an important step forward. The Paleolithic diet was very limited. People of that time didn't grow crops or herd animals. They hunted and fished for wild animals. They also gathered **edible** berries and roots. Using fire to cook food added new foods, such as wild grains, to their diet.

The basic pattern of Paleolithic culture seems to have remained unchanged for tens of thousands of years. Paleolithic people probably lived in small groups. Some experts think that each group might have numbered about 25 people. These groups most likely migrated to follow the animals they hunted.

Ancient Artists

The cave paintings made by Paleolithic people show how important animals were to them. One cave in Lascaux, France, shows a few stick-figure people, no plants, and about 600 paintings of animals.

Paleolithic artists often used different-colored clays or earth for their paintings. They also used wood charcoal for black. Chalk, bone, or shell made white. Stones with mineral **veins** gave them red and yellow. The ancient artists didn't use such materials by accident. They figured out which materials made the best colors. They passed their "recipes" down through the generations.

Kinds of Animals Shown in the Cave Art of Lascaux

Wild horses
Bison
Aurochs (a kind of ancient wild cattle)
Several kinds of deer
Several kinds of wild cats
Ibex (a kind of wild goat)
Mammoth (an extinct kind of elephant)
Bear
Rhinoceros
Fish

The Mystery of the Cave Art

The reason for the cave paintings is a mystery that archaeologists may never solve. They have some guesses. Maybe the pictures of animals were a way of telling about important hunts. Or perhaps the pictures were part of a religious ceremony, asking for successful hunts so the people could eat well.

The paintings do reveal something very important about Paleolithic people. They understood that they could use a **symbol** to stand for a real thing. They knew that a flat mark on a cave wall could show a living horse. This symbolic thinking was a huge leap forward for humankind. It was the beginning of art. It was also the beginning of using symbols to stand for ideas. One day this ability to make pictures would lead to written language.

STOP AND THINK

1. How can archaeologists tell what Paleolithic people ate?
2. Do you think art or fire was more important for early humans? Why?

Your Turn

Use Your Words:

accounts	glazed
angle	influence
artifact	irrigation
canal	keel
corrupt	nobles
dike	reign
domesticate	reservoir
elaborate	strait
employ	structure
feature	suspend

- Read the words on the list.
- Read the dialogue. Find the words.

MORE ACTIVITIES

1. Take a Survey

Graphic Organizer

There were many jobs in the city pictured above. Survey 12 of your classmates. Ask them which job they would like to do. Tally your results and share them with your class.

Jobs						
Ship Builder	Sailor	Construction	Farming	Pottery Maker	Ruler	Other

2. You Are the Author

Writing

Choose an artifact from the picture. Write a paragraph describing it in detail.

3. Describe Your Day

Listening and Speaking

Imagine you lived in the ancient city pictured above. Choose to be the ruler, a noble, or a worker. What would your life be like? Tell your partner about your typical day.

4. Draw a Diagram

Graphic Organizer

Draw a diagram of the irrigation system shown in the picture. Use the diagram to explain to your partner how the system worked.

5. Guess the Objects

Listening and Speaking

Choose an object in your school or classroom. Describe three or four features of the object. See if your partner can guess what the object is.

6. Make a List

Vocabulary

List eight animals that are domesticated. List eight animals that are wild. Share your list with the class.

Animals	
Domesticated	Wild

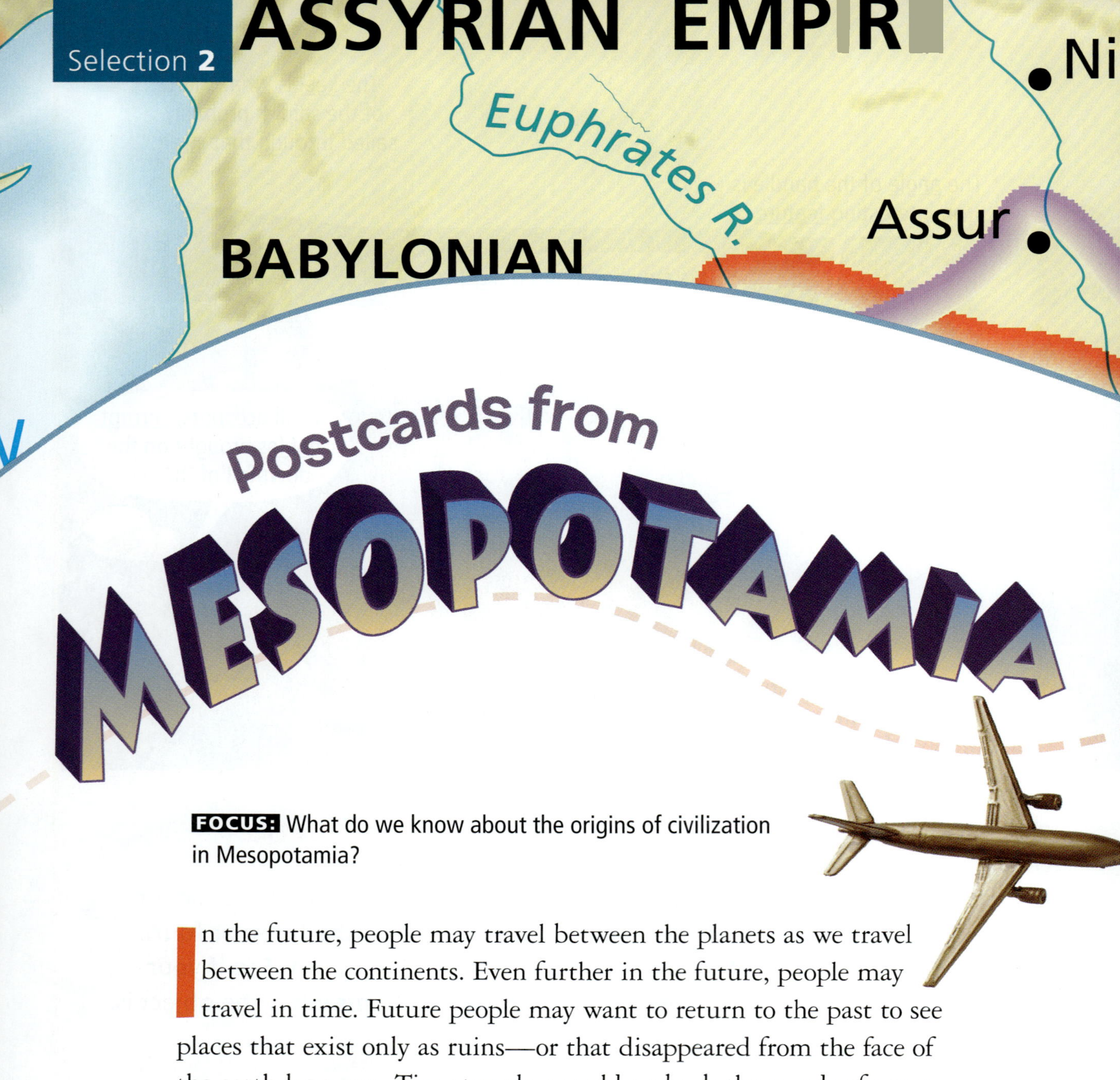

Postcards from MESOPOTAMIA

FOCUS: What do we know about the origins of civilization in Mesopotamia?

In the future, people may travel between the planets as we travel between the continents. Even further in the future, people may travel in time. Future people may want to return to the past to see places that exist only as ruins—or that disappeared from the face of the earth long ago. Time travelers could go back thousands of years to see the Egyptian pyramids in all their glory. Roman Empire buffs could visit Rome during its heyday.

These high-definition plasmatronic postcards were sent by a time traveler far in the future. The traveler visited one of the first great civilizations, in Mesopotamia. This fertile area was located between the Tigris and Euphrates Rivers in what is now Iraq. She got a great package—she toured 8,000 years of history in one week.

Cuneiform Writing

Dear Tanya,

The Mesopotamians have an incredible way of writing—they make marks in soft clay. Many of the **symbols** are pictures of the things they represent. A sheep, for example, has its own symbol, as does a bundle of grain, and a hand. In time, the symbol begins to stand for the sound of the word. These sounds are the beginnings of an alphabet. It all begins around 4000 B.C., but it will take another 2,000 years for this kind of writing to be widely used.

Love,
Grandma

The Ziggurat at Ur

Tanya,

This magnificent series of platforms is actually a mountain of bricks. The ziggurat is nearly ten stories high and 200 feet wide. There are about seven million bricks just in the first level. The bricks were baked hard enough to become waterproof, and each brick bears the stamp and name of the king. The soil in the area is soft from constant flooding, so each layer of bricks was laid in a different direction. Sand and reed mats were placed between the layers of bricks. This construction keeps the whole mass from slumping to one side like one of your layer cakes. Massive staircases lead to the top. A temple, built around 3000 B.C., forms the top layer. Each wall is slightly curved, which makes the **structure** seem even higher.

Love,
Grandma

The Ctesiphon Arch

Dear Tanya,

This may be the most fantastic sight I've seen so far. It's a gigantic, vaulted hall called the Taq Kisra. The Sasanina king, Shapur I, had the hall built in 400 C.E. for his throne room. It features enormous rooms with perfect archways. The workers used thin bricks that weren't baked hard, piling them up on a slant. Gradually, the bricks formed an arch. The ceiling is 110 feet high. And the structure doesn't even have a framework supporting it, because the bricks fit so well that they transfer the weight to the walls. The king's throne sits underneath. His crown is so heavy with gold and jewels that it needs to be **suspended** from the arch. The hall also has beautiful glass mosaics and a huge illustration of the king on a golden horse. Unfortunately, armies and floods will later destroy most of Taq Kisra. I'm glad I got to see it now, in the past, when it's still in perfect condition.

Best,
Grandma

The Royal Cemetery at Ur

Dear Tanya,

I was fortunate to happen across the burial of a rich man at the royal cemetery. What a ceremony! What wealth! He must have had a musical background, for they buried him with several harps that were covered with precious stones, gold, silver, and bronze. Maybe he had a lot of wives, because they also buried a number of women's headdresses, each very ornate. The outsides of the tombs are equally **elaborate**.

Kisses,
Grandma

The First Written Laws and Stories

Dear Tanya,

The tribes who live in Mesopotamia are the first people to leave records of their laws—on cuneiform tablets. These laws tell who has to pay taxes. They also command that silver be paid to the poor. Some laws outlaw **corruption** in government. Others protect widows and orphans from rich men who might take advantage of them. Medical texts and religious works have been written down. And the epic story of my personal hero, Gilgamesh, is being recorded even now. Maybe I can find out which of our versions is the original.

Best,
Grandma

THE HANGING GARDENS OF BABYLON

The Hanging Gardens of Babylon and the Ishtar Gate

Dear Tanya,

This gorgeous ziggurat has royal gardens growing on the terraces of each level. Water is pumped from the Euphrates River for the gardens. According to the locals, King Nebuchadnezzar II built this amazing structure to make his wife happy. Her faraway homeland was unlike the hot, dry, and brown plains of Mesopotamia. Later, the ancient Greeks will describe the ziggurat as a paradise of greenery. For me, it's certainly one of the seven wonders of the ancient world. The Ishtar Gate is massive, with beautiful **glazed** bricks in bright colors and horses in relief brickwork. These Babylonians really know how to decorate. See you soon.

Love,
Grandma

STOP AND THINK

1. How did Mesopotamians begin to write?
2. If you could travel back in time, where would you go?

Egyptian Life on the NILE RIVER

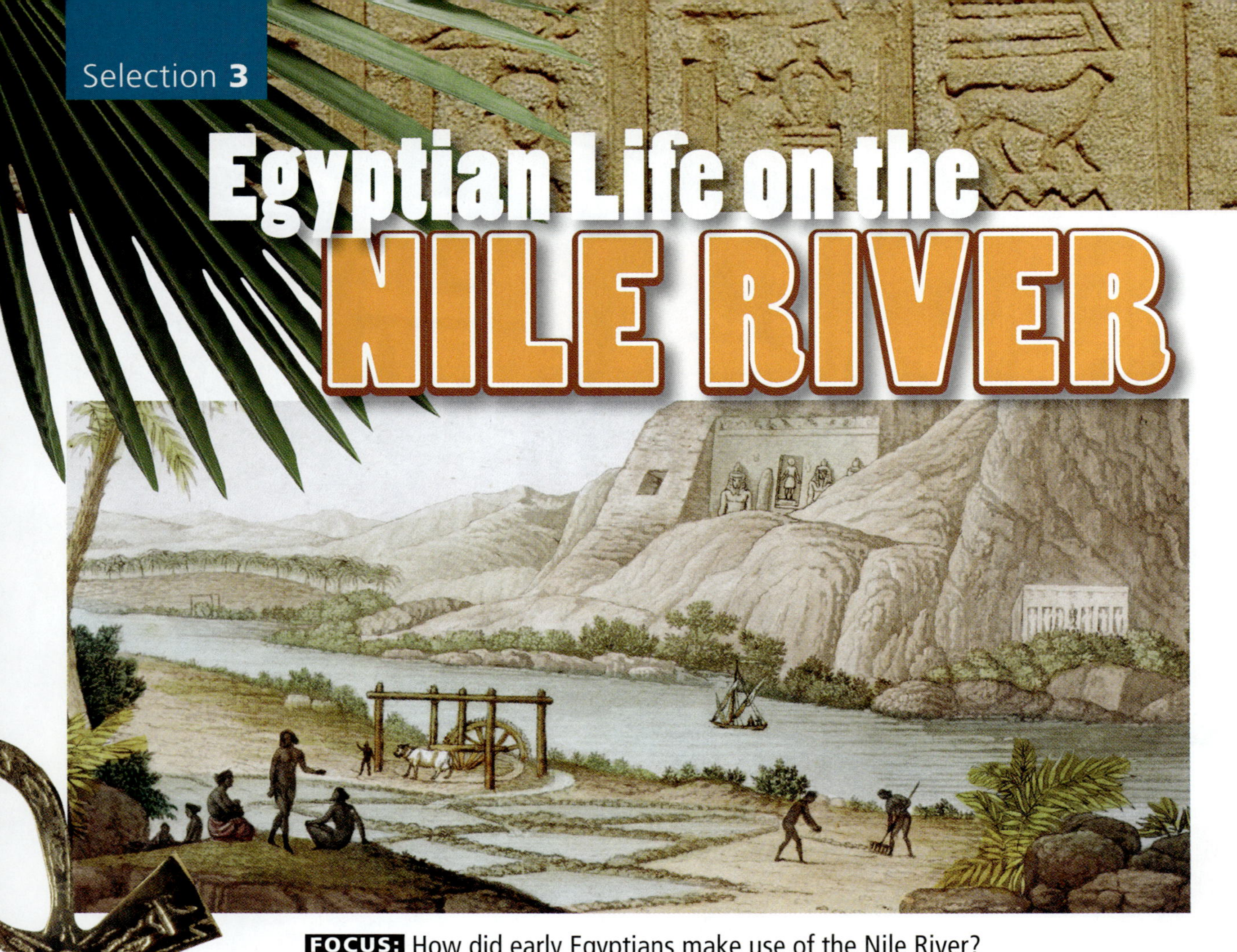

FOCUS: How did early Egyptians make use of the Nile River?

The Nile River has supported humans ever since hunters and gatherers began carving rocks along its banks. **Artifacts** from their campsites date long before 10,000 B.C. Most of Egypt is desert. Only the Nile Valley remains green year round. As the major source of water, it brought life to the early Egyptians.

The Three Seasons of the Nile River

Life in ancient Egypt was governed by the water flow of the Nile. During the season of Ahket, the Nile's floodwaters kept people away from their fields. This was a time for craftwork, construction, and commerce. People dug **irrigation canals** to spread floodwaters deeper into the deserts. People also made **dikes** and dams to create **reservoirs** and lakes. These bodies stored some of the floodwater for the dry season. The government controlled the canals and dikes.

In the season of Peret, the floodwaters drained away, leaving the soil fertilized by silt carried in the water. Farmers grew corn, wheat, barley, beans, chickpeas, and flax. Bow-shaped sticks served as plows. Four men pulled each plow. People spread seeds from baskets strapped to their heads. Hogs and sheep were used to trample the seeds into the soil. Egyptian farmers used their knowledge of mathematics to redraw boundaries of fields whose **features** were buried under silt each year. They **employed** measured rope and a knowledge of **angles** to find the length of the sides of their fields.

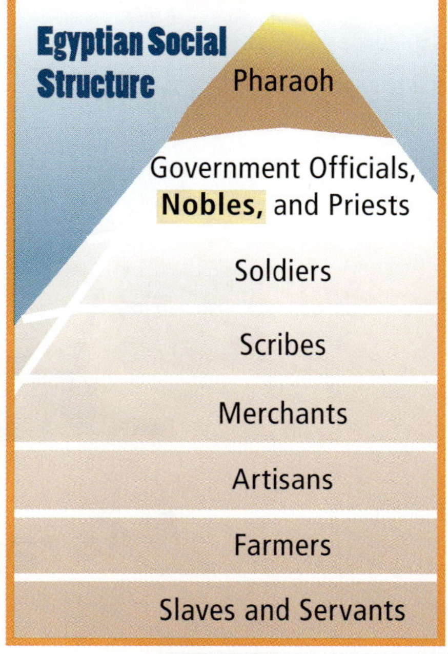

The government forced almost every citizen to help bring in the harvest during the season of Shem. For their labor, people were paid the amount of grain they could harvest in a single day. Everyone worked from sunrise to sunset. Men used wooden sickles with flint blades to cut the wheat. Women and children followed them, gathering sheaves of wheat into baskets. Poor people went last, picking up fallen sheaves and grains.

REREAD

Sequence of Events

What happened after the wheat was cut and before the fallen sheaves were packed up?

Vegetables and fruits were grown in separate gardens. People watered these gardens with shadoofs, an invention that has been in use since about 2000 B.C.E. A shadoof is a long pole balanced on a beam. A weight is on one end, and a bucket is on the other. The weight allows buckets of water to be lifted easily from a reservoir or irrigation channel.

Fish was the most important part of the ancient Egyptian diet. People caught fish in the Nile and raised fish in ponds. Waterfowl, cattle, and geese were **domesticated**. Oil from castor plants and sesame seeds was another important part of their diet.

STOP AND THINK

1. How were the agricultural fields fertilized each year?
2. What different activities do you do in each season of the year?

The Phoenicians

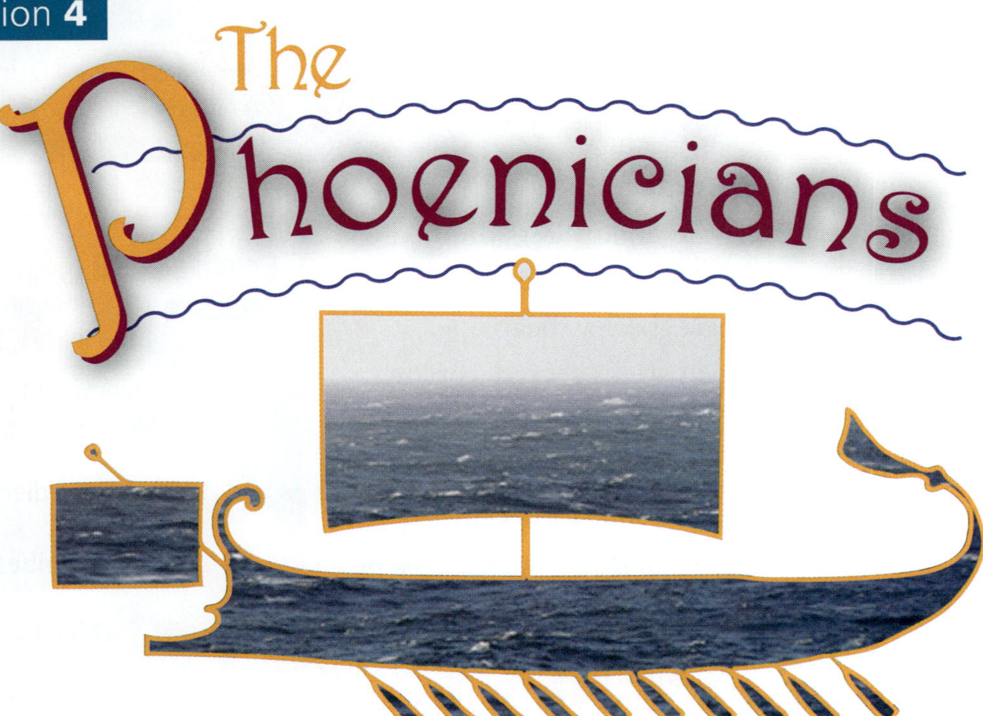

MASTER SAILORS & TRADERS

FOCUS: Why did Phoenicia have such an influence in the Mediterranean region?

Phoenicia's reign over the eastern Mediterranean lasted only from 1200 to 800 B.C. Yet the country had an important influence on other societies. Phoenicians built the first ships with keels. A keel is a central timber that runs lengthwise in a ship's hull. Keels made it possible to build larger ships. So Phoenician trading ships could carry more materials than other trading ships. Phoenicia became a great trading nation. Its merchants took over the old Egyptian trade routes. And its navy went on to establish colonies in Africa, Sicily, Carthage, Sardinia, and Spain.

Shipbuilding

Phoenicians could sail on the open seas because their ships were well built. They used a new method to join pieces of wood. Pockets were cut into heavy timbers. A piece of wood was fit into the pockets, joining two larger pieces. Finally, a peg was pounded into a hole drilled between the pieces. This construction held the ship together even in the worst storms.

Merchant Ships

The Phoenicians sailed across the Mediterranean Sea. They passed through the **Straits** of Gibraltar, then called the Pillars of Hercules. They journeyed to England to trade for tin. Some **accounts** claim that Phoenician merchants sailed around the Horn of Africa. Phoenician ships were about the same size as those that Columbus would use to cross the Atlantic—2,000 years later.

Trading Materials

Phoenician ships carried goods from port to port around the Mediterranean. Some of the most valuable goods were gold, glass, tin, cedar, and pine. One of Phoenicia's famous exports was fine linen, which was often dyed purple. (The dye was made from snail shells.) Returning merchants brought back papyrus, ivory, ebony, silk, amber, and many other goods.

Alphabet

The Phoenician alphabet used **symbols** to represent sounds. It was easier to read and write than cuneiform. This method of writing spread across the region and eventually developed into our alphabet.

STOP AND THINK

1. What made Phoenician ships better than other ships?
2. Which do you think is more important, trading goods or trading ideas?

Selection **5**

SCIENCE CONNECTION

The Disappearing Kingdom of KUSH

FOCUS: Do archaeologists have enough time to study the kingdom of Kush?

Imagine a friend has scratched you a message in the mud. It starts to rain. You rush over to read the message before it washes away.

Something like that is happening now in northern Africa, in a country called Sudan. Archaeologists are rushing to find and study the remains of the ancient African civilization of Kush. But it's not rain that is making them hurry. It's the construction of a huge dam.

The Merowe Dam on the Nile River is projected to create a **reservoir** about 2 miles wide and more than 100 miles long. The rising waters will cover everything—homes, villages, and farmland. Tens of thousands of people will have to be resettled in a new location. The rising waters will also cover our chance to know more about the past. The area is rich in archeological **sites** that have not yet been examined. Teams of archaeologists from many countries are trying to find and document as much as they can before it's too late. Already, their discoveries have changed what we know about the kingdom of Kush.

The ancient civilization of Kush was centered at the city of Kerma, a couple of hundred miles downstream from where the Merowe Dam is being built. Recently, archaeologists began working at Hosh el-Geruf, upstream from the dam site. In one area they found more than 55 large grinding stones. The stones were used for processing gold. The number of grinding stones and their design show that gold was not just for local use. The stones were dated to between 2000 and 1500 B.C.E. That's the period when the Kush civilization was at its height.

Nearby, archaeologists found delicate clay pots in a cemetery. The pots are of a style commonly found at Kerma.

These two discoveries make archaeologists believe that the kingdom of Kush controlled or influenced a much larger area than previously thought. New discoveries are making scientists change their ideas about the past.

There are an estimated 2,500 archaeological sites in the area behind the Merowe dam. As a result, teams of archaeologists are rushing to study as many sites as they can before the water arrives. For what gets covered by the reservoir's water will **remain** a mystery.

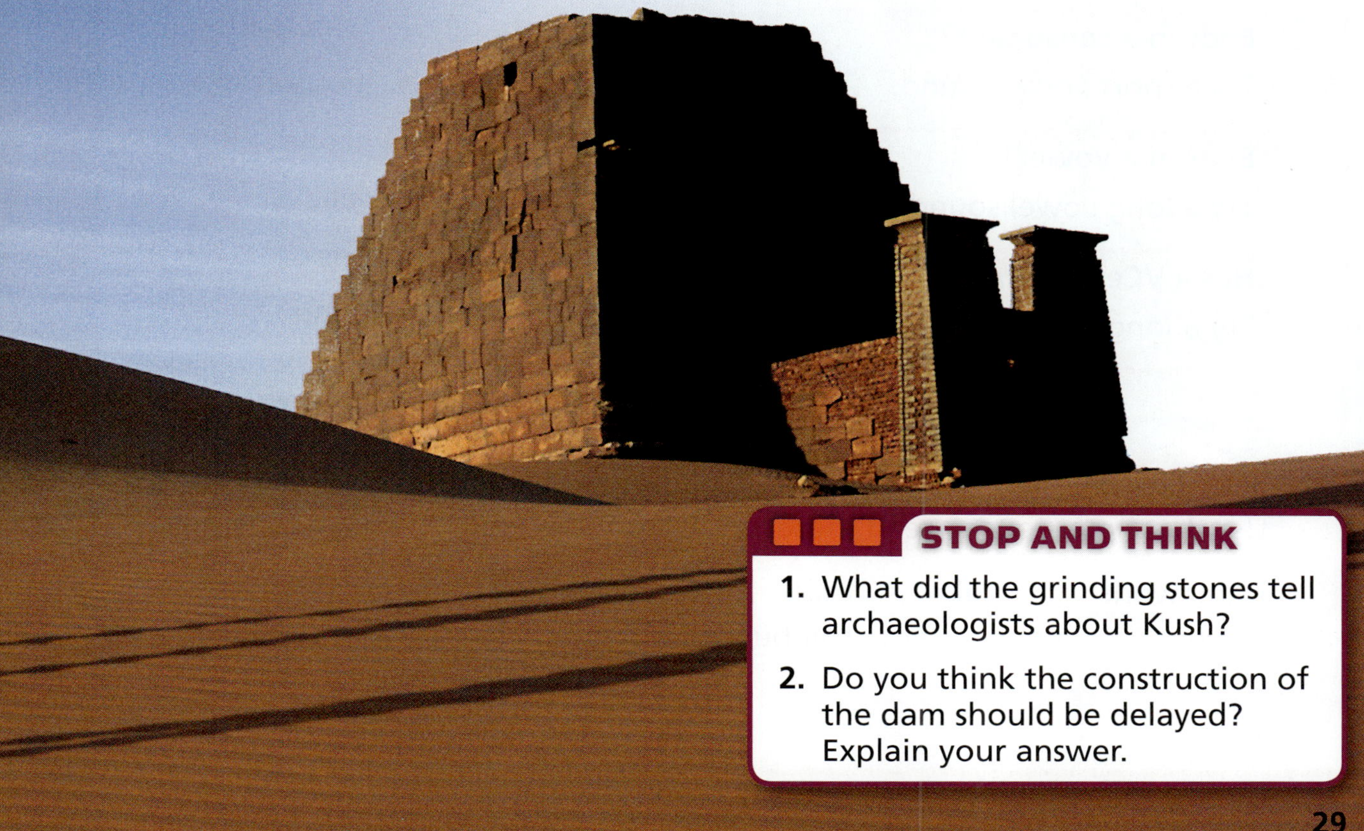

STOP AND THINK

1. What did the grinding stones tell archaeologists about Kush?
2. Do you think the construction of the dam should be delayed? Explain your answer.

Reading Longer Words

In this unit you learned more about how to read longer words.

Step 1: Divide the word into parts.

Compound word?
Divide between the words.

VCV letter pattern?
Divide before the consonant.
or
Divide after the consonant.

Step 2: Read each word part.
Step 3: Read the whole word.
Sound right? If not, try an alternative.

Ends in a consonant?
Try a short vowel sound.

Ends in a vowel?
Try a long vowel sound.

Has a VCe pattern?
Try a long vowel sound.

Divide the Words

green/house	back/pack
band/leader	step/lad/der
mouse/trap	o/zone
val/id	ti/dy
rhi/no	den/im

Read Word Parts		Read Whole Words
green house	→	greenhouse
back pack	→	backpack
band leader	→	bandleader
step lad der	→	stepladder
mouse trap	→	mousetrap
o zone	→	ozone
val id	→	valid
ti dy	→	tidy
rhi no	→	rhino
den im	→	denim

Read More Words

Use the three steps to read these words from the unit.

framework	musical	epic	homeland	craftwork
colony	floodwater	shipbuilder	navy	delicate

Vocabulary

Figurative and Metaphorical Language

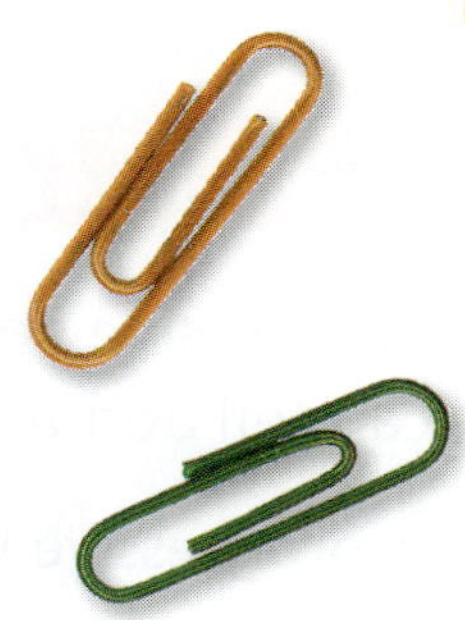

Figurative language is a way authors use words to make a picture in the mind. The words add up to more than the meaning of the words alone, or the *literal* meaning. Figurative language uses **figures of speech**, such as similes, metaphors, personification, and hyperbole.

Figure of Speech	Definition	Examples
Simile	Comparison between two unlike things using the word *like* or *as*.	The girl has cheeks **like roses.** The shoe is as light **as a feather.**
Metaphor	Comparison between two unlike things without using the word *like* or *as*.	An **army** of traffic blocked us. The fog is a **fluffy blanket** over the hill.
Personification	Language that describes animals, things, or ideas as if they were human.	Leaves **danced** in the street. The moon **smiled** down on us.
Hyperbole	Language that exaggerates to emphasize something.	I waited a **million years** for the bus. I'm so hungry I could **eat a horse**.

Progressive Verbs

Progressive verbs describe ongoing action. A progressive verb can tell about the present, the past, or the future.

A progressive verb—

- contains a helping verb that is a form of *to be*
- contains a main verb in the present participle form (ending in *-ing*)
- agrees with the subject in number (singular or plural verb form of *to be*) when applicable

The **present progressive** tense shows ongoing action taking place now. The helping verb *to be* is in the present tense.

Present Progressive Tense

	Singular	Plural
First Person	I am speaking.	We are speaking.
Second Person	You are speaking.	You are speaking.
Third Person	He is speaking.	They are speaking.

The **past progressive** tense shows ongoing action in the past. The helping verb *to be* is in the past tense.

Past Progressive Tense

	Singular	Plural
First Person	I was speaking.	We were speaking.
Second Person	You were speaking.	You were speaking.
Third Person	She was speaking.	They were speaking.

The **future progressive** tense describes action that will be going on in the future. The helping verb *to be* is in the future tense.

Future Progressive Tense

	Singular	Plural
First Person	I will be speaking.	We will be speaking.
Second Person	You will be speaking.	You will be speaking.
Third Person	He will be speaking.	They will be speaking.

The chart below shows that sentences in a simple tense can be changed into a progressive tense.

Simple Present	**Present Progressive**
I walk home from school.	I **am walking** home from school.
Simple Past	**Past Progressive**
Dana fought off a bad cold.	Dana **was fighting** off a bad cold.
Simple Future	**Future Progressive**
They will see you next week at the party.	They **will be seeing** you next week at the party.

Write a Personal Narrative

Sentence fluency is the rhythm and flow of the sentences that make up a story. A story should be enjoyable to read, and good sentence fluency really stands out when a piece of writing is read aloud. Sentences should sound "natural" to the reader, rather than mechanical or choppy.

First Draft

You've read the final draft of "Helicopters." Read the first draft.

My dad told me all about helicopters. He seemed to always have all of it pent up inside of him but now it was coming out. Finally I just said, Dad, why don't _you_ become a helicopter pilot? He became a pilot six months later. He took classes and read books. He also had me to coach him with HelicopterSim because I had been playing it for two years. He was a natural, the flight trainer said.

My dad told me about how he wanted to fly helicopters since he was a kid. He grew up in upstate New York, where there was a helicopter factory started by sikorsky. Sikorsky was a crazy russian who invented helicopters.

He is training now to be a helicopter pilot for hospitals. He takes me for rides sometimes. I think he's never been happier but I can't be sure.

Writing Traits Checklist

- **Ideas** Is the personal story told well?
- **Organization** Is the sequence of events clear?
- **Sentence Fluency** Are the sentence beginnings varied and interesting?
- **Voice** Does the writer engage the reader in the story?
- **Word Choice** Does the writer use vivid words?
- **Conventions** Are there any capitalization or punctuation errors?

Final Draft The writer made many revisions to complete this final draft.

My dad told me all about helicopters. How he wanted to fly them since he was a kid. How he used to live in upstate New York, where there was a helicopter factory started by some crazy Russian guy, Sikorsky, who invented them. It was like my dad had all this pent up inside and now it was coming out. Finally, I just said: "Dad, why don't <u>you</u> become a helicopter pilot?"

Six months later, he was. He took the classes and read the books. I coached him, too, with HelicopterSim and whatever I'd learned playing it for two long years. The flight trainer said Dad was a natural. Now he is training to be a helicopter pilot for hospitals. Sometimes he takes me for rides. To say my dad's never been happier would be more than I can be sure of.

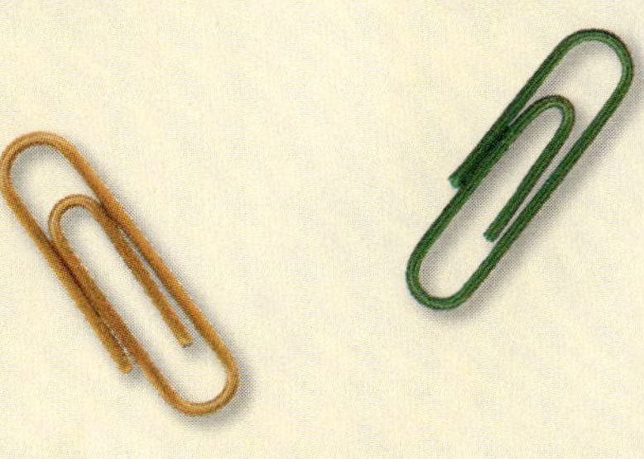

UNIT 2 ECO DISASTERS

THE BIG QUESTION:

HOW ARE HUMANS, PLANTS, ANIMALS, AND RESOURCES ON EARTH CONNECTED?

READINGS

Look at Environmental Issues

What does a food chain show?

A food chain shows...

- the sun as the source of energy.
- that plants use sunlight to grow and reproduce.
- that animals and insects eat plants.
- that some animals and insects are eaten by other animals.

How do invasive species threaten the environment?

Invasive species threaten the environment by...

- competing with native species for food.
- damaging the physical environment.
- killing native species.
- upsetting the food web.

What happens to animals when natural areas are destroyed?

When natural areas are destroyed, animals...

- are forced to move to a smaller, shrinking habitat.
- compete with other animals for limited food.
- try to stay and survive.
- begin to die off.

How are humans damaging the oceans' ecosystems?

Humans damage the oceans' ecosystems by...

- overfishing.
- dumping waste into the oceans.
- filling in wetlands and mangrove swamps.
- allowing fertilizers and pesticides to flow into the oceans.

What can humans do to help endangered species?

To help endangered species, humans can...

- make everyone aware of endangered animals living nearby.
- recreate a species' habitat.
- fight to preserve natural areas.
- discover what is threatening the species.

Science Words

decline
decompose
displace
exploit
fungi
organism
photosynthesis
physical
resource
species

decline

Decline means to follow a downward trend or course.

"The harsh winter caused a decline in the deer population."

decompose

Decompose means to rot or decay.

"Over time, a dead plant will decompose with the help of fungi and bacteria."

organism

An **organism** is a form of life, such as a plant or an animal.

"An amoeba is just one organism found in pond water."

photosynthesis

Photosynthesis is the process by which green plants use sunlight to produce carbohydrates.

"Photosynthesis relies on sunlight and carbon dioxide."

displace

Displace means to move or put out of the proper or usual place.

"Cutting down the forest will displace a lot of animals."

exploit

Exploit means to use to one's advantage.

"The government plans to exploit the river's current in order to produce electricity."

fungi

Fungi are organisms that include mushrooms, mildew, mold, and yeast.

"The fungi on that dead tree are helping to decompose the rotted wood."

physical

Physical means of or relating to material things.

"The pond, meadow, and forest made up the frog's physical surroundings."

resource

A **resource** is an available supply that can be used when needed.

"The country's main resource was oil."

species

Species refers to a class of individuals that have some common characteristics.

"The lake is home to a rare species of fish."

IT'S ALL CONNECTED

Think of a place such as a river, a plain, or a valley. Now think of all the **organisms** that live there, the relationships they have with one another, and their **physical** surroundings. That's an ecosystem. The living and nonliving parts are connected by two main processes. Energy flows through the ecosystem, and nutrients are cycled through it. The sun is the source of energy. Plants use **photosynthesis** to convert sunlight into sugars, which they use to grow and reproduce. Some animals eat plants. Other animals eat those animals. And still other animals eat those animals. Finally, bacteria and **fungi** consume dead plants and animals.

Scientists call this movement of nutrients and energy a food chain. A mouse might eat the seeds of a wildflower, a snake might eat the mouse, and a hawk might eat the snake. Then, when the hawk dies, it is **decomposed** by bacteria. Most food chains, however, are interrelated and overlapping. The mouse eats many kinds of plants and, in turn, may be eaten by many kinds of animals. Together, all the food chains in an ecosystem are called a food web.

Great blue heron

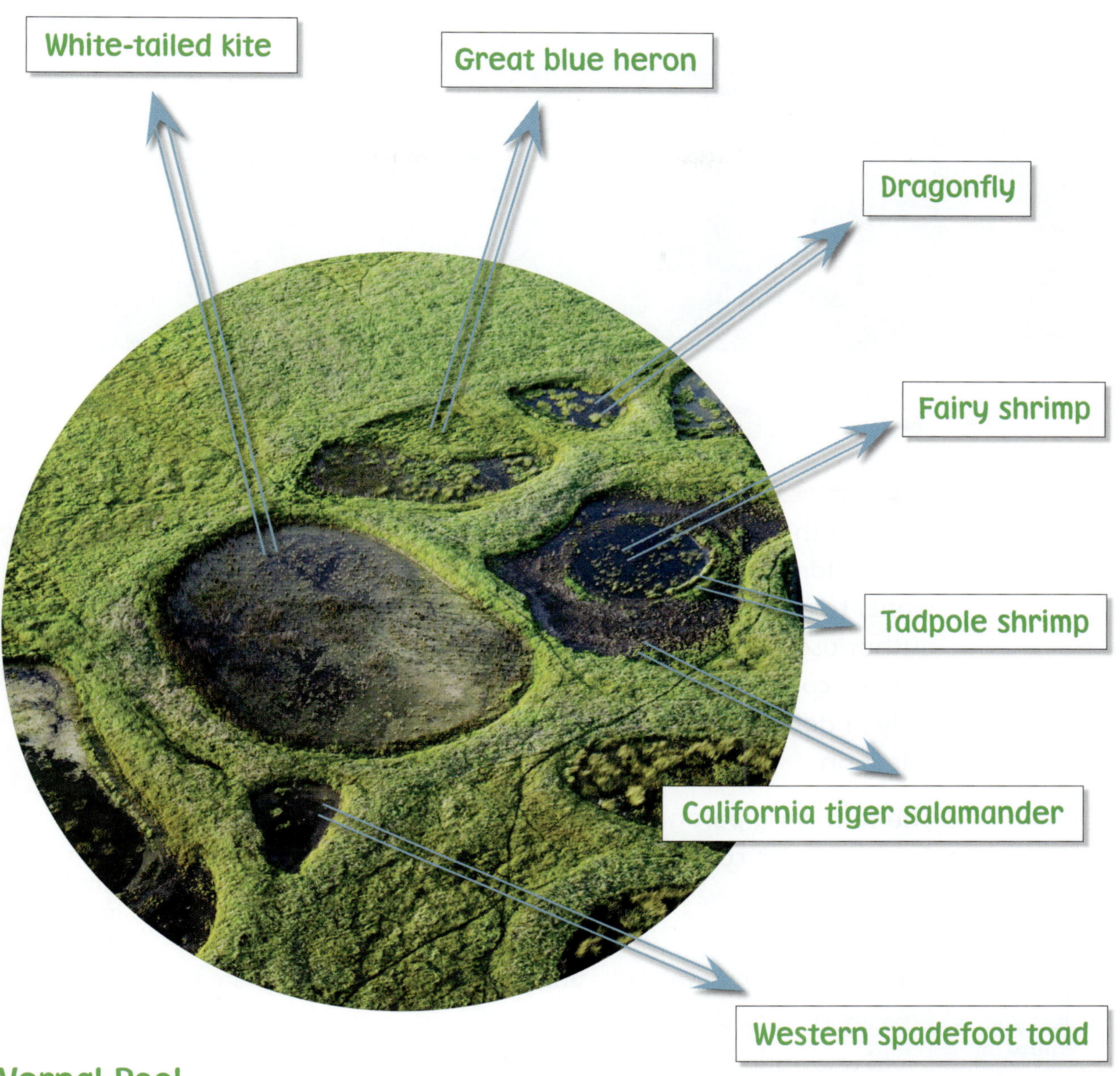

Vernal Pool

California's vernal pools are a unique ecosystem, providing habitats for plants and animals that live nowhere else. A vernal pool is a low spot, usually on an ancient valley floor, that floods each winter. During the summer, it dries out. Only plants and animals that have adapted to this pattern of flooding and drying out can survive there. But of course vernal pools are part of a larger, surrounding ecosystem. For many plants and animals, vernal pools are just one part of their habitat. Everything is connected.

Comprehension

TARGET SKILL **Main Idea and Details** Some passages begin with an important detail that helps prove a main idea. A **main idea** is the most important idea or point a writer wants to make. **Details** are small pieces of information that an author uses to support or tell more about a main idea. Good readers connect important details about related topics to more fully understand and evaluate the main idea of a passage or selection.

The following paragraph, taken from the selection "We're Surrounded!" contains a main idea and supporting details.

This clue phrase lets you know an example will help explain the main idea.

Humans also move plants and animals from one ecosystem to another. In the nineteenth century, for example, a group of New Yorkers brought 100 European starlings to Central Park. Today starlings live throughout North America. Their population is estimated at over 200 million. Biologists think the starling's success has led to declines in many native bird species.

This is an important detail that relates to the main idea of the passage.

A related topic can more fully explain or prove the main idea.

A concluding detail tells a result related to the main idea.

The main idea in the top circle tells what the paragraph is about. The details in the first row of small circles under the main idea help to explain and to prove the main idea. The second row of small circles shows related topics that can help readers understand more about the main idea.

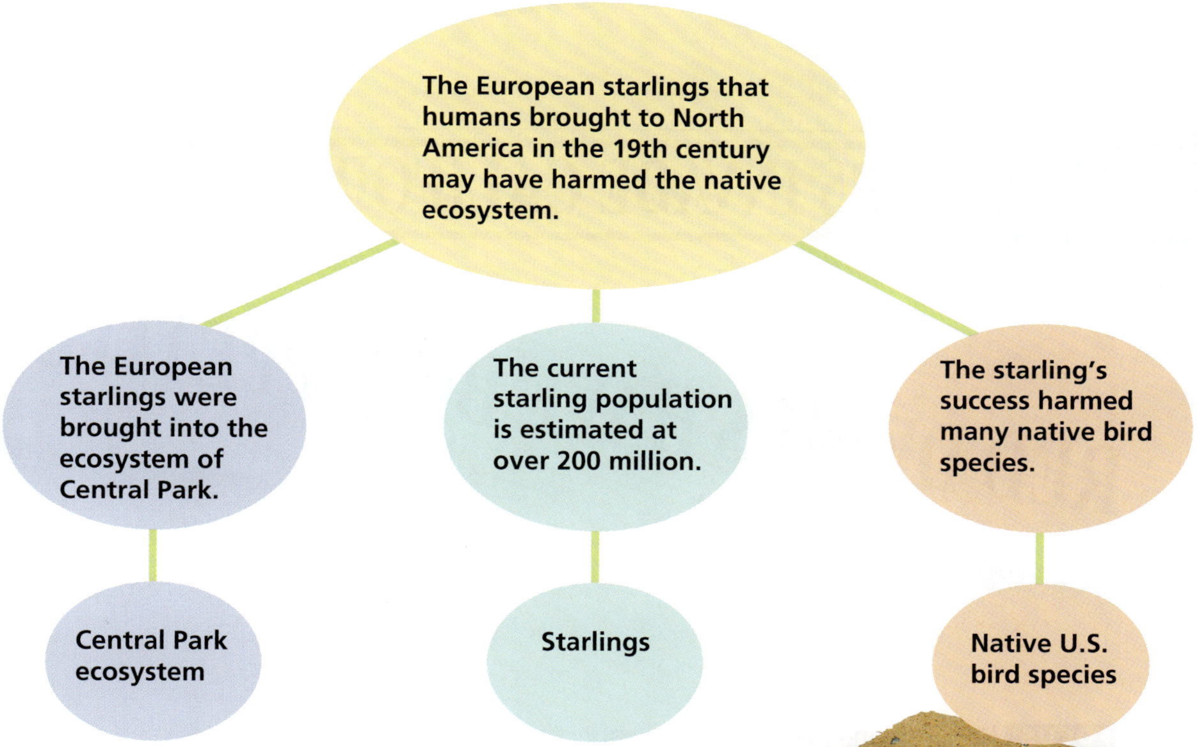

The European starlings that humans brought to North America in the 19th century may have harmed the native ecosystem.

The European starlings were brought into the ecosystem of Central Park.

The current starling population is estimated at over 200 million.

The starling's success harmed many native bird species.

Central Park ecosystem

Starlings

Native U.S. bird species

TARGET STRATEGY **Summary** As you read, keep the main idea and supporting details in mind. These facts can help you summarize the selection by using your own words to retell the most important events and ideas.

WE'RE SURROUNDED!

SEA MONSTERS INVADE CALIFORNIA COAST

RED DEVILS HAVE BIG APPETITES

FOCUS: How can one invading species affect an ecosystem?

These headlines may sound exaggerated, but they're serious. Animals and plants from one ecosystem can cause havoc when they are moved to a different ecosystem.

Plants and animals have always traveled to new lands. Seeds drift in the wind or float in water. Birds fly, wolves roam, and lizards swim. Most plants and animals don't survive very long in new environments. But some thrive. Their natural predators and competitors may not live in the new place. Or the new environment may have **resources** that the newcomer can **exploit** better than native **species** can. If the invading species does well enough, it can **displace** native species and change the ecosystem.

Humans also move plants and animals from one ecosystem to another. In the nineteenth century, for example, a group of New Yorkers brought 100 European starlings to Central Park. Today, starlings live throughout North America. Their population is estimated at over 200 million. Biologists think the starling's success has led to **declines** in many native bird species.

Monster Squid

The "red devil" of South American and Mexican waters has come to California. Humboldt squid have ten tentacles with suckers to grasp their prey. Each sucker has teeth. The squid has a razor-sharp beak as well. Humboldt squid are fierce predators. They grab and hold onto fish with their tentacles, and take bites with their beak. One diver reported seeing a squid attack a shark twice its size.

REREAD

Main Idea + Details

What makes Humboldt squid fierce predators?

When 1,500 monster Humboldt squid washed up on a California beach in 2005, it was national news. Scientists had already seen large numbers of the animals 20–50 miles off the coast. They concluded that the squid were in Monterey Bay to stay. There is evidence, however, that they are moving even farther north, along the coast of Oregon.

Humboldt squid

The squid may be venturing north because of the warming of the ocean. But some scientists believe that the squid is expanding its range because its predators—big fish such as tuna and swordfish—are disappearing. The decline of these predators is due to overfishing, which points the finger back at humans.

No one knows what effects Humboldt squid will have on their new ecosystem. But they will certainly upset the food web.

Injurious Crabs

Chinese mitten crabs are named for their claws, which are covered with soft bristles. They aren't exactly warm and fuzzy. The first Chinese mitten crab ever found on the East Coast of the United States was collected from the Chesapeake Bay in Maryland in 2006. The federal government immediately issued an alert, like one of the FBI's "Most Wanted" posters. It told anyone who found a mitten crab *not* to throw it back into the water. That's because the crabs can multiply and spread quickly. They cause serious damage to riverbanks, levees, and ecosystems.

REREAD

Main Idea + Details

What makes the mitten crab undesirable?

The Chinese mitten crab comes from East Asia and probably traveled by ship to the United States. They may have arrived in a ship's ballast water. The crabs are good to eat, so they may have been shipped to food markets. Or they may have been imported for the aquarium business. The crabs, which have already established themselves in California and Europe, create serious long-term impacts on the environment. Huge numbers of the crabs burrow into riverbanks, causing erosion and mudslides. They displace native species, out-competing them for food. They also get into fishing and shrimping nets, damaging the nets and ruining the catches.

Chinese mitten crabs

Some Invasive Species in the United States

Species	Bad Habits	Estimated Costs
Leafy Spurge Purple Loosestrife Garlic Mustard Star Thistle	These plants mix with crops, make livestock sick, damage rangeland, crowd out native species, and kill trees.	$20 billion to control invasive weeds in the 1990s
Zebra Mussels Asian Clams	These mollusks eat native species, clog waterways and pipes, and damage ecosystems.	$5 billion per year to control zebra mussels and repair the damage $1 billion per year for the Asian clam
Balsam Woolly Adelgids Red Fire Ants Formosan Termites	These insects kill trees, hurt livestock, and damage wooden buildings.	95 percent of the Fraser firs in the Southern Appalachians destroyed by woolly adelgids $1 billion each year in livestock losses and control of the fire ant $1 billion per year in damages and control of the Formosan termite

STOP AND THINK

1. Why is it national news when 1,500 monster squid wash up on a beach?
2. In what ways do invaders affect new homes?

Your Turn

Use Your Words:

aquatic	immense
balance	infinite
base	mechanize
compete	narrative
consequence	recover
decade	refine
deplete	respire
extinct	restore
extract	stock
fundamental	vast

- Read the words on the list.
- Read the dialogue. Find the words.

MORE ACTIVITIES

1. Venn Diagram

Graphic Organizer

In what ways can you help the environment at home? in school? in both places? Fill in the Venn diagram. Write the things you can do only at home. Write the things you can do only at school. Write the things you can do in both places. Then talk about the diagram with your class.

Helping the environment at home | Both | Helping the environment at school

2. Make a Drawing

Listening and Speaking

Suppose you could work, like the teenagers in the picture, to help restore a river. Draw a picture showing what job you would do. Show the picture to your partner. Talk about it.

3. Write a Letter

Writing

Is there a lake, pond, river, or stream in your area that needs help? Write a letter to an official, describing the body of water and what needs to be done to make it healthy. Share your letter with your class.

4. It's Immense!

Vocabulary

Immense means "huge or very great." With a partner, think of other words that mean the same or almost the same as *immense*. Make a list of the words and share them with your class.

5. You Are the Reporter

Writing

Suppose you were a reporter covering the story of the river restoration. What questions would you ask? Write down five questions that would help you understand the project better. Share the questions with your partner. Talk about ways they can be improved.

6. Make a List

Vocabulary

People working to restore a river need tools and supplies. With a partner, make a list of the tools and supplies they might need. Share the list with your class.

Tools and Supplies
1.
2.
3.

Selection **2**

WHAT HAPPENED HERE?

FOCUS: What "good idea" caused the Aral Sea disaster? What were some of the unexpected side effects?

Governments and companies often take advantage of natural resources or use them inappropriately. A government might decide to dam a river or allow gas exploration in a mountain range. A company might log a forest or build a mall on a wetland. The **consequences** of these decisions can affect many people for a long time.

The Story

In 1960, the Aral Sea, really a saline lake, was the fourth largest inland body of water in the world. It was the size of Southern California. The sea was rich with many kinds of fish, and it supported an important fishing industry. The sea regulated the icy winds from Siberia in winter and eased the fierce summer heat. The sea was also a great "evaporator" that kept moisture in the air.

In the 1960s, the Soviet Union decided to use the land around the Aral Sea to grow cotton. There were millions of acres of flat land. All the land needed was water. The government ordered that water should be diverted from the AmuDarya River and the SyrDarya River to irrigate **immense** new cotton fields. The region became one of the world's largest cotton producers.

KAZAKHSTAN
Aral Sea
UZBEKISTAN
Caspian Sea
TURKMENISTAN
IRAN

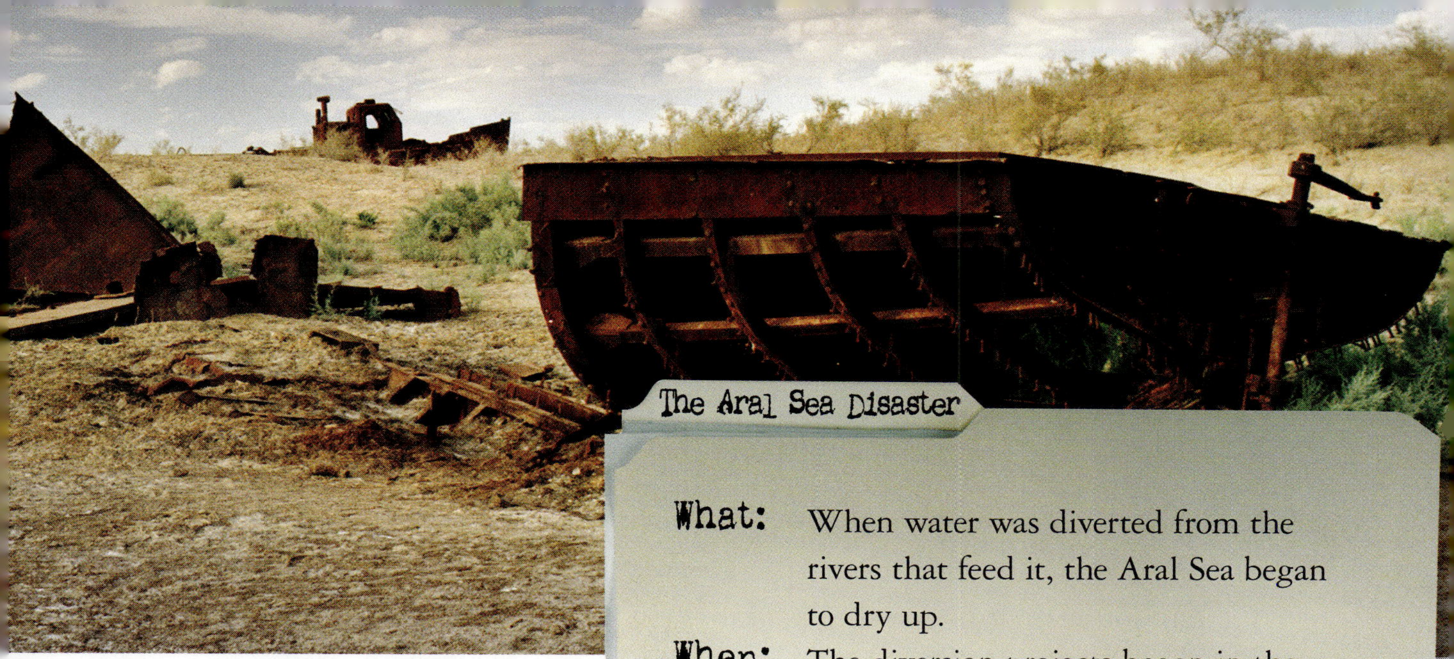

Abandoned boats rust near the Aral Sea.

The Aral Sea Disaster

What: When water was diverted from the rivers that feed it, the Aral Sea began to dry up.

When: The diversion projects began in the 1960s.

Where: Kazakhstan and Uzbekistan, in Central Asia

The Consequences

Once water was diverted from the rivers to the cotton fields, only a trickle was left to flow into the Aral Sea. The water in the sea kept evaporating. Salt does not evaporate with water, so as the sea shrank, it became more and more salty. The number of fish dropped. Four species became extinct. By the 1980s, there were not enough fish left to support a fishing industry. By 1995, seventy-five percent of the water in the Aral Sea was gone.

A huge salty desert has replaced the sea. Dust storms are frequent, and they carry the salt far. Without the sea, the local climate has become more severe. Winters are longer and colder, and the growing season is shorter and drier.

The impact on the people who live around the sea has been drastic. When the fishing industry collapsed, many families lost their livelihoods. Almost 5 million acres of once fertile land have become too salty to grow crops or vegetables. Grasslands where cows and sheep used to graze are now covered in toxic dust. Pesticides and fertilizers from the cotton fields have seeped into the groundwater, making people sick.

REREAD

Main Idea + Details

What is the main idea of this paragraph?

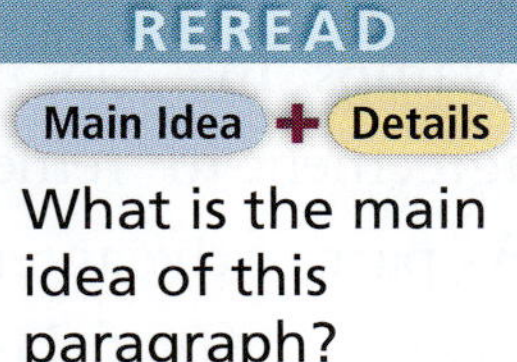

Toxic Waste in Ecuador

What: As oil was **extracted** from Ecuador's rain forest, enormous amounts of toxic waste were spilled and dumped.

When: Drilling began in 1964, but most of the spills occurred between 1971 and 1992. Oil extraction is still going on in the area.

Where: In eastern Ecuador, a country in South America

Some of the rivers in Ecuador are polluted with oil and toxic waste.

The Story

Ecuador was in the middle of an oil boom in the early 1970s. The world was demanding more and more oil for industry and personal use. Large oil companies, including Ecuador's national oil company, were drilling and extracting oil in an area near the city of Oriente. The companies dumped large quantities of toxic wastewater into pits and swamps. In 1995, the companies signed an agreement to "remediate" the damage done. As part of the agreement, the company would clean up 160 of the more than 600 waste-filled pits. That part of the job was completed in 1998.

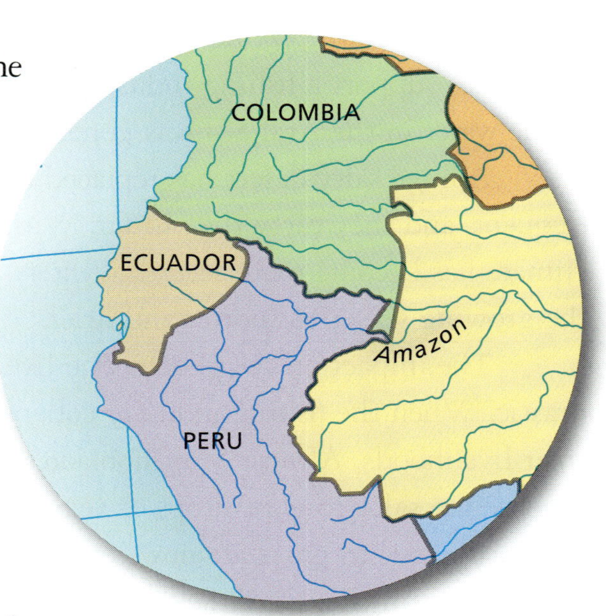

However, many large pits of toxic waste remain. Today, the surface of a river that feeds the Amazon River shimmers with an oily sheen. Children swim in the water; people eat fish caught in it. Some of the waste pits are in people's backyards. The fumes make them sick with **respiratory** infections and rashes.

The Future

Now a group of Ecuadorian citizens is suing the big oil companies again. They say that the oil waste has seeped into rivers and streams, poisoning animals and humans. They cite the cancer rate in the region, which is several times the nation's rate. The oil companies claim that the charges are unfounded. They refuse to negotiate a settlement. One way or another, two and a half million acres of rain forest have been damaged—or ruined. Many experts doubt whether the land can ever be cleaned up, since much of the toxic waste has already seeped into the ground.

What Can You Do?

We all need to make choices every day. Do we toss something away or recycle it? Do we walk to the corner store or ask for a ride in a car? How do these choices affect the world? If we recycle paper and clothing, not as much cotton has to be grown. If we walk to the corner store, not as much oil needs to be extracted and **refined**. Do you feel as though you should live "green"? What can you do to make a difference?

STOP AND THINK

1. What are some of the negative effects caused by wastewater from oil drilling?
2. What does toxic wastewater in Ecuador have to do with your life?

FERRET DOESN'T LIVE HERE ANYMORE

FOCUS: What ecosystem is as seriously threatened as the rain forest, and why?

Native to North America, the black-footed ferret is an endangered species. Less than two percent of its original grassland habitat still exists.

Following is the personal **narrative** of Oscar Anderson, an imaginary retired farmer from North Dakota, who might have seen some of the last black-footed ferrets in that state.

I was born in North Dakota in 1906. When I was growing up, there was still some prairie around here. I liked it. Used to lie on my back in the grass and watch the clouds sail by, listening to the meadowlarks.

I heard that the American prairie might be more endangered than the tropical rain forest that people make such a fuss about. We sure lost a lot of prairie, and we have to admit, we did it ourselves. There used to be grass as far as you could see, like an ocean of grass. Long ago, they say the prairie was black with buffalo. There were millions of those animals. Between the settlers and the government, they killed all but a few. Now people raise buffalo on ranches and sell them for meat, like beef. I've heard it's good, but I don't care to try it.

So what happened to the prairie? Folks like my grandparents are what happened. They settled here in the 1870s and 1880s and started their farms and ranches. Naturally, they came to make a living for themselves and their families, so they plowed the prairie under. And they drained the ponds and marshes where the ducks used to live. The problem is, all those wheat fields and cornfields were the end of the prairie.

Now, the ferret doesn't live here anymore. I heard there are a couple of groups out in Montana and Wyoming now. The ferrets nearly died out, you know. When that last group in South Dakota died, everyone thought they were ***extinct****. Then in 1981 someone found 130 ferrets living in Wyoming. The conservationists got real excited, but most of those animals died of disease. Finally the scientists took the last eighteen and started breeding them in captivity.*

What happened to the ferrets has a lot to do with what happened to prairie dogs. They're not related to dogs, but people call them dogs because they bark. When a prairie dog sees a hawk or a badger or a ferret, it jumps up and down and barks, "Yip, yip, yip!" to warn the others. Then they all dive into their holes. The prairie dogs are mostly gone now. Ranchers killed them. They thought prairie dogs were ***competing*** *with their cattle for grass.*

The ferrets used to eat prairie dogs, and they lived in old prairie-dog burrows. So when the prairie dogs disappeared, the ferrets did, too. It's all connected.

STOP AND THINK

1. The ferrets lost more than their land. What was the real cause of their disappearance?
2. Do you think it's important to keep animals like prairie dogs and ferrets alive? Explain your answer.

TECHNOLOGY CONNECTION

Oceans in Danger

Green sea turtle

Forum: What's Happening to Our Oceans?

FOCUS: How are oceans affected by human activities?

For most of human history, people have considered the oceans too large to damage. The number of fish living in oceans was practically limitless, so we didn't have to worry about them disappearing. Pollution that made its way into the oceans would be so diluted that it wouldn't matter. The ecosystems were **vast** and stable, so there wasn't any danger of upsetting the natural **balance**. But now we know that this isn't true. The oceans are not **infinite**. They are affected by human activities, and their ecosystems are surprisingly delicate.

OVERFISHING Since the 1970s, the number of factory fishing ships has risen dramatically. These giant, **mechanized** trawlers can sweep miles of ocean clean of fish. They have led to the collapse of many fisheries. When an important fish **stock** disappears, the food web is torn apart.

POLLUTION Runoff from crop fertilizers flows down rivers into the ocean. This leads to algae blooms that **deplete** the oxygen in the

Forum, cont.: What's Happening to Our Oceans?

water, creating "dead zones" that extend for miles. When oil tankers run aground, the spills can damage coastal ecosystems for **decades**.

RISING TEMPERATURES Along with atmospheric temperatures, ocean temperatures are rising. The warmer temperatures cause damage to coral reefs. Warmer temperatures may also force some **aquatic** animals to move to colder waters. Scientists have also noticed a decline in the amount of tiny ocean organisms called plankton and krill, but they aren't sure what the cause is. Plankton and krill are **fundamental** to ocean food chains.

COASTAL DEVELOPMENT Much of the world's population now lives in coastal regions. Wetlands, estuaries, and mangrove forests, which act as nurseries for many ocean species, are filled in or paved over. Bays and beaches are polluted, further damaging coastal ecosystems.

Comments

1. Nikos (November 6)

I live in Athens, Greece. I know that industrial waste and raw sewage are dumped into the ocean here. It's bad enough that our coastal waters are filthy and that fish are dying. It hurts to think that what we do here hurts the ocean in other places, too.

2. Darlene (November 8)

I live in Greenville, near the Mississippi River. We aren't even close to the ocean. But I know that the water that flows from our land to the river is loaded with chemicals from fertilizers and pesticides. And the amount of animal waste a hog farm produces in a week is astonishing! All of it goes down the Mississippi and into the Gulf of Mexico. I've seen pictures of parts of the Gulf that are now officially dead. No sea creatures can live there because of the pollution.

3. Ben (November 11)	I'm really proud of my state, Washington. We are part of a project to **restore** the Olympia oyster. It's the only oyster native to the Pacific Northwest. Landowners, tribes, community groups, and the shellfish industry have all worked together. More than 5 million oysters have been placed, or "seeded," in different areas across Puget Sound.
4. Maneh (November 15)	In Bali, we have had a problem with sea turtles. Four of the five kinds of great sea turtles live around Indonesia. They have been hunted or accidentally killed in fishing nets, and now they are endangered. There is a big illegal trade in turtles and turtle meat here. And turtles are also used in some religious ceremonies. The World Wildlife Federation is working with Hindu priests to tell people that turtles don't have to be killed for the ceremonies. It is making a difference, I think.
5. Brenda (November 21)	Doesn't everybody realize that the main danger for oceans right now is the decline of plankton and krill? Without plankton and krill, everything goes. They're the **base** of all the ocean's food chains. And scientists still don't know why the plankton and krill are declining, just that they are. I'm writing from Australia.

6. Derek
(November 29)

I live near Mombasa in Kenya. We are losing coast and wetlands that are important to the health of our communities. In many places, the plants that held the soil in place have been cut down, so now the waves drag the soil into the ocean. Also, our beaches are very important to tourism. The United Nations and the Kenyan government are studying what to do about it.

7. Abigail
(December 3)

I'm from Massachusetts. Overfishing really cut the amount of cod all along the East Coast. Fishers have had to change the kind of fish they look for until the cod population **recovers**—if it ever does. I've heard that sometimes, when too many of a species die, the population can't recover. It's called a "tipping point." I really hope that hasn't happened.

STOP AND THINK

1. Why can fertilizers that help things grow create dead zones in the ocean?
2. Notice that the students who commented are aware of what's happening in the oceans near them. What do you know about what's happening to the oceans in North America?

Turning It Around

FOCUS: What did David Ogilvie do that helped preserve endangered species?

The Return of the Willow Flycatcher

It seems that David Ogilvie has proven the doomsayers wrong. He has created one of the healthier riverbank ecosystems in arid New Mexico.

Scientists knew that populations of southwestern willow flycatchers had been declining. They also knew that two endangered fish, the loach minnow and the spikedace, lived in New Mexico's rivers. Conservationists believed that all three animals are threatened wherever cattle are raised.

David Ogilvie's U Bar Ranch has shown this idea to be wrong. The largest known populations of all three endangered animals now live on the U Bar, along with his cattle.

What's the story? In 1994, Ogilvie decided to use some irrigation ditches from the old days, before the U Bar. When water flowed in the ditches, dying willow trees began to flourish. The same year, the U.S. government put the flycatcher on the endangered species list. Ogilvie was interested. He thought he had seen some willow flycatchers near the old ditches.

The rancher got a biologist to do a bird survey. The biologist found that there were indeed southwestern willow flycatchers on the ranch, and that it was the largest known population anywhere—64 pairs. Since then, Ogilvie has opened up more irrigation ditches. The willow trees have continued to thrive, and the bird population has grown. Now there are healthy forests and grasslands along the Gila River where it flows through the U Bar Ranch.

Some conservationists still think cattle should be removed from land where endangered birds and fish live. But Ogilvie's experience may lead to changing opinions. In his stretch of the Gila River, 99 percent of the fish are native species. That's not true elsewhere in the Southwest. And the U Bar supports what may be the healthiest habitat for songbirds in North America.

Willow flycatcher

New Mexico | Endangered Species List

Bat, Mexican long-nosed (Leptonycteris nivalis)
Bear, grizzly lower (Ursus arctos horribilis)
Chub, Chihuahua (Gila nigrescens)
Falcon, northern aplomado (Falco femoralis septentrionalis)
Flycatcher, southwestern willow (Empidonax traillii extimus)
leopard (Rana chiricahuensis)
Pecos (Gambusia nobilis)
hermosphaeroma thermophilus)
r (Panthera onca)
loach (Tiaroga cobitis)
de silvery (Hybognathus amarus)
Owl, Mexican spotted (Strix occidentalis lucida)
Rattlesnake, New Mexican ridge-nosed (Crotalus willardi obscurus)

STOP AND THINK

1. Some conservationists believe in an idea that Ogilvie's ranch disproves. What is the idea?
2. What does the story suggest to you about animals and ecological systems?

Reading Longer Words

In this unit you learned more about how to read longer words.

Step 1: Divide the word into parts.

VCCV letter pattern?

Divide between the consonants.

Step 2: Read each word part.

Step 3: Read the whole word. Sound right? If not, try an alternative.

Ends in a consonant?

Try a short vowel sound.

Ends in a vowel?

Try a long vowel sound.

Has a VCe pattern?

Try a long vowel sound.

Ends in *-le, -al,* or *-el*?

Try dividing before the consonant preceding the *l*.

Divide the Words

con/test	crim/son
sub/mit	cul/prit
vel/vet	scra/mble
cym/bal	tem/ple
grum/ble	vo/cal

Read Word Parts			Read Whole Words
con	test	→	contest
crim	son	→	crimson
sub	mit	→	submit
cul	prit	→	culprit
vel	vet	→	velvet
scram	ble	→	scramble
cym	bal	→	cymbal
tem	ple	→	temple
grum	ble	→	grumble
vo	cal	→	vocal

Read More Words

Use the three steps to read these words from the unit.

travel	animal	newcomer	human	burrow
company	immense	trickle	industry	tropical

Vocabulary and Morphology

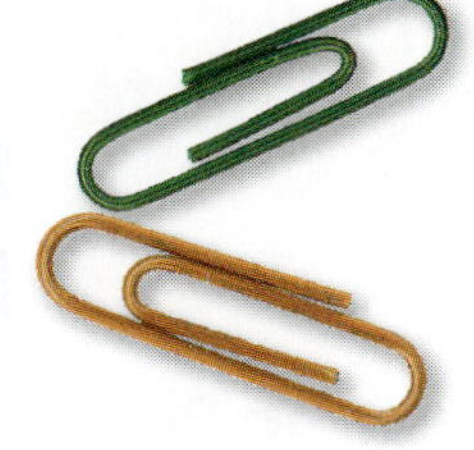

Greek and Latin Roots

Many subjects that are studied in schools and colleges have Greek and Latin roots in their names. Understanding how these words are put together will help you understand their meaning.

music	+	*ology*	=	*musicology*

Ology is a Greek root that means "the science of" or "the study of." *Musicology* means the study of music, or the science of music.

musicology	+	*ist*	=	*musicologist*

The suffix *ist*, which comes from Greek through Latin, means "one who does or practices." *Musicologist* means one who practices the study or science of music.

Some words ending in *ology* are not fields of study, but have to do with speaking or saying, such as the word *apology*.

The suffix *-ist* can have shades of meaning. A *pianist* does need to practice, but a pianist is a person who plays the piano. A *novelist* doesn't practice or study a novel. A novelist produces or writes novels.

Regular Present and Past Perfect Verbs

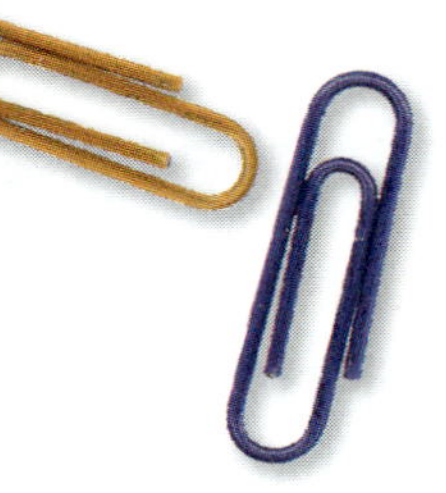

Regular Present Perfect Verbs

A verb in the **present perfect** tense describes an event that occurred at an unspecified time before now.

A present perfect verb—
- contains the helping verb that is a form of *to have* in the present tense
- contains a past participle (the *-ed* form)
- agrees with the subject in number (singular or plural verb form of *to have*)

Present Perfect Tense

	Singular	Plural
First Person	I have helped them.	We have helped them.
Second Person	You have helped them.	You have helped them.
Third Person	She has helped them.	They have helped them.

Notice how sentences in the regular present tense can be changed into the regular present perfect tense.

Regular Present	Regular Present Perfect
I call you every night.	I **have called** you every night.
My favorite program starts.	My favorite program **has started**.
The children play with their new toys.	The children **have played** with their new toys.

Regular Past Perfect Verbs

A verb in the **past perfect** tense describes an action that happened before a different, more specific, action in the past.

A past perfect verb—

- contains the helping verb *had* in the past tense
- contains a past participle (the *-ed* form)

Past Perfect Tense

	Singular	Plural
First Person	I had waited until ten o'clock.	We had waited until ten o'clock.
Second Person	You had waited until ten o'clock.	You had waited until ten o'clock.
Third Person	She had waited until ten o'clock.	They had waited until ten o'clock.

Look at how sentences in the regular present tense can be changed into the regular past perfect tense.

Regular Present	Regular Past Perfect
The team travels to Chicago for their away game.	The team **had traveled** to Chicago for their away game.
The nurse examines the baby more than once.	The nurse **had examined** the baby more than once.
Lakisha focuses her attention on winning the contest.	Lakisha **had focused** her attention on winning the contest.

Punctuation: Using Commas in Compound Sentences

A group of words that can function as a complete sentence on its own is called an independent clause. Sometimes, two independent clauses are linked together to make a **compound sentence**.

When the two clauses are linked with one of the coordinating conjunctions (*and, but, for, or, so*), place a comma after the first independent clause, right before the conjunction.

I am going home. I am definitely going to stay there.
I am going home, and I am definitely going to stay there.

It rained all afternoon. We still had our picnic outdoors.
It rained all afternoon, but we still had our picnic outdoors.

It was very dark. Juan had to use a flashlight.
It was very dark, so Juan had to use a flashlight.

Two clauses may also be linked using a pair of conjunctions (either/or, both/and).

Either you keep quiet, or I will leave the room.

Writing Traits Checklist

☑ **Punctuation and Capitalization**
Are commas used correctly in compound sentences?

Sometimes two clauses have the same subject. You don't have to repeat the subject, and you usually don't need a comma.

The crew worked for hours. The crew couldn't repair the damage.
The crew worked for hours but couldn't repair the damage.

Hank was tired. He stayed at home.
Hank was tired and stayed at home.

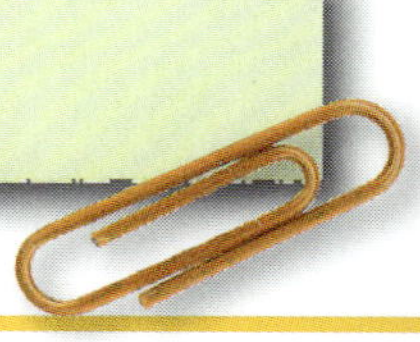

Only one of each three sentences is written correctly.

1. a. I sat next to Omar, and Rachel sat next to Joan.
   b. I sat next to Omar and, Rachel sat next to Joan.
   c. I sat next to Omar, and Rachel, sat next to Joan.

2. a. The summers are long and hot and bitter winters usually follow them.
   b. The summers are long and hot, and bitter winters usually follow them.
   c. The summers are long, and hot and bitter winters usually follow them.

3. a. I made my famous stew and the captain played a song.
   b. I made my famous stew and, the captain played a song.
   c. I made my famous stew, and the captain played a song.

4. a. He did invite us but we couldn't go.
   b. He did invite us but, we couldn't go.
   c. He did invite us, but we couldn't go.

5. a. She could call Gregor, or she could call Fiona.
   b. She could call Gregor or, she could call Fiona.
   c. She could call Gregor, or, she could call Fiona.

6. a. We picked them up early, but they still missed their plane.
   b. We picked them up early but, they still missed their plane.
   c. We picked them up early but they still missed their plane.

7. a. Yuliya came to the party, and brought dozens of gifts.
   b. Yuliya came to the party and, brought dozens of gifts.
   c. Yuliya came to the party and brought dozens of gifts.

8. a. He said that he wanted to stay behind but, he really wanted to come with us.
   b. He said that he wanted to stay behind but he really wanted to come with us.
   c. He said that he wanted to stay behind, but he really wanted to come with us.

UNIT 3

IDENTITY

THE BIG QUESTION:
HOW DO PEOPLE FIGURE OUT WHO THEY REALLY ARE?

READINGS

Looking at Identity

What makes up a person's identity?

A person's identity is made up of his or her...

- personality.
- heritage.
- beliefs.
- individuality.

What questions might an adopted child have about his or her background?

An adopted child might have questions about...

- the country he or she came from.
- his or her original culture.
- what the people were like in the place he or she was adopted from.
- how the background is part of his or her identity.

What traditions can help people express their identity?

People can express their identity through...

- ☐ their traditional music.
- ☐ their language.
- ☐ their clothing.
- ☐ family stories and memories.

What does Chinese opera include?

Chinese opera includes...

- ☐ singing.
- ☐ dancing.
- ☐ speaking.
- ☐ acrobatics.

How did American Indian soldiers help during World War I and World War II?

During World War I and World War II, American Indian soldiers helped by...

- ☐ being fierce fighters.
- ☐ going behind enemy lines.
- ☐ using their native languages to send secret messages.
- ☐ rescuing soldiers who were captured.

Literature Words

acquaintance

amber

common

convince

dusk

identify

pale

remote

rhythm

unusual

acquaintance

Acquaintance refers to a person one knows, but who is not a close friend.

"The football star is an acquaintance of mine."

amber

Amber refers to a brownish-yellow color.

"Her eyes were the color of amber."

identify

Identify means to recognize a particular person or thing.

"The lost dog had a tag that helped us identify its owner."

pale

Pale means lacking intensity of color; colorless, whitish.

"A barn owl's face is almost as round and pale as the moon."

common

Common means ordinary, or usual.

"It was common for our dog Rocky to chew on my homework."

convince

Convince means to persuade.

"Dad could not convince me to ride the roller coaster."

dusk

Dusk is the period of partial darkness between day and night.

"At dusk we lit the campfire and started cooking dinner."

remote

Remote means far apart or located at some distance away.

"The tiny island was in a remote part of the world."

rhythm

Rhythm is the pattern of musical movement through time.

"The rhythm of the music made everyone get up and dance."

unusual

Unusual means not typical, or uncommon.

"It was unusual to see snow falling in Florida."

Final Curve

by Langston Hughes

When you turn the corner
And you run into *yourself*
Then you know that you have turned
All the corners that are left.

The Drum

by Nikki Giovanni

daddy says the world is
a drum tight and hard
and i told him
i'm gonna beat
out my own rhythm

Celebration

by Alonzo Lopez

I shall dance tonight.
When the **dusk** comes crawling,
There will be dancing
  And feasting.
I shall dance with the others
  in circles,
    in leaps,
      in stomps.
Laughter and talk
      will weave into the night,
Among the fires
  of my people.
Games will be played
And I shall be
  a part of it.

GET READY TO READ

Comprehension

TARGET SKILL **Story Structure**

Story structure means the way that events are put together to form the plot, or what happens in a story. Plots involve a problem, or conflict, that must be resolved, or solved. When you read, look for the problem or problems in the story and how they are solved.

The following paragraph is from the selection "A Song for Ba." Ba is Wei's father. Ba is a singer in a Chinese Opera company. Women were not allowed to sing in Chinese operas at that time, and Ba must sing a woman's part. But Ba is having problems singing in a woman's voice. Ba and Wei are in their home.

The author introduces the problem. Ba is not able to sing in a woman's voice.

Ba's voice kept cracking as he tried singing the higher notes…Early the next morning… Wei began to sing in a clear, strong voice. It was a woman's song, full of high, ringing tone. [*Ba grabs Wei and asks where he learned to sing like that.*] "Grandfather taught me," Wei said. "Shall we sing together?"

[*Wei shows his father how to move his mouth and tongue.*] Over and over they practiced the woman's melody until Ba sang it perfectly.

Wei teaches his father how to sing in a woman's voice. The problem is resolved.

You can show problem and resolution with a graphic organizer.

Problem	Resolution
Ba must be able to sing in a woman's voice. He is not able to do so.	Wei, Ba's son, teaches Ba how to sing in a woman's voice.

TARGET STRATEGY **Analyze and Evaluate** As you read, ask yourself:

- Does the setting of the story affect the problem and/or resolution in the story? If so, how?
- What is your opinion about how the setting affects the problem in the story?

These questions will help you to better understand the conflict and resolution in the story. Understanding the conflict and resolution will help to make the story structure clear.

Out of Her Past

From *Finding Miracles*
by Julia Alvarez

FOCUS: How can your past be part of your identity if you know almost nothing about your past?

Most people find it easy to identify themselves as a son or daughter of their parents, and as a member of the community in which they live. This sense of identity doesn't always come as easily to children who were adopted, especially if they were adopted from another culture. Sometimes they feel as though they are two people instead of one. If that feeling happens, they must think deeply to figure out how their parts fit together.

Milly Kaufman knows that she's adopted, and she knows that she was born in a Latin American country, but she thinks of herself as an ordinary American teenager. Then one day, Pablo Bolivar, a new student, arrives at her high school, and he sees something other than an ordinary American teenager when he looks at her. He is convinced that she is from somewhere else. What he sees in Milly is closer to the person she started out as—Milagros, a child born in what might as well be another world.

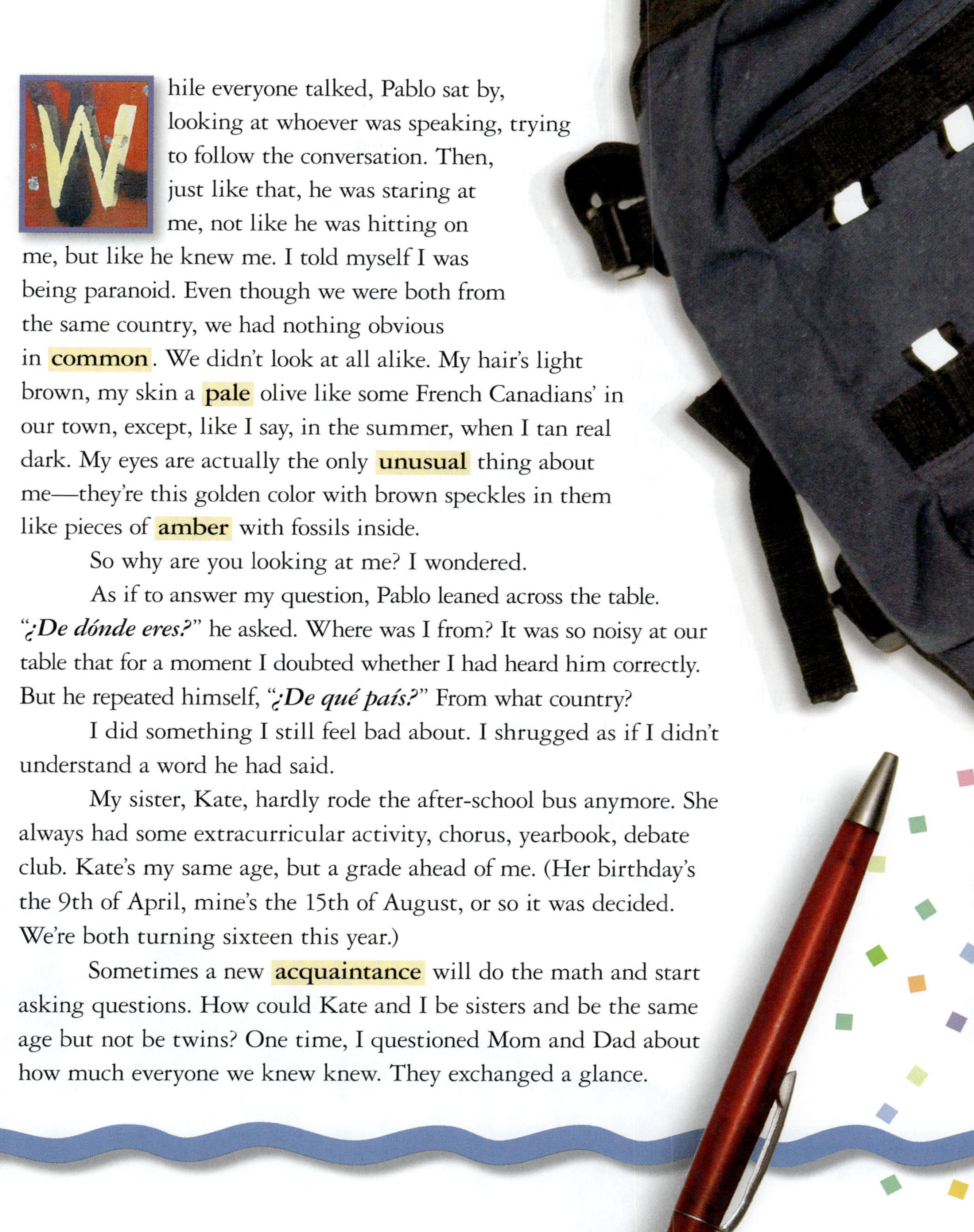

While everyone talked, Pablo sat by, looking at whoever was speaking, trying to follow the conversation. Then, just like that, he was staring at me, not like he was hitting on me, but like he knew me. I told myself I was being paranoid. Even though we were both from the same country, we had nothing obvious in **common**. We didn't look at all alike. My hair's light brown, my skin a **pale** olive like some French Canadians' in our town, except, like I say, in the summer, when I tan real dark. My eyes are actually the only **unusual** thing about me—they're this golden color with brown speckles in them like pieces of **amber** with fossils inside.

So why are you looking at me? I wondered.

As if to answer my question, Pablo leaned across the table. "***¿De dónde eres?***" he asked. Where was I from? It was so noisy at our table that for a moment I doubted whether I had heard him correctly. But he repeated himself, "***¿De qué país?***" From what country?

I did something I still feel bad about. I shrugged as if I didn't understand a word he had said.

My sister, Kate, hardly rode the after-school bus anymore. She always had some extracurricular activity, chorus, yearbook, debate club. Kate's my same age, but a grade ahead of me. (Her birthday's the 9th of April, mine's the 15th of August, or so it was decided. We're both turning sixteen this year.)

Sometimes a new **acquaintance** will do the math and start asking questions. How could Kate and I be sisters and be the same age but not be twins? One time, I questioned Mom and Dad about how much everyone we knew knew. They exchanged a glance.

"We've just told a few friends," Mom said, then hesitated. "Honey, I hope you know there's nothing to be ashamed of. Children come to families in different ways."

That inspirational stuff always sounds great, but it doesn't take the feelings away. I wanted to be just another Kaufman. Was that so hard to understand?

"It's private, that's all," I tried explaining.

The funny thing is that Kate looks more Latin than I do. She's got our grandmother Happy's chocolate brown eyes and brown-black hair (Grandma's is from a bottle now) and olive skin that was common, Grandma says, on her mother's side, before they all got wiped out in the Holocaust. Grandma Happy actually has a lot to be sad about. But that's a whole other story.

Kate is also smart. I should know. We shared a room for years, before I begged for my own attic cubbyhole, where I didn't have to watch Kate put together a report the night before and come home a week later with an A. Meanwhile, I was lucky if I could hang on to a B minus with some assignment I'd struggled over for weeks.

Milly has always had to work with tutors to overcome a reading disability. Once, she overheard a tutor telling her mother that her learning challenges may have resulted from traumas in her early life, before her adoption. He said that it was often a miracle that children who endured such a difficult early life survived at all.

Was he referring to me? Was I a *survivor*?

How could I claim credit for something I couldn't even remember?

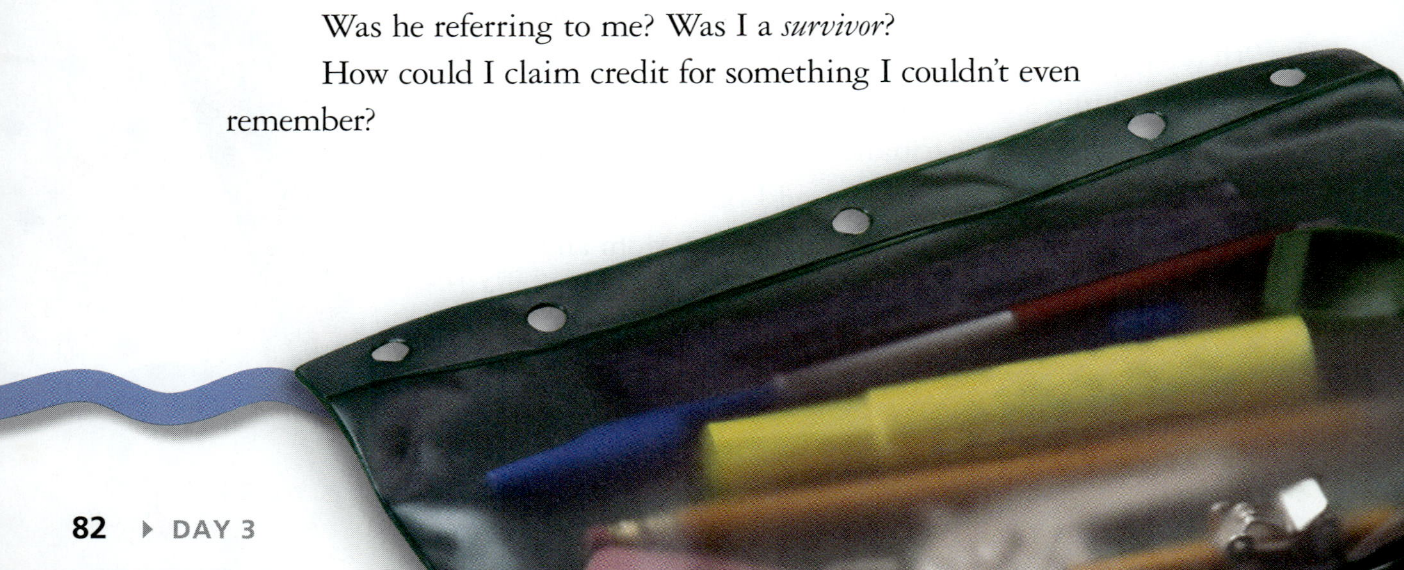

Milly gets to know Pablo better when she agrees to help him learn English, and he says he will help her improve her Spanish. They work together at her house after school.

"Where are you from?" Pablo was reading from his workbook. When I didn't respond, he looked up.

"You asked me that same question the first day I met you," I reminded him. It was high time I admitted I had understood him.

He nodded, then repeated what he had said. "*¿De dónde eres?*"

"I'm sorry that I pretended...I...I didn't know why you were asking me where I was from." Even now, two months later, it was still hard to talk about.

Pablo was staring at me again with that intense look of his. "I explain why I ask. Your eyes...they are eyes from Los Luceros."

It was a good thing I was sitting down. I felt lightheaded. My hands were tingling. "What do you mean, eyes from Los Luceros?" I managed to get out.

Moving back and forth, English to Spanish, Pablo told me about a small town high in the mountains of his country. "It is called Los Luceros, *muy remoto*, very **remote**. That is why the revolutionaries hide there. These people from Los Luceros, they all have eyes like yours."

As he spoke, my eyes filled with tears.

In time, Milly travels back to her first country and learns a lot about her beginnings. She finds a way to make her past a part of who she is.

STOP AND THINK

1. What does Milly learn about her identity from Pablo?
2. Why might finding out something about your past be exciting? Why might it be frightening?

Your Turn

Use Your Words:

communicate	interview
courage	jostle
delicate	logical
elegant	military
ethnic	opportunity
express	relief
fellow	stationed
fluent	term
former	translate
imperial	transmit

- Read the words on the list.
- Read the dialogue. Find the words.

MORE ACTIVITIES

1. Make a Venn Diagram

Graphic Organizer

What things can you think of that are elegant? What things can you think of that are delicate? What things are both elegant and delicate? Write the things you think of in the Venn diagram.

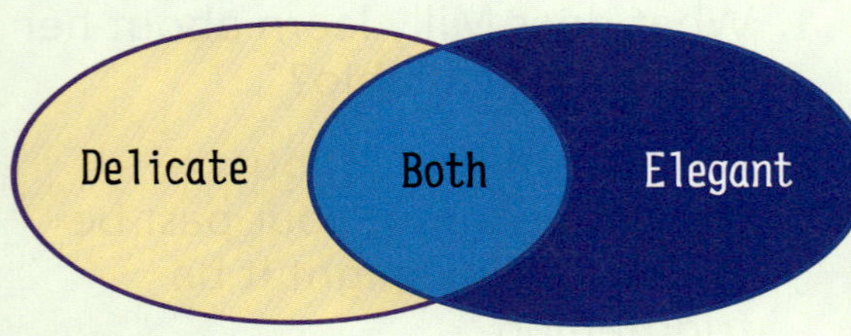

2. Conduct an Interview

Speaking and Listening

Suppose your partner was a volunteer in the picture. Ask your partner five questions about what he or she is doing. Then change places and have your partner ask you five questions.

3. Write a Paragraph

Writing

Have you ever done or witnessed something that took courage? What was it? Write a paragraph describing your experience. Share your paragraph with your partner.

4. Can You Communicate?

Vocabulary

Communicate means "to express thoughts, feelings, or information." With a partner think of all the ways people communicate. Make a list of the words and share them with your class.

5. Play "What Am I?"

Speaking and Listening

Chose a person or object from the picture. Have your partner ask five or six yes-or-no questions to try to guess the person or object. Then trade places.

6. Make a List

Vocabulary

Suppose your town was hit by a storm and homes were destroyed. What things would people need in order to survive? Look at the chart below. List items that would be needed in each category. Share the list with your class.

Shelter	Food and Water	Clothing	Furniture	Energy source

A Song for Ba

by Paul Yee, illustrated by Jan Peng Wang

FOCUS: How can music that is hundreds of years old help a young boy express his identity?

Chinese opera began more than a thousand years ago. It blends singing, speaking, and dancing, along with acrobatic fights. Chinese operas tell exciting stories based on events from history or old stories. The singers always play the same kind of character: one singer might always play a king or a leader, another might always play a young woman, while another might play a clown. The singers' clothes, makeup, and hand movements show which parts they are playing. Each kind of performer even walks in a different way. In the past, only men performed this kind of opera, singing both men's and women's roles.

Wei Lim is a Chinese boy in North America. His father, Ba, sings opera, and his grandfather is a ***former*** *singer. At this time, around 1925, Chinese opera is losing popularity in North America. Wei thinks of himself as a singer, carrying on a family tradition, even though he doesn't know whether this tradition will continue.*

Wei loved to go to the opera. When the curtain lifted, drums and cymbals crashed. An emperor and **imperial** princess shook out their generous sleeves and lit the stage with dazzling colors. White-painted faces showed scarlet-red around the eyes, robes glittered with metallic embroidery and sequins, and headdresses gleamed from bands of pearls and beads and millions of tiny mirrors.

Wei listened to the tuneful melodies gliding off the Chinese cellos and the sharp beats clicking from the woodblocks. He heard the high voice of the princess dancing around the lower voice of the emperor. He knew that women did not perform in the Chinese opera, so men played both the men's and women's roles. His grandfather had always played the female parts, and he had taught Wei many of the songs. Wei had a high, clear voice, but he thought he would rather play the general. In his mind, he saw himself doing acrobatic jumps, spins, and twists just like his father.

One day, Grandfather announced, "I'm returning to China. I'm old now, and I want to see my hometown one last time."

Wei felt as if he were losing his best friend. "Please don't go," he cried.

Grandfather shook his head. "You shouldn't worry," he said. "Your father will take good care of you."

Wei flung the tears from his eyes. "Ba? He doesn't care about me! He doesn't even want me to learn opera."

"He is only looking out for your future."

A few weeks later, Grandfather sailed for home, and then Ba's troupe went touring to seven towns. Wei stayed behind with the wardrobe master. He went to school and studied hard, hoping that high marks would please his father.

The opera troupe stays away for several weeks. When it returns, Wei is shocked to see that his father, Ba, has lost weight and has a cough. The company didn't make money, and worse, several of the performers have quit and returned to China. So the remaining performers must play several roles.

To raise money, the performers plan to stage a new opera. Wei hopes the company doesn't go out of business. How can he ever become an opera performer if there is no place to perform?

One evening close to opening night, Wei sneaked into the theater and hid behind the rows of seats. On the stage, musicians lined one side while singers filled the center with smooth, **elegant** movements. Wei saw two jeweled maidens hiding coyly behind **delicate** fans, a scholar and a porter carrying books and umbrellas, a boatman with long white whiskers, and a priest wearing a golden crown.

But he didn't see Ba anywhere.

Wei crept under the seats to move closer and squinted at the faces.

He gasped. Ba wore a woman's robe and waved its long sleeves. His face had been painted pink; his eyes were lined with black. But his voice kept cracking as he tried singing the higher notes. The other actors muttered impatiently, and the troupe master stopped the music again and again.

Wei hurried home and pretended to be asleep when Ba returned. He heard his father sigh and curse. He heard him hum the new melody and then lose it in a fit of coughing.

That night, neither father nor son slept.

Early next morning, just when the black sky loosened into gray, Wei began to sing in a clear, strong voice. It was a woman's song, full of high, ringing notes.

Ba jumped from his bed and grabbed him. "Where did you learn that?"

"Grandfather taught me," Wei answered. "Shall we sing together?"

Wei let his jaw drop and waggled it loosely. Several times he curled his top lip like a pig's snout. He opened his mouth and let his tongue dart up and down, sideways and around in circles.

Grinning, Ba imitated him. Then they opened their mouths to sing.

After a few lines, Wei stopped and said, "Grandfather says the higher voice comes from the head, not the throat or the chest. He always told me to roll the notes through my forehead."

Louder and louder the two pushed their voices. Over and over they practiced the woman's melody, until Ba sang it perfectly.

When they stopped for a rest, Ba told Wei the government had stopped Chinese immigration. Audiences were shrinking and actors now had to sing more than one role.

On opening night, Wei could hardly sit still. The crowd streamed in, **jostling** for good seats. An eager buzz filled the air, for a new show always excited the audiences. They brought in bags of dried plums and crunched on peanuts and sunflower seeds. A brass horn sounded and bright lamps lit the stage. Wei rubbed his cold hands to warm them.

A hush fell over the hall.

Two women glided onto the stage, rocking on tiny shoes. The audience murmured with approval at their dainty movements. Wei didn't recognize his father under the jeweled headdress, under the layers of make-up, under the flowing silks of pink and scarlet. But when Ba started to sing, Wei heard his grandfather's voice and his own, soaring through the hall like a bell.

He didn't know whether there would still be a Chinese opera when he grew up, but on that night he, too, was a star.

STOP AND THINK

1. Why does Wei try so hard to help his father?
2. How else besides from family members can people learn traditional art forms of their culture?

Warriors: Navajo Code Talkers

by Kenji Kawano

FOCUS: How can an ancient language help change the modern world?

Background

One way an **ethnic** group **expresses** its identity is by speaking a common language. There are hundreds of American Indian languages. Many are spoken by only a few thousand people.

In World War I and World War II, some American Indian languages helped save lives and win battles. The United States used them to develop several codes that the enemy simply could not understand or break.

In 1918, during World War I, fourteen Choctaw men traveled to Europe to handle battlefield **communications**. Over field telephones, they **transmitted** messages in their own language.

Starting in 1942, during World War II, the idea of "code talking" was brought back. Choctaw and Comanche code talkers were sent to Europe. Navajo code talkers were **stationed** in parts of the Pacific.

Navajo Word	Original Meaning	Military Term
gini	chicken hawk	dive bomber
ne-as-jah	owl	observation plane
atsah	eagle	transport plane

Bronze sculpture of a Navajo Code Talker.

Navajos formed the largest group of code talkers. About 400 Navajos served in this top-secret program. These young men had to be in good physical condition, because they would become U.S. Marines. They also had to be **fluent** in both English and Navajo. The first group of 29 code talkers helped construct the code.

One problem was coming up with Navajo words for **military terms**. The solution was to use traditional words that had some kind of **logical** link with the military words. For example, words for naming various birds became the code words for different kinds of planes.

The word for "submarine" was *besh-lo*, or "iron fish." The word for "battleship" was *lo-tso*, or "whale." The word for "tank" was *chay-da-gahi*, or "tortoise."

The code also used Navajo words for alphabet letters to spell out any additional words that they needed to transmit.

To send a message, a code talker first **translated** it from English into the code. Another code talker then received the message and translated it back into English. This whole process might take less than half a minute.

Code talking was dangerous work. In the Pacific, Navajo code talkers talked by field telephone or walkie-talkie, often right on the battlefield. And they often did more than just report on troop movements—they might even direct those movements. In fact, the entire military operation to capture the island of Iwo Jima was directed by orders sent through code talking. ◆

Forty-five years after World War II, Kenji Kawano interviewed Navajo code talkers about their experiences. His work is especially meaningful. Kenji Kawano grew up in Japan. Japan fought against the United States in World War II. Now the two countries are friends.

"The Iwo Jima sand was ashy and hard to walk on, but I had to carry my radio and other equipment across it. I was sent to replace Pfc. Paul Kinlacheeny, who was killed on the beach."

—Thomas H. Begay

"We went to the front lines, most of the time carrying the radio, talking in our own language."

—Wilmer Belinda

"The shouts and screams of fellow soldiers were all around us, and we thought these were our last minutes on earth. Suddenly I heard a deep THUMP next to me, where my fellow code talker was lying, and I was scared I would be next. It took every ounce of courage I had to look over at him—I expected blood and guts. To my relief—and the relief of my foxhole partner—I saw one of the biggest bullfrogs I'd ever seen on my partner's back."

—Samuel Tom Holiday

“Throughout the war against the Japanese in the Pacific, we code talkers had to brush up on our codes at every opportunity. When the fighting got bad, words would fail us for a second; it was a good thing we have so many sounds in our language.”

—William Kien

“What I remember is carrying messages to the front line, night and day, for eighty-two days.”

—Deswood R. Johnson Sr.

“I walked the full length of Saipan and Tinian islands carrying maps and escorting replacements, prisoners, and farmers. At the same time, I operated the radio for the riflemen and was under fire myself while delivering messages.”

—Albert Smith

“Early one morning I went to the top deck of our ship and looked left and right. As far as I could see there were ships and I thought to myself ‘How can we lose this war?’”

—Samuel N. Tso

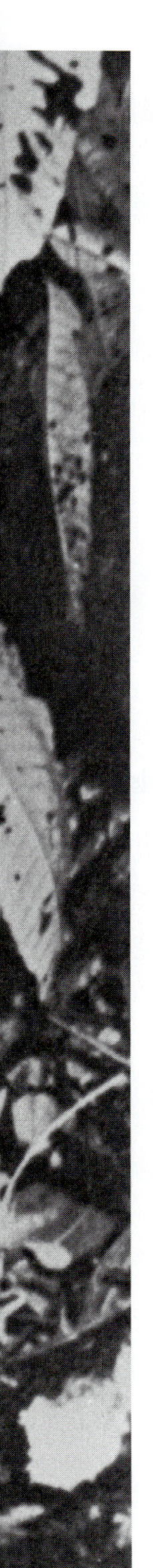

"One experience that stands out in my memory is being on combat patrol in Okinawa; our patrol was pinned down for two days—the antenna of my radio was shot off, but I was able to get a message through [in code] for reinforcements."

—Roy O. Hawthorne

"My language was my weapon."

—David E. Patterson

"I was seventeen and in high school at Fort Wingate in 1942. I wanted to protect my country. For thirty-two days, I was radio war chief at Iwo Jima. If I had the chance, I'd like to go back to some of the islands I was on during the war."

—Harold Y. Foster

"We moved from place to place with our radios. Even if we were scared, we just went on until we finished our duty."

—George Edward Yoe

STOP AND THINK

1. How did knowing their traditional language let these Marines help the United States?
2. What elements besides a person's culture can be important parts of his or her identity?

Reading Longer Words

In this unit you learned more about how to read longer words.

Step 1: Divide the word into parts.

Compound word?
Divide between the words.

Prefix?
Divide after the prefix.

Suffix?
Divide before the suffix.

VCCV letter pattern?
Divide between the consonants.

VCV letter pattern?
Divide before the consonant.
or
Divide after the consonant.

Step 2: Read each word part.

Step 3: Read the whole word.
Sound right? If not, try an alternative.

Ends in a consonant?
Try a short vowel sound.

Ends in a vowel?
Try a long vowel sound.

Has a VCe pattern?
Try a long vowel sound.

Ends in *-le, -al,* or *-el*?
Try dividing before the consonant preceding the *l*.

Divide the Words

dis/o/bey
en/tan/gle
em/brace
mov/able
im/pos/si/ble
en/code
trans/mit/tal
con/ver/sa/tion
spec/u/la/tion
com/mis/sion

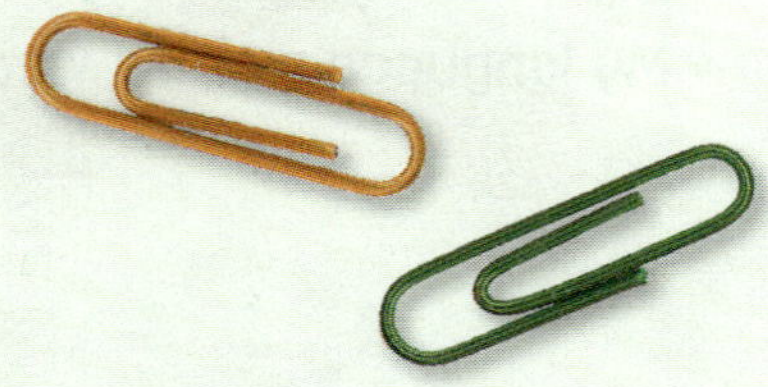

Read Word Parts		Read Whole Words
dis o bey	→	disobey
en code	→	encode
en tan gle	→	entangle
trans mit tal	→	transmittal
em brace	→	embrace
con ver sa tion	→	conversation
mov able	→	movable
spec u la tion	→	speculation
im pos si ble	→	impossible
com mis sion	→	commission

Read More Words

Use what you learned in Units 1–3 to read these words from the unit.

correctly	melodies	immigration	movements	logical
submarine	replacements	unusual	chocolate	wardrobe

Vocabulary and Morphology

Foreign Origins of English Words

Online dictionaries can be used to study the origins of words.

Words evolved over time from different languages. Read the following online dictionary entry. Look at the part that gives the origin of the word *china*.

> **chi·na** (chī nə) *n.* porcelain or ceramic ware, originally made in China [Persian *chīnī*]
>
> An online dictionary may also include this additional information:
>
> **Etymology:** from Chinese *Qin* to Persian *chīnī*
>
> **Word History:** The word *china* and the name of the country China are identical in spelling. The name of the country, however, comes from the Sanskrit word *cīnāh*, Chinese people. Both the Persian word *chīnī* and the Sanskrit word *cīnāh* go back to the Chinese word *Qin*, the name of a dynasty that ruled China from 221 to 206 B.C.E.

Etymology is the history of the word and its parts. The word *china* was first used in 1579.

The origins of a word can be given before or after the definition or definitions of the word, and terms such as *American Indian, French,* and *Italian* are sometimes abbreviated.

To find an online dictionary, open a search engine and look for *dictionary*. Some dictionaries do not include word origins at all. If the dictionary you find does not include word origins, try another dictionary. You can also find a dictionary in your school's Library Resource Center.

Regular Future Perfect Verbs & Possessive Nouns, Adjectives, and Pronouns

The Future Perfect Tense of Regular Verbs

A verb in the **future perfect** tense describes an action that will happen before another future action happens.

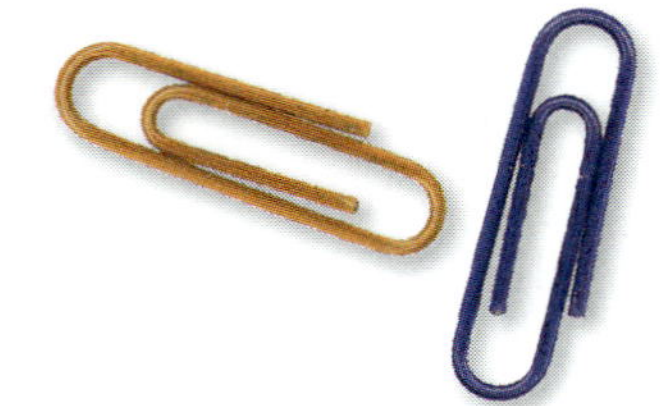

A regular verb in the future perfect tense—

- contains the helping verb *will have*
- contains a past participle (the *-ed* form)

Future Perfect Tense

	Singular	Plural
First Person	I will have cleaned the basement.	We will have cleaned the basement.
Second Person	You will have cleaned the basement.	You will have cleaned the basement.
Third Person	He will have cleaned the basement.	They will have cleaned the basement.

Look at how sentences in the simple future tense can be changed into the future perfect tense.

Simple Future	Future Perfect
By the time we are done, we will collect 1,000 cans of food for the food drive.	By the time we are done, we **will have collected** 1,000 cans of food for the food drive.
Before you fly home, you will visit all the major tourist attractions in New York.	Before you fly home, you **will have visited** all the major tourist attractions in New York.
I will review all the chapters of my English textbook in time for the exam.	I **will have reviewed** all the chapters of my English textbook in time for the exam.

Plural Nouns vs. Possessive Nouns

If you start with a singular noun, you can create one of three forms of the noun:

- the plural form of the noun (add *-s*)
- the singular possessive form of the noun (add *-'s*)
- the plural possessive form of the noun (add *-s'*)

Singular Noun	Add . . .	Make It . . .	Sentence
teacher	*-s*	plural	Our school has three sixth-grade **teachers**.
teacher	*-'s*	singular possessive	My **teacher's** desk is very tidy.
teacher	*-s'*	plural possessive	The **teachers'** meeting started at 6:30 P.M.

With words that do not form a regular plural that ends in *-s*, such as *children, men, women, mice*, and *geese*, add an apostrophe and *-s*.

the **children's** room   the car belonging to the children

Possessive Adjectives vs. Possessive Pronouns

A **possessive adjective** modifies a noun that is an item owned. A **possessive pronoun** replaces both the adjective and the noun.

Sentence	Possessive	Possessive Adjective or Possessie Pronoun?
My dentist wants to see me again in six months.	my	possessive adjective
Sarah likes her new dress, but **yours** is even prettier.	yours	possessive pronoun

Its vs. *It's*

Sometimes people confuse *its* with the word *it's*. The word *its* is a possessive adjective. *It's* is a contraction meaning "it is."

Our house is very old. **It's** on the National Register of Historic Places. (**It is** on the National Register of Historic Places.)

Our property is very large. **Its** backyard goes on for more than a mile. (**The backyard of our property** goes on for more than a mile.)

Write a Response to Literature

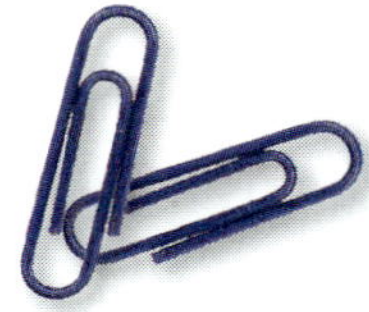

Organization is the road map that directs the reader through your writing. It gives an essay a sense of structure. A response to literature should begin with a clear statement of the writer's position on the text, and supporting details and examples should be presented in a logical, orderly fashion.

First Draft

You've read the final draft of "Where Courage Is King." Read the first draft.

He "didn't have an office, he didn't have many medical supplies."

When Ivarapa says a cheif with so many warriors must not be very strong we learn a lot about where he comes from. Ivarapa's people must give a pretty high value to individual courage and self-relience. Anywhere else in the world, having many warriors would just add to a leader's status. In Ivarapas world, a cheif who needs so many warriors to protect him is seen as week and afraid!

We know that Ivarapa's home is very remote from the rest of the world. Probably it takes great personnal courage to live there. Over time, Ivarapas people must have grown to value this quality—especially in their leaders. Dr. Hernandez is very self-relient. This may also be why they seem to like him so much and even why he finds it so easy to learn their language.

Clearly, we learn a lot about Ivarapa in just those few words!

there isn't "anything for hundreds of miles"

The forest he lives in is "outside the walls of civilization."

Writing Traits Checklist

Ideas
Does the response show full understanding of the story?

Organization
Does the writer provide good reasons for his or her response that include examples and details?

Sentence Fluency
Are the sentence beginnings varied?

Voice
Do facts and details support the position?

Word Choice
Does the writer choose clear, persuasive language?

Conventions
Are there any errors?

Final Draft

The writer made many revisions to complete this final draft.

When Ivarapa says a chief with so many warriors must not be very strong, we learn a lot about where he comes from. Ivarapa's people must give a pretty high value to individual courage and self-reliance. Anywhere else in the world, having many warriors would just add to a leader's status. In Ivarapa's world, a chief who needs so many warriors to protect him is seen as weak and afraid!

We know that Ivarapa's home is very remote from the rest of the world. There isn't "anything for hundreds of miles." The author tells us the forest Dr. Hernandez lives in is "outside the walls of civilization." Probably it takes great personal courage to live there. Over time, Ivarapa's people must have grown to value this quality—especially in their leaders. The fact that Dr. Hernandez must rely on his own skills when he is in the forest and "didn't have an office, he didn't have many medical supplies" shows that he has this quality of self-reliance, too. This may be why they seem to like him so much, and even why he finds it so easy to learn their language.

Clearly, we learn a lot about Ivarapa in just those few words!

UNIT 4 LOOK TO THE EAST

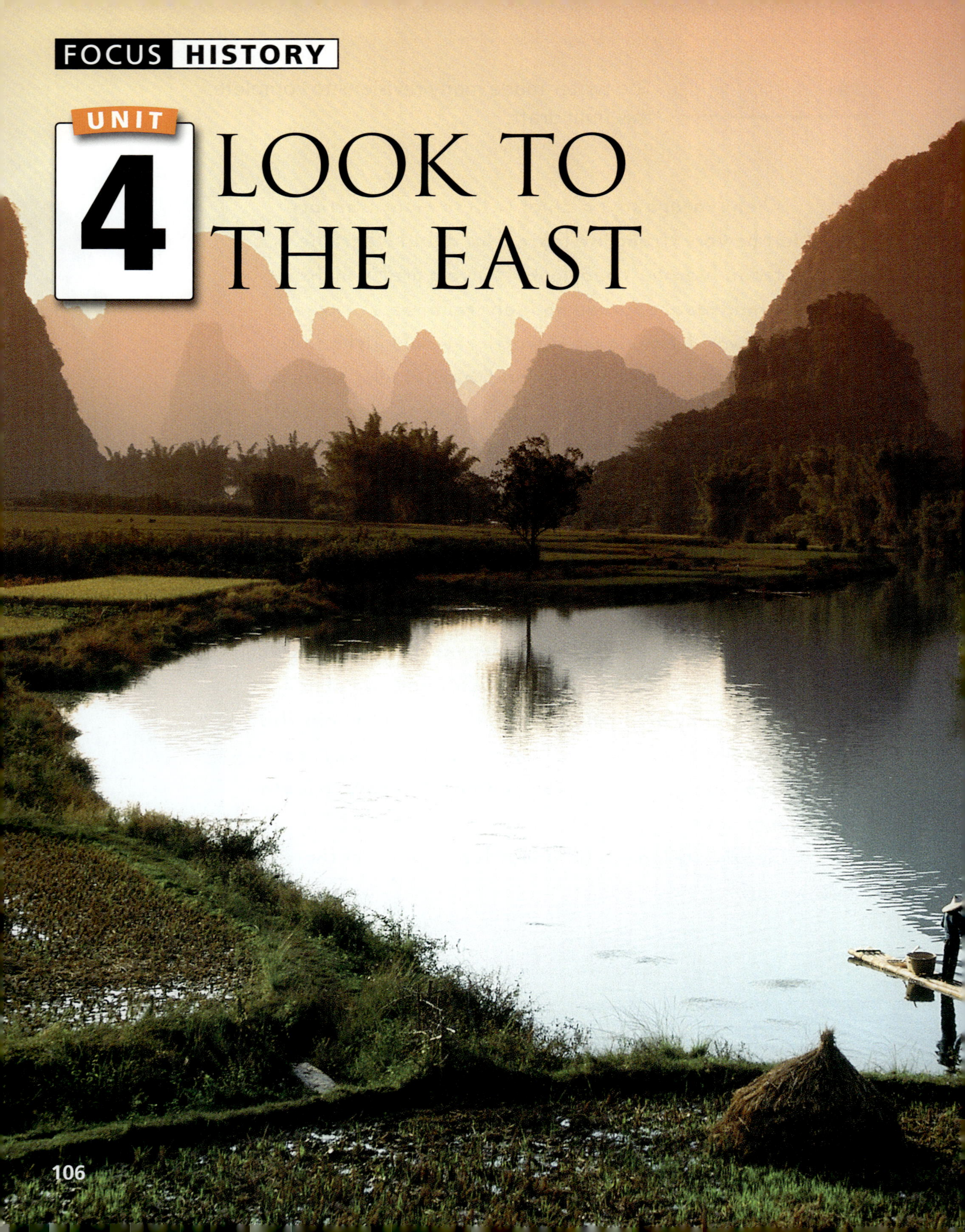

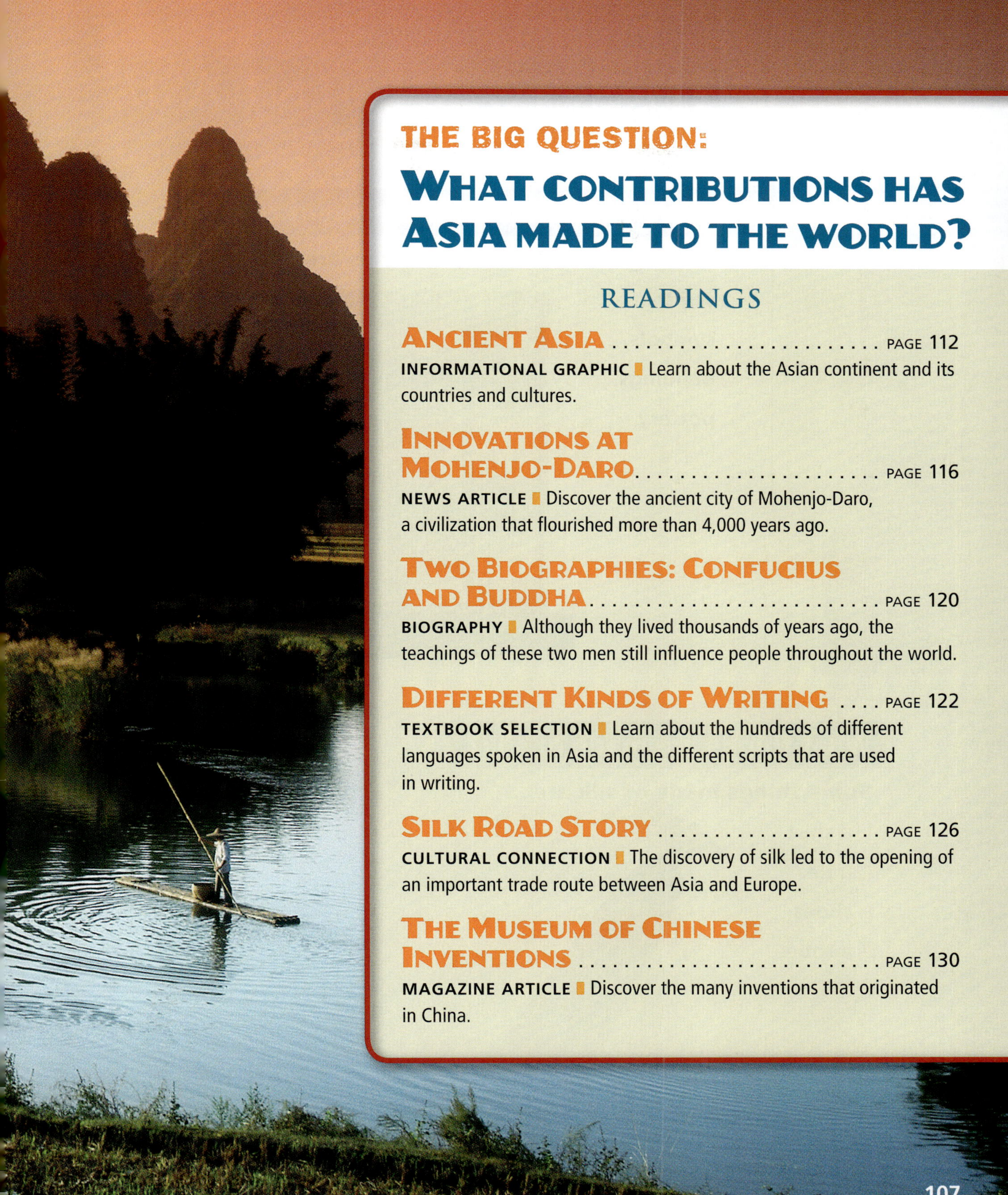

THE BIG QUESTION:

WHAT CONTRIBUTIONS HAS ASIA MADE TO THE WORLD?

READINGS

Look to Ancient Asia

What things are found in ancient cities?

The things found in ancient cities are...

- ☐ writing.
- ☐ symbols.
- ☐ buildings.
- ☐ pottery.

What things are made of silk?

Some things made of silk are...

- ☐ a shirt.
- ☐ a tie.
- ☐ shoes.
- ☐ a robe.

How many forms of writing (scripts) are found in Asia?

Asian writing uses...

- ☐ only one script.
- ☐ two scripts.
- ☐ four scripts.
- ☐ more than four scripts.

Which Asian teachers wanted to make the world a better place?

The Asian teachers who wanted to make the world a better place are...

- ☐ Buddha.
- ☐ Confucius.

What inventions originated in China?

The inventions that originated in China are...

- ☐ the kite.
- ☐ the abacus.
- ☐ rope.
- ☐ the wheelbarrow.

History Words

archaeology
collectively
decipher
flourish
globalization
linguistic
manner
populous
promote
scholar

archaeology

Archaeology is the study of ancient people and their cultures.

"I love archaeology because I love figuring out what life must have been like long ago."

collectively

When people work **collectively**, they work together.

"We get so much more done when we work collectively."

linguistic

The word **linguistic** refers to language.

"English has undergone many linguistic changes."

manner

Manner is a way of doing something.

"John wrote his name in a sloppy manner."

decipher

When you **decipher** something, you figure out its meaning.

"I'm amazed that anyone was able to decipher hieroglyphics."

flourish

To **flourish** means to grow and thrive.

"With care, sunlight, and water, a plant will flourish."

globalization

Globalization is a process by which a business becomes international.

"People around the world communicate easily because of the globalization of the telephone industry."

populous

A place is **populous** if many, many people live there.

"The city is a populous place."

promote

When you **promote** something, you work to make it happen.

"The two countries were against war and worked together to promote and encourage peace."

scholar

A **scholar** is someone who has much knowledge about a subject.

"An Asian scholar has great knowledge of Asia and its culture and history."

Ancient ASIA

This map of Asia shows some of the trade routes that were known as the Silk Road.

ASIA is the world's largest and most **populous** continent. It is a huge and varied region, with many countries and cultures. Today, Asia includes countries as distant geographically and culturally as Kazakhstan and Cambodia, Iran and Japan, Afghanistan and Singapore.

Some of the earliest and most sophisticated civilizations developed in Asia. For example, by 2500 B.C.E., a well-organized civilization prospered in the Indus Valley—located in part of present-day Pakistan and India. And more than 2,000 years later, the Han dynasty in China began an extraordinary period of advancement in technology and the arts. Asia was also the birthplace of some of the world's most important religions, including Hinduism, Buddhism, and the belief system known as Confucianism. Many technological, scientific, cultural and **linguistic** developments that originated in Asia traveled to the western world along the trade routes known **collectively** as the Silk Road. Today, **globalization** is bringing Asia and the West into even closer contact.

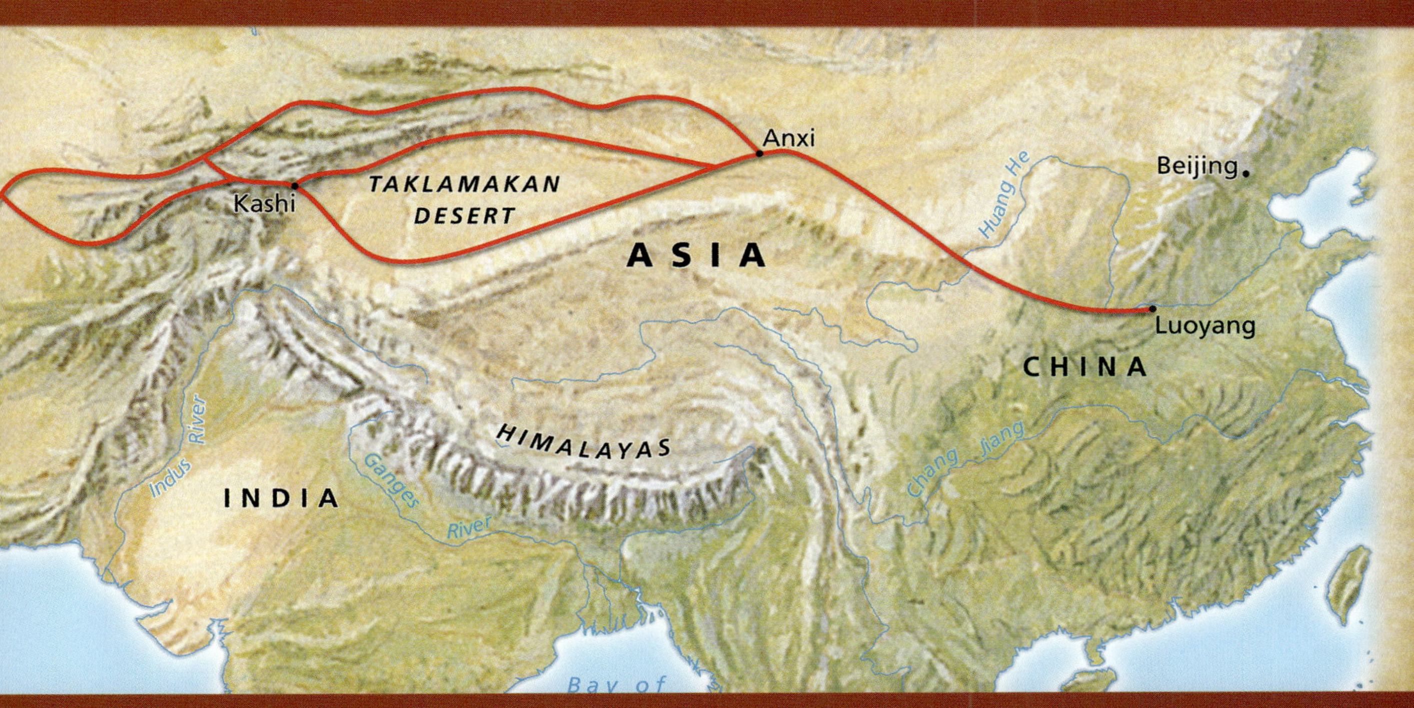

GET READY TO READ

Comprehension

TARGET SKILL **Compare and Contrast** Many selections include information that can be compared or contrasted. When you **compare** things, you show how they are the same. When you **contrast** them, you show how they are different. **Clue words and phrases** help tell you that things are being compared or contrasted.

The following paragraph, taken from the selection "Different Kinds of Writing," contains clue words and phrases that give hints about which things are being compared and contrasted.

Sometimes, one script is a clue phrase that tells you one script will be contrasted with one or more other scripts; the example of one such script is Devanagari.

This clue word lets you know that _some_ languages will be different from others.

Sometimes, one script is used to write several languages. For example, a script called Devanagari is used to write Sanskrit, Hindi, Marathi, and at least half a dozen other languages. Some scripts, however, are used to write only one language. For example, the Telugu script is used to write only the Telugu language. Some languages in India can be written in many different scripts. Although Sanskrit is now usually written with Devanagari, at different times it has been written with many other scripts. Finally, a few Indian languages are only spoken, with no written form at all.

The clue words _some_, _however_, and _only one_ let you know how these scripts are different from a script like Devanagari; the example of one such script is Telugu.

Here, a clue word and phrase contrast or tell about two different time periods.

Devanagari

used to write Sanskrit, Hindi, Marathi, and at least half a dozen other languages

Both

Indian scripts

Telugu

used to write only the Telugu language

The left part of the Venn diagram gives information that shows how Devanagari is different from Telugu. The right part of the diagram gives information that shows how Telugu is different from Devanagari. The center area shows how Telugu and Devanagari are the same.

Vowels	Hindi	Punjabi	Bengālī	Gujarātī
A	अ म	ਅ ਮ	অ ম	અ મ
Aa	आ मा	ਆ ਮਾ	আ মা	આ મા
I	इ मि	ਇ ਮਿ	ই মি	ઇ મિ
Ee	ई मी	ਈ ਮੀ	ঈ মী	ઈ
U	उ मु	ਉ ਮੁ	উ মু	ઉ
Oo	ऊ मू	ਊ ਮੂ	ঊ মূ	ઊ
E	ए मे	ਏ ਮੇ	এ মে	એ
Ey	ऐ मै	ਐ ਮੈ	ঐ মৈ	ઐ

TARGET STRATEGY **Evaluate** Ask yourself questions about the information in the chart. For example: *Which script is probably used by more people? What might happen to the Telugu script if fewer and fewer people speak Telugu?*

Innovations at Mohenjo-Daro

FOCUS: What do archaeologists know about Mohenjo-Daro?

Archaeologists are studying the remains of the ancient city of Mohenjo-Daro, located in present-day Pakistan. Mohenjo-Daro was part of the Indus Valley Civilization, which **flourished** between about 2500 and 1900 B.C.E., more than 4,000 years ago. The city was carefully planned and constructed, with straight streets

▼ The Great Bath

and many two-story brick houses. A good number of the houses had their own wells, from which residents could draw water. Some houses had indoor bathing areas, and a few even had a kind of toilet. Houses and streets had covered drains and sewers to carry away dirty water and waste. For such an ancient civilization, Mohenjo-Daro seems to have been clean, tidy, and well-organized.

Archaeologists can only guess about the **manner** in which the Great Bath at Mohenjo-Daro was used. Most think it was for rituals and ceremonies. It was about 39 feet long, 23 feet wide, and 8 feet deep. A layer of sealant under the brick floor made the bath watertight.

Scholars have to guess about the bath's purpose because they don't know much about the religion or rulers of Mohenjo-Daro. They have found no evidence that the rulers **promoted** warfare. Trade and agriculture, on the other hand, were key parts of the culture.

The writing used in Mohenjo-Daro—found on tablets, stamps, and seals like the ones shown here—has not yet been **deciphered**. Maybe you can help figure out what these signs mean.

▲ Many seals found at Mohenjo-Daro look like this one. The writing is backward so that when the seal was pressed into wet clay, the writing in the clay would appear correctly.

STOP AND THINK

1. What do you think life was like at Mohenjo-Daro?
2. Why do archaeologists think Mohenjo-Daro was a planned city?

Your Turn

Use Your Words:

despite	originate
dialect	philosophy
disciple	pillar
enlighten	privilege
generally	rank
haggle	relatively
horizontal	standardize
impact	unique
inscription	unravel
moral	vertical

- Read the words on the list.
- Read the dialogue. Find the words.

MORE ACTIVITIES

1. Make a Chart

Graphic Organizer

How are an ancient city and your town alike? How are they different? Write your ideas in the chart.

Alike	Different

2. You Are the Author

Writing

Imagine you are part of a team. You are working in the ruins of an ancient city. Write a diary entry telling about your day.

3. Play "What Is It?"

Listening and Speaking

Make a sketch of something you might find in an ancient city. Challenge your partner to ask up to six yes-or-no questions to try and figure out what the object is. Then change places.

4. Decipher the Inscription

Writing

Number each letter of the alphabet from 1 to 26. Write a message using the numbers instead of letters. Trade messages with a partner. Decipher the new message.

5. Time Travel

Speaking and Listening

Suppose you could travel back in time to an ancient city. Think of one thing you would teach the people to do. Share your idea with your partner.

6. Make a List

Vocabulary

List eight things you see that are in a vertical position. List eight things you see that are in a horizontal position. Share your list with the class.

Vertical	Horizontal

Two Biographies: Confucius and Buddha

FOCUS: Who were the men behind Confucianism and Buddhism?

Confucius and Buddha were real people who were born about 2,500 years ago. They lived far apart and never knew of each other. Both were teachers who believed that the world would be a better place if people lived according to certain ideas. The ideas of these men have had a huge influence on the lives of people in Asia. Buddha's followers developed the Buddhist religion, while the followers of Confucius **promoted** a system of thought called Confucianism.

Confucius and Confucianism

Confucius was a **scholar**, teacher, and **philosopher**. He was never very rich or powerful; he never held a high position in government. Nevertheless, he became one of the most educated and respected men of his day.

When Confucius was born, Chinese states were frequently at war. Their rulers were often dishonest and oppressive. Confucius believed that the problems of government, society, and individuals could be solved if each person became educated and took responsibility to live and act in a better manner.

Confucius believed that everyone had the right to an education. He was the first private teacher in China. People sent their sons to study with him. Over the years, he taught thousands of young men. After Confucius died, his followers spread his ideas, which

Confucius is believed to have lived from 551 to 479 B.C.E.

became known as Confucianism. Most of what we know about Confucius's life and teachings comes from books written by his followers. Historians can't say for sure whether these books recount exactly what Confucius said, thought, or did. But we do know that the ideas of Confucianism have had a lasting **impact** on China and other Asian societies.

Buddha and Buddhism

REREAD

Compare + Contrast

Compare and contrast Buddha's lifestyle before and after he turned 29.

Buddha was born a Hindu prince named Siddhartha Gautama. He lived a **privileged**, pampered, and protected life until he was 29 years old. Then he witnessed old age, illness, poverty, and death for the first time. Siddhartha gave up his wealth and position and set out to try to understand the meaning of life. He lived as a beggar, wandering the countryside.

But his suffering did not bring **enlightenment**. Siddharta came to believe in a "middle way"—a balance between luxury and self-denial. When he began to teach what he had learned he was called Buddha, which means "enlightened one."

Buddha is believed to have lived from 563 to 483 B.C.E.

Buddha believed people suffered because they wanted things they could not have. His teachings described a way of life to end this wanting. As a great teacher, he soon had many **disciples**. After his death, Buddha's disciples, or monks, collected his teachings. They continued to develop his ideas, spreading Buddhism through much of Asia.

STOP AND THINK

1. What were the differences between the lives of Confucius and Buddha?
2. How do you think Confucius or Buddha would react to the modern world?

Different Kinds of Writing

FOCUS: How has writing evolved in Asia?

Scripts of India

Can you read what the tablet to the right says? No? Well, don't worry. No one else can either. The tablet was found at Mohenjo-Daro, one of the cities of the ancient Indus Valley civilization, which **flourished** between 2500 and 1900 B.C.E. **Archaeologists** are sure that the marks and shapes on the tablet are a kind of writing. If they're correct, the Indus script is one of the earliest forms of writing ever used. More than 4,000 objects with this writing have been discovered. The problem is, no one has been able to figure out what the writing says. This adds another layer of mystery to a civilization that disappeared almost 4,000 years ago. If **linguists** or archaeologists ever crack the code, we will surely learn a lot about the Indus Valley culture.

Writing from Mohenjo-Daro

Later, in the third century B.C.E., King Ashoka ruled most of what is now India, Pakistan, and Bangladesh. He had **inscriptions** carved on stone **pillars** and rocks throughout his kingdom. The inscriptions often gave **moral** advice to his subjects. Sometimes they were carved in two scripts so that people who knew either language could read what was written. The scripts chosen for a particular pillar or rock depended on what languages the local people could read. For example, at the eastern edge of Ashoka's kingdom was inscribed in Greek and Aramaic, a Middle Eastern language. The educated people in that region could read those scripts.

One of the most important scripts used on Ashoka's pillars and rocks was Brahmi. This ancient writing system was used for about 1,000 years, and most of the dozens of modern scripts in India today evolved from Brahmi.

Today, people in different parts of India speak many different languages. There are 15 or so main languages, but hundreds of other languages and **dialects**. More than 50 Indian languages are taught in schools! And to make things more complicated, these languages are written with many different scripts.

REREAD

Compare + Contrast

Compare the number of languages taught in American schools to the number of languages taught in an Indian school.

Sometimes, one script is used to write several languages. For example, a script called Devanagari is used to write Sanskrit, Hindi, Marathi, and at least half a dozen other languages. Some scripts, however, are used to write only one language. For example, the Telugu script is used to write only the Telugu language. Some languages in India can be written in many different scripts. Although Sanskrit is now usually written with Devanagari, at different times it has been written with many other scripts. Finally, a few Indian languages are only spoken, with no written form at all.

One of Ashoka's pillars

Some Indian scripts

Vowels	Hindi	Punjabi	Bengāli	Gujarātī
A	अ म	ਅ ਮ	অ ম	અ મ
Aa	आ मा	ਆ ਮਾ	আ মা	આ મા
I	इ मि	ਇ ਮਿ	ই মি	ઇ મિ
Ee	ई मी	ਈ ਮੀ	ঈ মী	ઈ મી
U	उ मु	ਉ ਮੁ	উ মু	ઉ મુ
Oo	ऊ मू	ਊ ਮੂ	ঊ মূ	ઊ
E	ए मे	ਏ ਮੇ	এ মে	એ
Ey	ऐ मै	ਐ ਮੈ	ঐ মৈ	ઐ

Writing in China

Oracle-bone writing

Scratched onto tortoise shells and animal bones, the earliest writing in China **originated** about 1300 B.C.E. The writing is known as "oracle-bone script" because the shells and bones were used in ceremonies that were meant to foresee the future. Soothsayers heated the oracle bones until they cracked. They then made predictions based on the shape and placement of the cracks.

In the nineteenth century, people thought pieces of burnt and scratched bone were from dragons. They believed the bones had special curing powers, so they used them in medicines.

In 1899, two **scholars** came across some oracle bones. They realized the scratches were writing. Since then, over 100,000 pieces of oracle bones have been found. More importantly, the oracle bone script has been fully **deciphered**.

Some of the characters used to represent words in oracle-bone script are similar to characters used in modern Chinese writing. In the more than 3,000 years since oracle-bone script was used, many more forms of writing have developed in China. Several are still in use today. Chinese is considered the oldest written language in continuous use.

Rulers and governments of China have tried to make the Chinese writing system easier to read and write. They have **standardized** and simplified the written characters. **Despite** their efforts, Chinese is still a difficult written language to learn. Most characters have two parts—one that shows the meaning of the word and another that tells how to pronounce it. Together, these two parts help the reader figure out what the character is. But since the language doesn't have an alphabet based on sounds, students **generally** have to learn and remember each character separately.

Traditional Chinese was written **vertically**, in columns that were read from top to bottom, starting with the column on the right and moving left. Old Chinese also used little or no punctuation. Today, much Chinese is written using the Western system of **horizontal** lines, reading from left to right. And modern Chinese writing often includes punctuation.

REREAD

Compare + Contrast

Compare traditional Chinese writing and modern Chinese writing.

It takes a working knowledge of about 3,000 characters to be able to read a newspaper in Chinese. There are about 49,000 separate characters in Chinese. That's a lot to remember!

STOP AND THINK

1. What is a script?
2. Do you think learning to write Chinese would be harder than learning to write English? Why or why not?

Chinese calligraphy

CULTURAL CONNECTION

SILK ROAD STORY

FOCUS: Why was the Silk Road important?

Here's a little riddle.
Answer if you can.
I'll tell you of my story,
You tell me who I am.

Legend has it I was invented when a cocoon fell into the teacup of a Chinese empress. As she pulled it out, a long thread **unraveled**. Seeing how strong and shiny the thread was, she decided to weave it into cloth. This happened around 3000 B.C.E., or so the story goes. I became a favorite of the emperor and his family, and later of high-**ranking** nobles and officials. Common people could be punished if they were found wearing me.

The Chinese realized I was an excellent trade item. I was **relatively** light, not breakable, beautiful (of course), and **unique**. They were the only ones in the world who knew how to make me. They guarded their secret for 3,000 years. People outside China were willing to pay a lot for something so special. Big rolls of me were loaded onto camels and sent west. I became such an important trade item along the many roads from China to the West that the route was named after me.

Camel caravan

Okay, you may have guessed my name by now. I'm silk, and the trade route was called the Silk Road.

Now you know my name
And understand my fame.
Hear of places I've been through,
And people that I knew.

The Silk Road began in the ancient Chinese capital of Chang'an (called Xian today). By about 200 B.C.E., goods were traveling all the way from China to Persia and Europe. But one trader didn't carry me the whole 5,000 miles. It was more like a relay race, with different merchants each taking me part of the way, in stages. I got used to being **haggled** over, bartered, bought and sold, and handed off from one peddler to the next. I might pass through half a dozen hands along the many years of one journey.

Signpost in the Gobi Desert

I usually traveled in large baskets strapped to the side of a camel. It was too costly to make the long journey with anything but the most valuable merchandise. So I shared the same space with items such as tea, exotic spices, furs, porcelain, and paper. In the opposite direction, baskets might be filled with sacks of gold coins, precious gems, ivory, or colored glass.

Musical instruments that would have been carried by traders on the Silk Road

The farthest west I usually went was Rome. You should have seen how those rich Romans competed to buy the best pieces of me! They say Emperor Heliogabalus (218–222 C.E.) would wear nothing but silk. Over the centuries, the Roman demand for silk kept growing, until even the common people were wearing me.

Traveling on the Silk Road was dangerous. Bandits were common. It was best to travel when there was peace and a strong central government to protect my traders. Perhaps the best years were during the Mogul Empire (1206–1368 C.E.), when the government controlled and patrolled the entire trade route.

Even without bandits or war, it was a tough journey. There were deserts and mountain ranges to cross. The merchants could never have managed without camels. A camel can carry as much as 400 pounds, traveling 15 to 30 miles a day. It's not fussy about eating or drinking on a regular schedule, and it doesn't mind hot or cold weather. You might see caravans of 300 camels traveling together for safety and company.

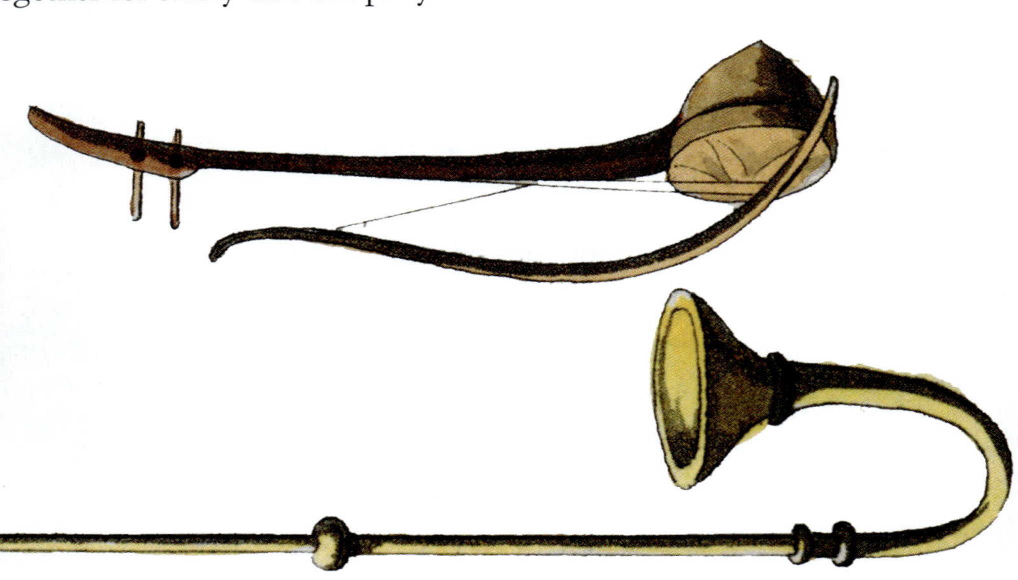

Those camels took us to some wonderful cities such as Samarkand, Bactria, Tashkent, and Khotan. In the cities, silk merchants found a mix of peoples, cultures, and languages. We would stop to rest the camels and get new supplies. In the evenings, all the traders would gather around a fire. The smells of Chinese, Persian, and other foods drifted in the air. Sometimes there was music or dancing, with a variety of instruments and dancing styles.

Chinese silk dress

You see that I was not the only thing that traveled along the dusty trails of the Silk Road—the traders also carried ideas. They spread customs about how to dress, cook, build houses, dance, and play music. They spread languages and scripts to write them. They spread inventions such as paper, the compass, and gunpowder. And they spread scientific and technological ideas.

At times, the armies of expanding empires moved along the Silk Road, too. We also saw many people carrying ideas about new religions. There were Buddhist monks, Christian missionaries, Hindu holy men, Jews, Zoroastrians, Muslims, and disciples of Confucius.

REREAD

Compare + Contrast

Compare and contrast the types of ideas that traveled along the Silk Road.

Even though I'm still around and still being produced in China, I don't get traded along the Silk Road much now. By the 1700s, ships had replaced camels as the way to trade goods from East to West.

STOP AND THINK

1. Why were only the most valuable goods carried in the camel caravans?
2. What do you think was the most important thing that traders carried on the Silk Road?

The Museum of CHINESE Inventions

FOCUS: What are some of China's contributions to science and technology?

MUSEUM GUIDE: Greetings! Welcome to our exhibit of milestones in the history of invention. What do these inventions all have in common? They all come from ancient China.

China is the home of many important inventions. Some of them were figured out so long ago that nobody knows their exact beginning. In history and legend, Chinese emperors are said to have encouraged scientists and given them a free hand to work out their ideas. That's probably why there were so many groundbreaking Chinese inventions. A few of these inventions were discovered independently in other countries, too. But most of them were China's gift to the rest of the world.

Quick—do you know where you're standing? Which direction are you going next? Once, people had to use the sun or the stars to find north, south, east, or west. A lot of people—and ships—got lost on cloudy nights. The first Chinese compasses used a magnetic stone that always points the same way. This kind of compass probably dates from about the second century B.C.E. The Chinese took several more centuries to perfect this important invention.

This compass of today uses a lightweight magnet that can easily pivot around the dial.

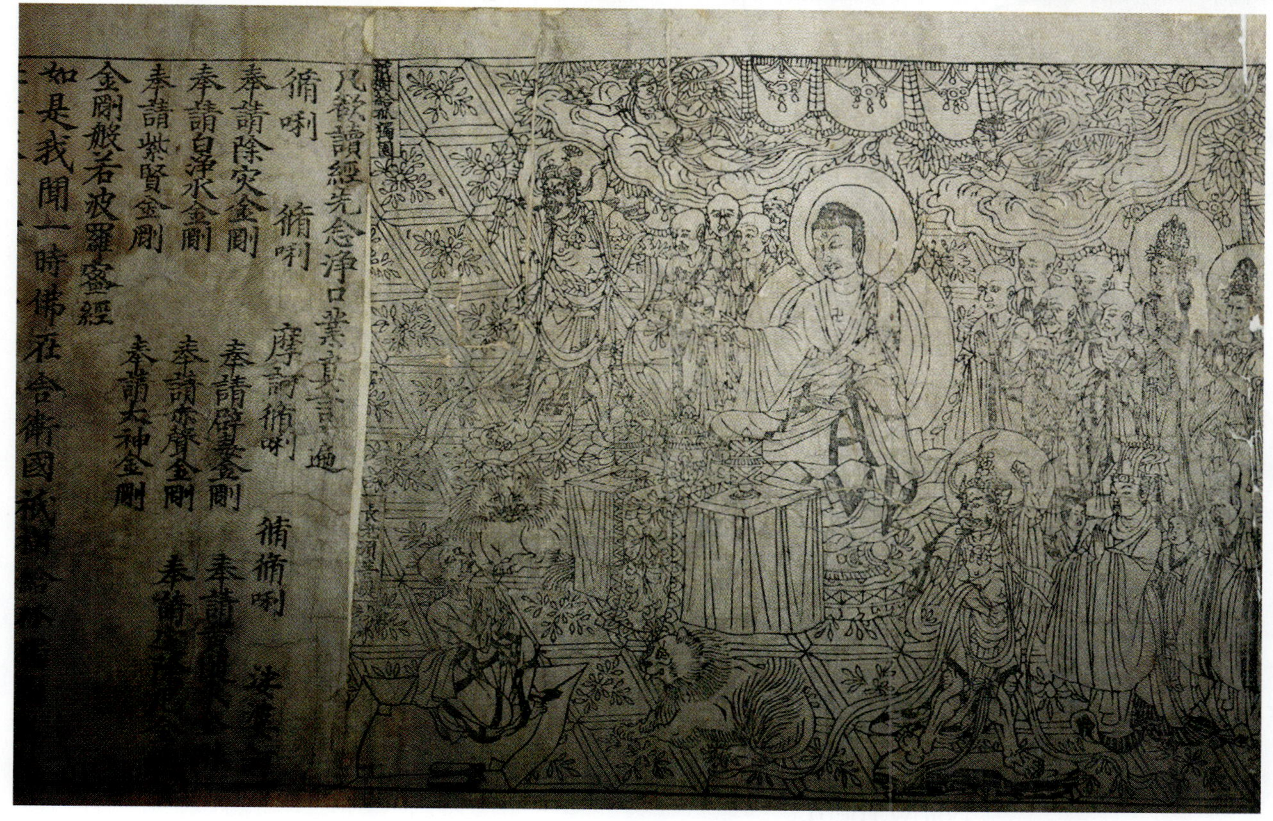

This book was published in about 868 C.E. It is the oldest known book made by a printing method instead of written out by hand.

Whenever you read a book or write on a sheet of paper, you're using Chinese inventions. According to Chinese legend, paper was invented by a man named Ts'ai Lin in 105 C.E. The earliest form of the printing press was a kind of block printing used in China by about 850 C.E. Block printing could make the same page over and over. This made it possible to make multiple copies of a book more quickly and cheaply. Chinese block printing methods led to the invention of the printing press in Europe in the fifteenth century.

For years there has been a worldwide argument over who invented noodles. Italy, the Arab world, and China all claim to be the home of pasta. Now archaeologists have found the oldest noodle dish so far. They dug up a pot of noodles in China that had been buried by an earthquake about 4,000 years ago. So far, nobody in Italy or Arabia has been able to top this.

Modern noodles like these don't look much different from the noodles of thousands of years ago.

The Chinese were flying kites as early as 500 B.C.E. Don't think of these just as toys. The Chinese used them for military communication. Also, the technology used in kites led the way to the invention of gliders and parachutes. That's pretty good for a kid's toy!

The wheelbarrow doesn't seem very exciting. But it was the first way that one or two people could move a heavy load without the help of an ox or other strong animal. The Chinese were using an early kind of wheelbarrow by the first century C.E. Wheelbarrows weren't used in Europe before the eleventh century C.E.

Kite flying is still a popular sport throughout Asia.

Today, scientists use a seismograph to give information about the strength and location of an earthquake. The Chinese had the earliest known earthquake detector, in about 130 B.C.E. Each bronze dragon held a ball in its mouth. When a quake happened, the dragons would drop the balls into the mouths of the frogs sitting below them.

This modern wheelbarrow doesn't look very different from the first Chinese wheelbarrows.

You can see the dragons and the frogs on this ancient earthquake detector.

This is what the first calculators looked like! The abacus was a wooden frame with rows of beads on thin metal rods. They helped people compute large numbers. The abacus may have been invented in China as early as 3000 B.C.E. That's about 5,000 years ago!

This modern abacus doesn't look very different from ancient ones.

Just about every culture figured out how to make pottery. Pottery is made of clay, baked until it becomes hard. Porcelain was a step up from regular pottery. It was unusually thin, hard, and smooth. The Chinese created an early kind of porcelain before 200 B.C.E. They used a very fine clay called kaolin to make porcelain. Kaolin is found in only a few places in the world. Chinese potters also figured out how to fire their clay at an unusually high temperature, and to fire it with the glaze already on. Today, we have a name for fine porcelain. We call it china. By now, you can guess why.

The incredible inventions you see here are just the tip of the iceberg! Chinese inventors also came up with silk, the stirrup, matches, the umbrella, paper money, and many other objects.

Artists in China made porcelain objects like this one hundreds of years ago.

STOP AND THINK

1. How is a modern calculator different from an abacus? How are they alike?
2. Which of these inventions are most important to your life? Why?

Reading Longer Words

In this unit you learned more about how to read longer words.

Step 1: Divide the word into parts.

Compound word?
Divide between the words.

Prefix?
Divide after the prefix.

Suffix?
Divide before the suffix.

VCCV letter pattern?
Divide between the consonants.

VCV letter pattern?
Divide before the consonant.
or
Divide after the consonant.

Step 2: Read each word part.

Step 3: Read the whole word.
Sound right? If not,
try an alternative.

Ends in a consonant?
Try a short vowel sound.

Ends in a vowel?
Try a long vowel sound.

Has a VCe pattern?
Try a long vowel sound.

Ends in consonant + *-le, -al, -el*?
Try dividing before the consonant preceding the *l*.

Has a syllable with vowel + *r*?
May change the sound of the vowel.

Divide the Words

gen/er/a/tion	re/hearse
in/tern/ship	per/mit/ted
dic/ta/tor/ship	rel/e/vant
re/pug/nant	hap/pi/ly
sum/mar/y	a/gil/i/ty

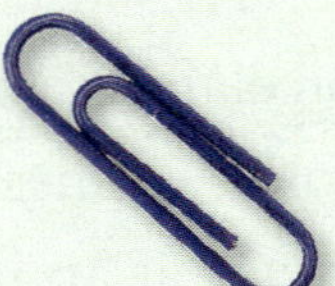

Read Word Parts	Read Whole Words
gen er a tion →	generation
re hearse →	rehearse
in tern ship →	internship
per mit ted →	permitted
dic ta tor ship →	dictatorship
rel e vant →	relevant
re pug nant →	repugnant
hap pi ly →	happily
sum mar y →	summary
a gil i ty →	agility

Read More Words

Use what you learned in Units 1–4 to read these words from the unit.

decipher	promote	globalization	enlightenment	inscription
generally	unraveled	merchants	inventions	wheelbarrows

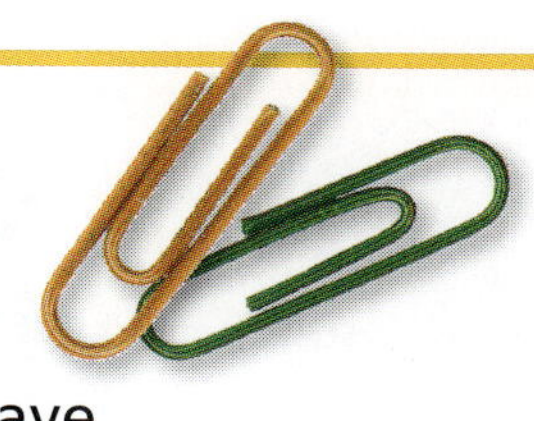

Vocabulary

Shades of Meaning

Most words that seem to have the same meaning actually have meanings that differ slightly from each other. This is referred to as *shades of meaning*.

Writers carefully choose the words they use, paying attention to the "shades of meaning" between words, so that their writing says exactly what they intend it to say.

There are many different words that mean *angry*.

angry						
mad	irate	upset	annoyed	irritated	furious	raging

The word the writer chooses depends upon what he or she is trying to express or what kind of character he or she is trying to portray.

There is no single correct word; the word you choose depends on what you want to convey in your writing. Read the following sentences. Think about how the word choice affects the meaning of the sentence and the character of Sarah.

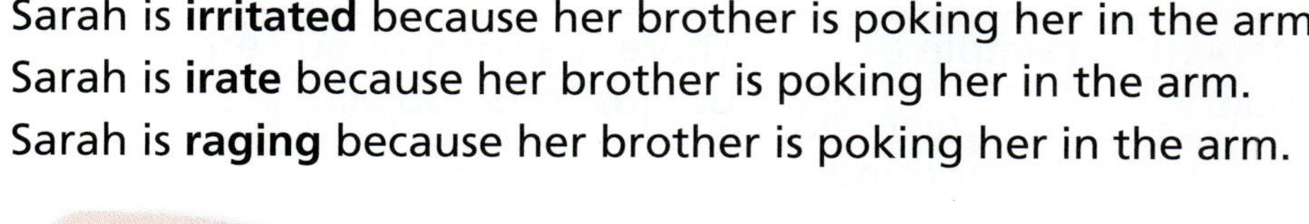

Sarah is **irritated** because her brother is poking her in the arm.
Sarah is **irate** because her brother is poking her in the arm.
Sarah is **raging** because her brother is poking her in the arm.

Compound Sentences & Independent Clauses

Compound Sentences

A **compound sentence** is made up of two **independent clauses** joined by a **coordinating conjunction**. An independent clause has a subject and a verb and can stand on its own, but it is part of another sentence. A coordinating conjunction (like *and, but,* and *or*) links the two clauses of a compound sentence.

Be careful! A simple sentence may have a **compound** (more than one) **subject, object,** or **verb**, but that doesn't make it a compound sentence. A compound sentence must have two independent clauses. In the following chart, all subjects are underlined, and all verbs are in red.

Sentence	Compound or Simple?	Why?
Jo **listened** to the speaker, and she **applauded** afterward.	compound	There are two independent clauses.
My mother and father **celebrated** their twentieth anniversary last month.	simple	There is a compound subject but just one verb.
The tennis player **served** and **volleyed** the ball.	simple	There is a compound verb but just one subject.
The old building **will be renovated**, or it **will be destroyed**.	compound	There are two independent clauses.

The Relationship Between Independent Clauses

In a compound sentence, the kind of conjunction you use signals how the two independent clauses are related.

Conjunction	What It Signals
and	signals two similar ideas
or	signals a choice (one or the other)
but	signals two contrasting ideas

First Independent Clause	Second Independent Clause	How They Are Related	Conjunction	Compound Sentence
The main course was delicious.	The dessert was wonderful.	similar ideas	and	The main course was delicious, **and** the dessert was wonderful.
The car engine can be rebuilt.	It can be scrapped.	a choice	or	The car engine can be rebuilt, **or** it can be scrapped.
I want to be in the school play.	I have trouble memorizing lines.	contrasting ideas	but	I want to be in the school play, **but** I have trouble memorizing lines.

Diagramming Compound Sentences

A diagram of the compound sentence below shows that there are two independent clauses related by a coordinating conjunction.

The main course was delicious, and the dessert was wonderful.

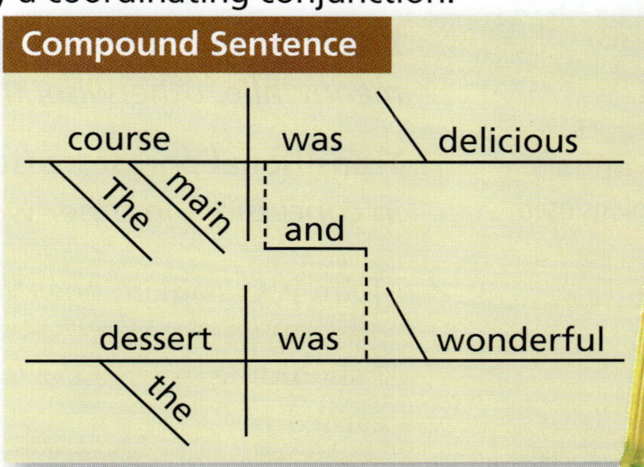

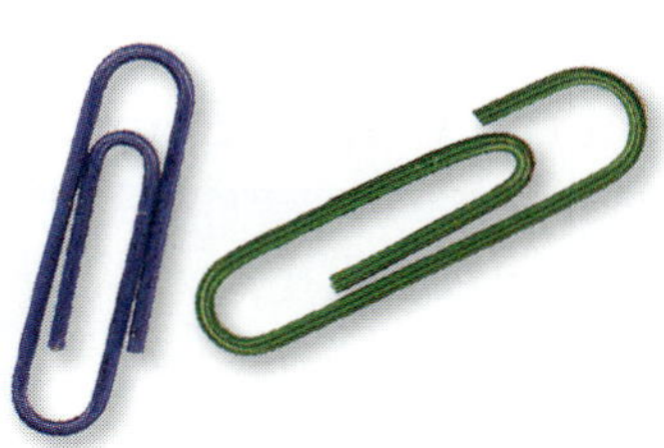

Using Semicolons

Semicolons are used to connect **independent clauses.** An independent clause is a group of words that could stand as a complete sentence by itself.

Semicolons are only used to connect independent clauses when there is no coordinating conjunction (for example, *and*).

Sam has lived in Rome all his life; he seems to love it there.

Sam has lived in Rome all his life, and he seems to love it there.

When we use a semicolon, we're suggesting that there is a relationship between the two clauses. Usually, you can tell the relationship from the context.

Cause	We have a championship game next week; **therefore**, we have extra practices this week.
Contrast	My family has always had dogs; **however**, we decided to get a guinea pig this time.
Cause/Effect	The camera didn't work at all; **as a result**, I returned it to the store.

Semicolons are often used between independent clauses when there is an adverb or a transitional phrase. These can be used to explain the relationship between the two clauses.

Adverbs: *also, anyway, besides, finally, however, meanwhile, otherwise, therefore*

Transitional phrases: *after all, as a result, for example, in conclusion, in other words*

John is Canadian; however, he lives in the United States.

I should be given a car for graduation; after all, I've earned it!

Writing Traits Checklist

☑ **Punctuation and Capitalization**

Are semicolons used correctly?

Only one sentence of each pair is written correctly.

1. a. Michael got a raise this week, in fact, his salary doubled.
   b. Michael got a raise this week; in fact, his salary doubled.
2. a. Soon-Yi practices every day; as a result, she's an amazing singer.
   b. Soon-Yi practices every day, as a result, she's an amazing singer.
3. a. Three countries were negotiating however; only two signed the treaty.
   b. Three countries were negotiating; however, only two signed the treaty.
4. a. Mahalia is going to Paris, because she's always dreamed of going.
   b. Mahalia is going to Paris; because she's always dreamed of going.
5. a. This project appears impossible; nevertheless, it can be done.
   b. This project appears impossible; nevertheless; it can be done.
6. a. I do want to go out tonight; on the other hand, I have so much work to do.
   b. I do want to go out tonight, on the other hand, I have so much work to do.
7. a. Lenore was washing the dishes, meanwhile, Frederique was dancing.
   b. Lenore was washing the dishes; meanwhile, Frederique was dancing.
8. a. Sophie stays up too late, she's afraid; she's going to miss something.
   b. Sophie stays up too late; she's afraid she's going to miss something.
9. a. I make toast every morning, and my brother eats it all.
   b. I make toast every morning; and my brother eats it all.
10. a. I love this house; and I have no plans to move.
    b. I love this house, and I have no plans to move.

UNIT 5

EARTH ON THE MOVE

THE BIG QUESTION:

HOW DOES THE MOVING EARTH AFFECT US?

READINGS

LOOK AT EARTH

Look at Earth. What can you see?

When I look at Earth, I can see...

- ☐ a mountain.
- ☐ a valley.
- ☐ a river.
- ☐ an ocean.

What is Earth covered with?

Earth is covered with...

- ☐ only land.
- ☐ only water.
- ☐ land and water.
- ☐ only mountains.

What is a continent?

A continent is...

- ☐ a planet.
- ☐ a large body of water.
- ☐ a big city.
- ☐ a large body of land.

What events show that Earth is a constantly changing planet?

Events that show Earth is constantly changing are...

- ☐ volcanic eruptions.
- ☐ snowstorms.
- ☐ tornados.
- ☐ earthquakes.

Where do earthquakes and volcanic eruptions occur?

Earthquakes and volcanic eruptions occur...

- ☐ on land.
- ☐ on mountains.
- ☐ in valleys.
- ☐ under the ocean.
- ☐ on land and under the ocean.

Science Words

- disturbance
- fatality
- fault
- magnitude
- prone
- stationary
- subsequent
- tectonic
- temporary
- tsunami

disturbance

A **disturbance** is an event that interrupts or unsettles.

"When Earth's crust moves it can cause a disturbance, such as a tremor or an earthquake."

fatality

A **fatality** is a death resulting from an accident or disaster.

"A broken beam on the Ferris wheel resulted in one fatality."

stationary

Stationary means to be unable to move.

"A house is stationary, but a motor home can travel anywhere."

subsequent

Subsequent means coming after or following in time or order.

"After making the first free throw, Jill was awarded a subsequent attempt."

fault

A **fault** is a crack in Earth's crust caused by the shifting of tectonic plates.

"Even though we were many miles from the fault, the earthquake still knocked us off our feet."

magnitude

Magnitude is a measurement of size or strength.

"The earthquake had such a low magnitude that we could hardly feel it."

prone

To be **prone** to is to have a tendency toward, or to be likely to happen.

"Barry was prone to knee injuries while playing football."

tectonic

Tectonic is a word that refers to the structure and movement of Earth's crust.

"Today we learned that all of Earth's crust, including its lands and oceans, rests on tectonic plates that are constantly moving."

temporary

Temporary means to last for only a certain amount of time.

"Substitute teachers are only temporary, and usually the regular teacher returns within a day or two."

tsunami

A **tsunami** is a huge wave caused by an underwater earthquake or volcanic eruption.

"The tsunami was over 40 feet tall, but thankfully the beach was empty when it hit."

READ TOGETHER

The Puzzle of PLANET EARTH

How Hard Is the Puzzle?

Take the same bike ride each day, and you'll think that the surface of our planet doesn't change. Fall off your bike, and you'll be convinced that Earth is solid to the core. Well, take a look.

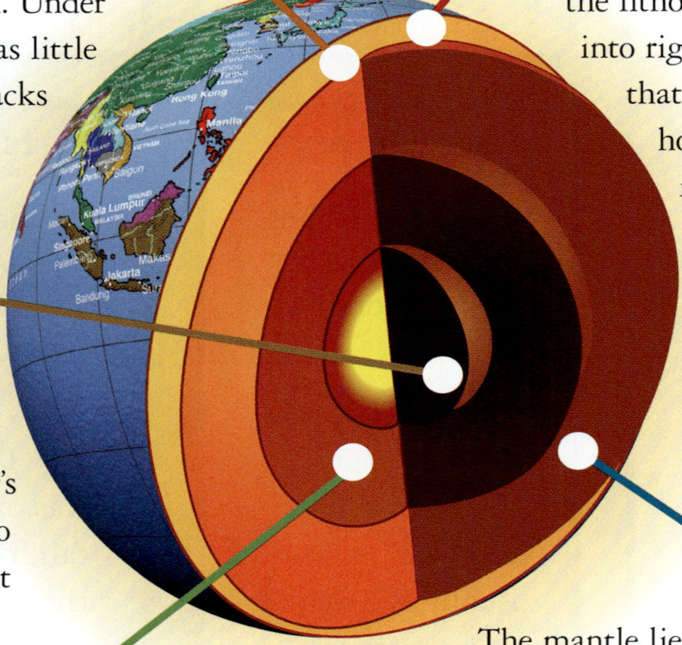

CRUST

The outer layer of the planet is called the *crust*. It can be up to 40 miles thick. Under the ocean, it can be as little as 3 miles thick. Cracks in the crust are called **faults**.

LITHOSPHERE

The crust and the hard top layer of the mantle make up the lithosphere. It's broken into rigid **tectonic** plates that "float" on the hotter, more liquid mantle beneath. When these plates move, the land above may shake, quake, or even erupt!

INNER CORE

The solid center of Earth is metallic rock. Even though it's very hot, it's under so much pressure that it stays solid.

MANTLE

The mantle lies below the crust, and it's made of liquid magma and rocks. It is hottest close to the core, and less hot close to the crust. Parts of the mantle circle slowly.

OUTER CORE

The hot, liquid rock of the outer core is mostly made up of melted iron and other minerals. This liquid rock is called *magma*.

Fitting the Pieces Together

Have you ever noticed that some of the continents look like puzzle pieces that might fit together—or that maybe once did fit together? Earth's tectonic plates have moved slowly over hundreds of millions of years. Let's see what time has done to the way our world looks.

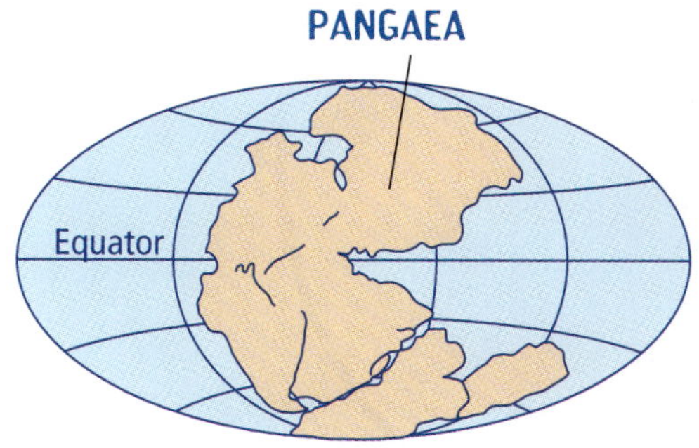

PANGAEA

Earth 200 Million Years Ago

Earth had just one huge landmass, known as Pangaea, 200 million years ago. This was the **temporary** shape of Earth's land masses.

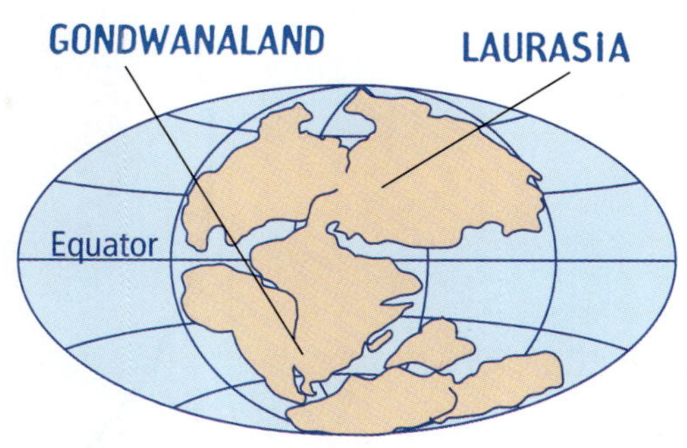

BREAKING APART

Earth 100 Million Years Ago

Pangaea broke up into Laurasia and Gondwanaland. If you look carefully, you can see the shapes of the continents as we know them today.

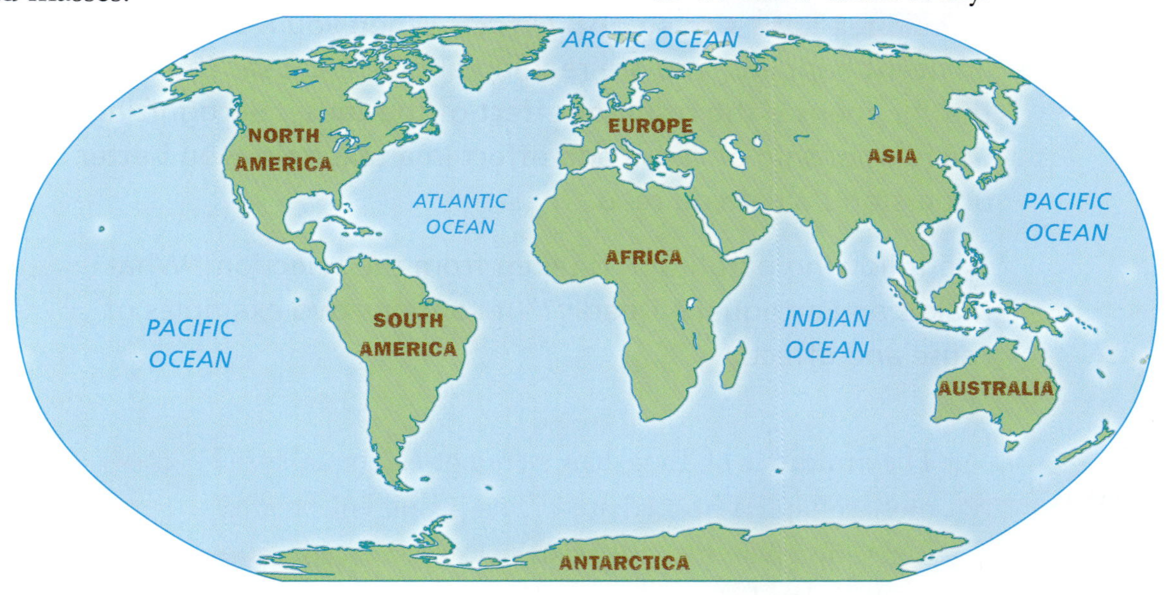

DOES THIS LOOK FAMILIAR?

Earth Today

Disturbances continue to cause Earth's plates to drift and shift. They carried the continents into the places where they are today. But they are not **stationary**. The continents will continue to move.

GET READY TO READ

Comprehension

TARGET SKILL **Cause and Effect** When you read about why an event happens, you are reading about its **cause**. The event that happens is the result or **effect** of the cause. Recognizing the relationship of **cause** and **effect** in a text helps you better understand what you read.

The following paragraph is taken from the selection "What Makes an Earthquake Deadly?" It contains two examples of cause and effect.

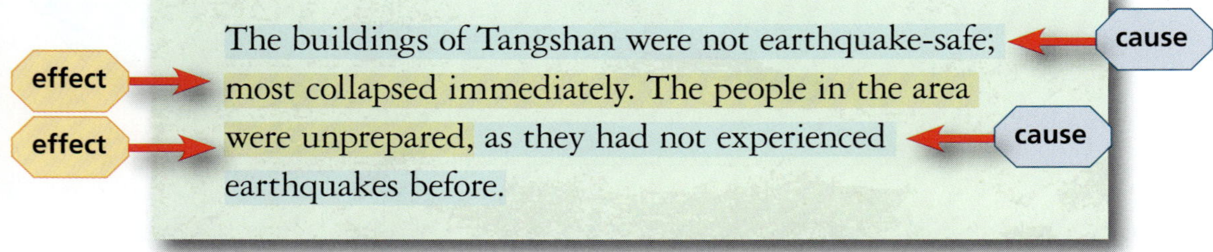

You can show cause and effect with a graphic organizer.

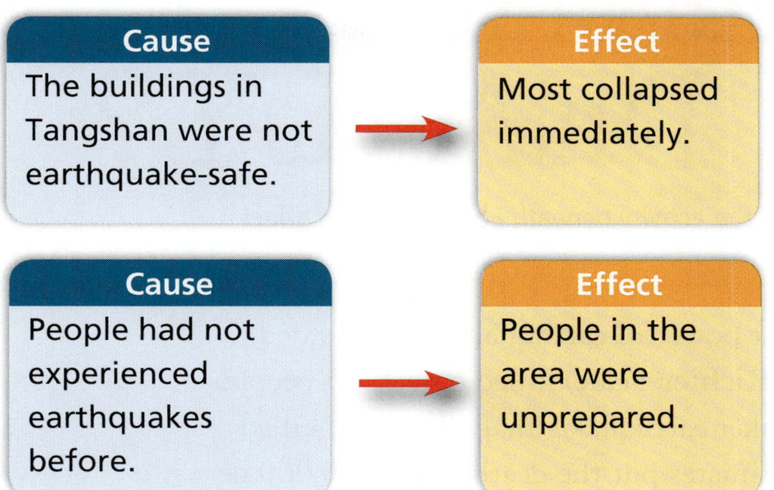

Writers sometimes signal cause and effect with words such as *because*, *as*, *therefore*, *since*, and *so*. Notice that the writer used a semicolon instead of a signal word in the first sentence of the text.

TARGET STRATEGY **Question** As you read, ask yourself questions about why events happen. Ask yourself what the cause might be.

- Ask: What happens?
- Ask: Why does it happen?

These questions will help you uncover cause and effect.

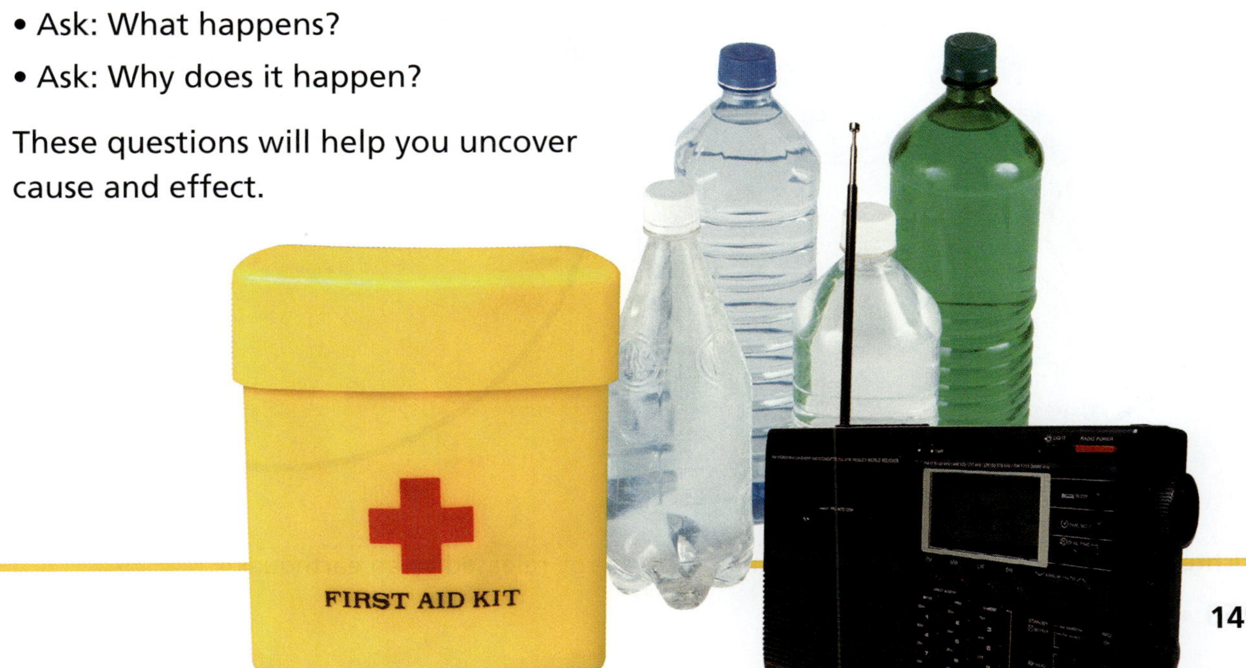

What Makes an Earthquake DEADLY?

FOCUS: What factors, other than the activity beneath Earth's surface, affect how deadly an earthquake is?

In Chile in 1960, the most powerful earthquake ever recorded (magnitude 9.5 on the **Richter Scale**) killed only 1,655 people. In China in 1976, a much weaker earthquake (magnitude 7.5) killed at least 255,000, and some estimates put the death toll at 655,000 or more. What made the weaker quake so much more deadly?

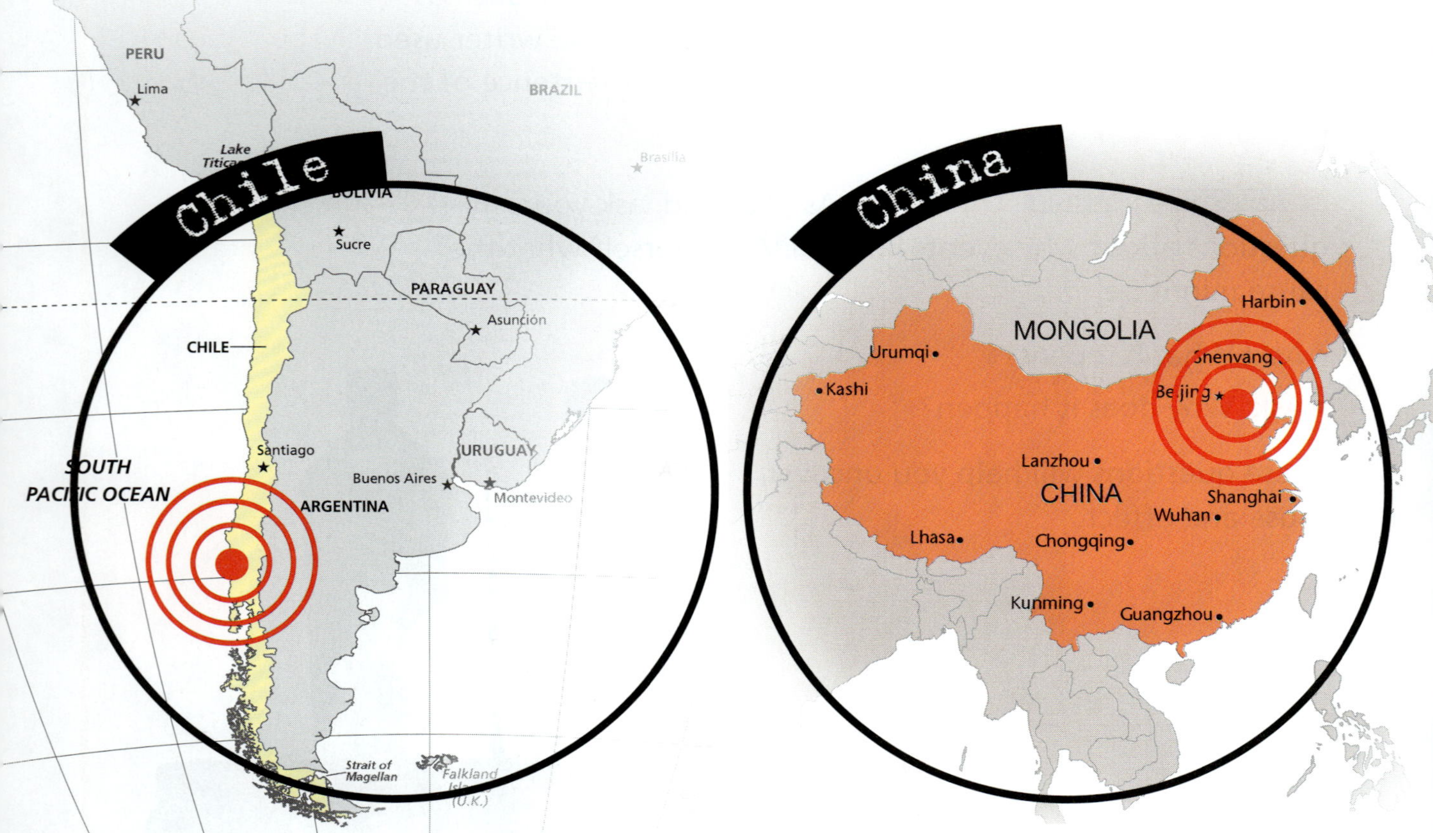

Richter Scale Scale for measuring the amount of energy released by an earthquake.

	Valdivia, Chile, 1960 Strong, but not as deadly	Tangshan, China, 1976 Weaker, but a terrible killer
Population Density	Several towns were severely affected by this quake, but none had a high population **density**.	The epicenter of the quake was near Tangshan, an **industrial** city with a population of about 1 million.
Surprise	Several strong foreshocks made the population wary.	There were no foreshocks. People were taken by surprise.
Time of Day	The earthquake struck in the afternoon. People were outside.	The earthquake struck at 4 A.M. Most people were asleep.
Aftershocks and Other Aftereffects	Although there were aftershocks and **tsunamis**, they caused more structural damage than loss of life.	Many people who might have been rescued were killed when powerful aftershocks shook the city. Survivors had no water or electricity, the sewage system didn't function, and there was limited **access** to food and health care.
Building Construction and Soil Conditions	The quake happened in an area that had experienced earthquakes before. Many of the **facilities** were constructed with earthquake safety in mind. People were better prepared.	The buildings in Tangshan were not earthquake-safe; most **collapsed** immediately. The people in the area were unprepared, as they had not experienced earthquakes before.

STOP AND THINK

1. Why was the earthquake in China so deadly?
2. If you had lived through the earthquake in Chile, how might you plan for a possible future earthquake?

Your Turn

Use Your Words:

access	observe
antiseptic	possessions
bureaucrat	proof
certificate	reliable
collapse	revitalize
density	section
distant	sense
earthly	slump
facility	suspicious
industry	tremor

- Read the words on the list.
- Read the dialogue. Find the words.

MORE ACTIVITIES

1. Dialogue

Listening and Speaking

What kind of building would you like to build? What would it be used for? Create a presentation that shows all about your building. Tell your partner about it.

2. You Are the Author

Writing

Working on a building can be dangerous. Think about how people working on a building need to protect themselves. Then make a poster that tells one way workers can stay safe.

3. Make a List

Vocabulary

Make a list of the materials that are used in buildings. Look at the drawing on this page. Look around your school. Share your list with the class.

Materials Used in Buildings

In the drawing	In the school

4. Activities to Observe

Writing

What activities occur around your neighborhood? Which do you like to watch? List your two favorites. Then tell why you enjoy watching them.

5. Play "Find It"

Listening and Speaking

Work with a partner. Take turns finding items in the drawing that begin with each letter of the alphabet.

6. Make a Plan

Listening and Speaking

Plan a new building for your town. What would the building be used for? How tall would it be? How would it benefit your town? Present your plan to your class. Be ready to answer questions about your building.

SAN FRANCISCO EARTHQUAKES

1906, 1989, AND WHO KNOWS WHEN?

FOCUS: What kind of stories do earthquakes leave in their aftermath?

Shara and her mom sat staring at the television. Every station was showing the same images over and over again—a **section** of the Bay Bridge **collapsed**, Highway 880 a twisted mess, roads covered with debris, houses tilted over and **slumping** crazily toward the sidewalk. It was like a weird dream.

"I just can't believe all that happened today, right here in the city where I live," said Shara. "It's scary, but exciting, too. I mean, it's part of history. When I grow up, I can tell my kids I survived the *Big One*, the earthquake of '89!"

"Honey, this was bad, no doubt about it, but I'm not so sure it was the *Big One*," said Mama. "This city has had bigger ones in the past. And they say an even bigger one is coming in the future."

"Well, it's the biggest one you were ever in, isn't it?"

"That it is," agreed Shara's mom. "But my grandfather, Old Pops, was here in 1906 during the great quake and fire. Now THAT was a big one. About 3,000 people lost their lives, and some 28,000 buildings were destroyed. That was most of the city. With the high population **density**, that meant maybe 250,000 people were left homeless. Of course, most of the destruction was from the fire after the quake."

"But people chose to stay in the city afterward?" asked Shara.

"Oh yes! The officials and **bureaucrats** were worried that folks would get scared and move away, and that San Francisco itself would die. So they tried to make it seem like it wasn't so bad—gave out false information about the number of people who had died, that sort of thing. But they didn't need to worry. People didn't give up on the city. They pulled together and helped each other like you wouldn't believe! Just look how much the city has grown since then. The population of the Bay Area in 1906 was about 650,000. Today it's 7 million."

REREAD

Cause → Effect

Why did city officials try to make the quake seem less serious than it was?

"Hey," said Shara **suspiciously**. "How do you know all this?"

"When I was in school," Mama said, "I was very curious about earthquakes. Probably because we live so close to the San Andreas **Fault**. So, I did a big project on the 1906 earthquake. I read ALL about it. I even interviewed my grandfather. He wrote his story for me—everything he could remember about the quake and what it was like afterward. I could probably find it if you want to take a look at it."

"Yes, please!" cried Shara.

Shara's mom turned off the television and went to search through a box of letters, **certificates**, newspaper clippings, and other papers.

"Here it is," said Mama. "Read it over. Then you can take it in to your class, if you like. I'm sure Old Pops would like to know he was still teaching young folks about the Great San Francisco Earthquake and Fire of 1906."

Grandfather's Story

In 1906 I was just a boy, seven years old, when the earthquake hit San Francisco. Papa was away working on the railroad. It happened early in the morning, just after 5 o'clock. My two brothers and I were sleeping when suddenly the whole world began to shake. It shook the three of us right out of bed into a tangled heap on the ground. The floor, the walls—the whole room and everything in it were shaking and rocking like a ship in a storm.

REREAD

Cause → Effect

Why was the room shaking?

Mama stumbled in carrying the baby, shouting and pushing us toward the door. We could hardly stand, and the door itself was tilting and stuck tight. But Mama kicked it open, and we all spilled out just in time to see the roof of our little house fall in—right where we had been standing just seconds before. They say the quake lasted less than a minute, but it felt like an hour.

When the shaking stopped, there were clouds of dust in the air. Lots of folks were outside, wearing nothing but their nightclothes. Many houses had fallen down, were leaning, or had partly sunk into the ground. People started to go inside to see what of their **earthly possessions** they could save. They hauled out clothes, food, and the strangest things—an old picture frame, an empty birdcage, a feather hat, a clothes iron and ironing board. I think that earthquake shook up their brains some, and they weren't thinking straight. I wouldn't **recommend** going into an earthquake-damaged building.

There were big fires burning downtown—we could see flames and clouds of black smoke. The air was full of the smell of burning buildings. But that was far away, and nobody was too worried about the fire coming near us.

Some men and older boys were putting out small fires and trying to help people who had been trapped in their houses or were injured. Some people had been killed, for sure. But there was nothing that could be done for them, and we didn't speak about it much. Of course, we all got a bit scared every time we felt an aftershock.

Later that day, Mama realized the big fire wasn't going to stop before it got to us, so it was time to get moving. We had been watching people going by all day. The lucky ones had carts or wheelbarrows. Some had bags, bundles, or baby carriages. Mama tied our bundles to the ends of some sturdy sticks, and we joined the march. I don't think she knew exactly where we were headed. We just followed the **multitudes** away from the smoke and flames. We ended up in Golden Gate Park along with thousands of others, all mixed up. Rich, poor, old, young—the fire hadn't stopped for anyone. Papa found us there a week later. He was so happy to see us alive and uninjured, except for a few scrapes and scratches.

After the fire, many people left San Francisco on boats—they traveled over to Berkeley or Oakland or other areas farther away. They stayed with relatives and friends or sometimes even with total strangers. It's amazing how a disaster will make folks open up their hearts and homes to those in need.

For those of us left behind in the city, life wasn't too bad at all. Golden Gate Park became a regular "tent city." The Red Cross and city officials handed out whatever supplies they had—clothing, blankets, **antiseptics**, and food. They had taken all the stock from grocery stores in the city that were about to burn up in the fire anyway. Sometimes they handed out strange foods that we had never eaten before, but we never complained. One day we had candy for breakfast, and there was porridge for supper many nights. We cooked around fires outside. Someone had saved his banjo, another his fiddle, and so there was plenty of music and laughter.

My brothers and I ran riot over that camp all spring and summer. Finally we were able to move back into a **revitalized** part of the city, where they had started to rebuild. Do you know, we didn't have school until the end of October? April to October… that was the longest summer vacation any of us ever had!

REREAD

Cause → Effect

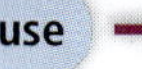

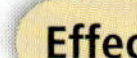

Why did summer vacation last from April until October?

STOP AND THINK

1. How was the fire worse than the earthquake in 1906?
2. What would you want to save from your house in an earthquake?

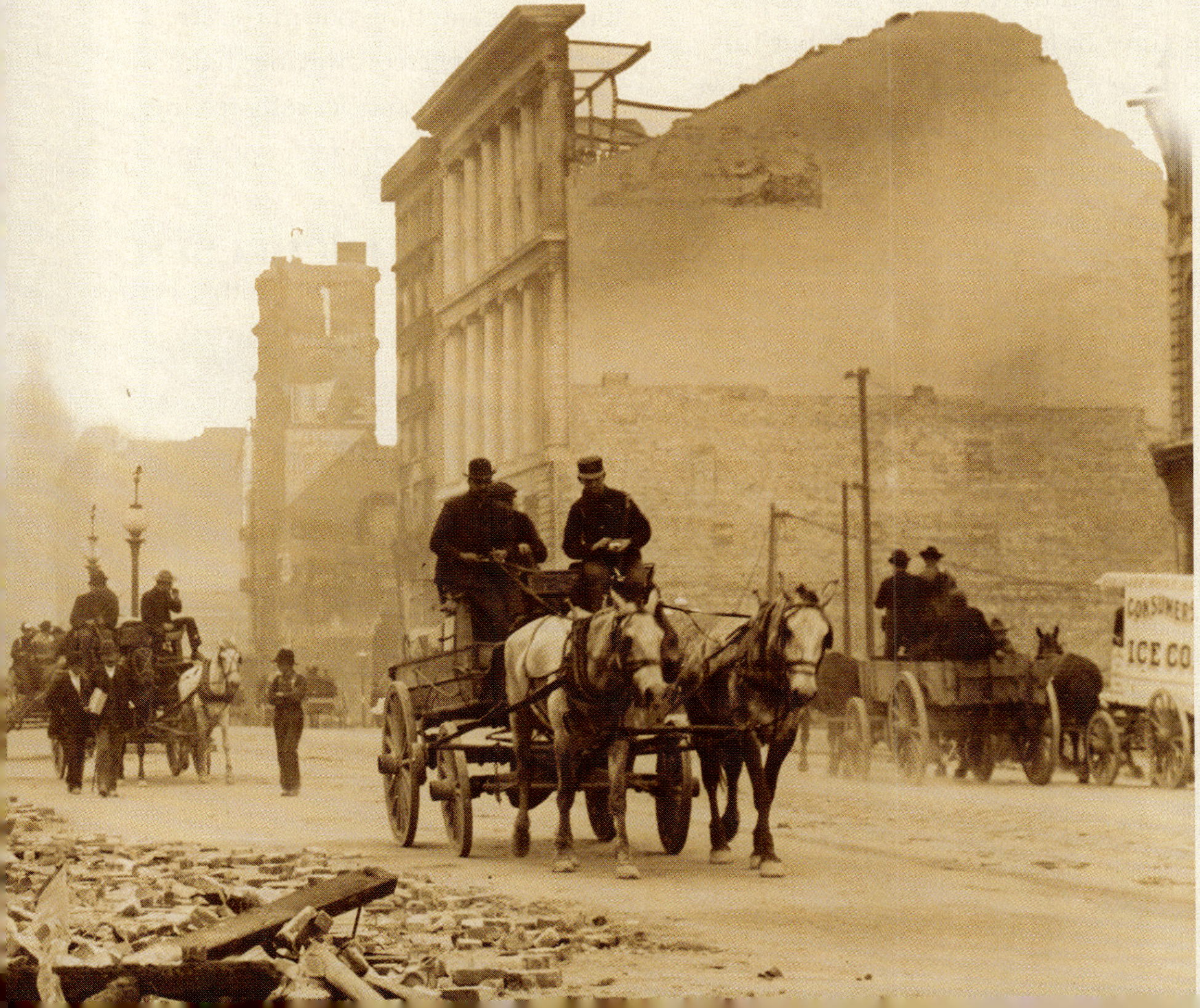

EYEWITNESSES

FOCUS: How do people who are used to earthquakes react to a big one?

These eyewitness accounts were posted on a news organization's website **subsequent** to an earthquake in Peru, in August 2007. There were roughly 500 **fatalities** from this quake. For people who live in this earthquake-**prone** area, feeling an earthquake is nothing new. However, this one made quite an **impact** on the people affected.

"We are used to **tremors** that happen about three or four times a year, but this was different. The ground started to move and it seemed to continue without end. We all rushed into the street but it just continued and we knew immediately that it was something big. The vehicles rocked from side to side and all the windows rattled."

JOHN UDRIS, Lima, Peru

"It was a frightening experience. I have experienced tremors before, but never standing out in the street watching the trees swaying, light posts bending, and actually feeling the waves under my feet, with my knees shaking."

MARION MICHELSEN, Lima, Peru

TO AN EARTHQUAKE

"It was terrible. It's the first time that an earthquake here has lasted more than two minutes. There were many people in the streets crying, shouting, hugging each other. It was awful."

ROXANA, Lima, Peru

"This earthquake is the strongest I've ever felt, and the longest one as well, at two minutes. For some it seemed like the end of the world, and most people I know are still nervous. Some were too scared to sleep all night because they feared another one. After the earthquake, most people stayed outside their houses for at least an hour."

BERENICE, Lima, Peru

"We were thrown out of bed and ran into the streets. We thought we were being bombed or something. It was very frightening, and my wife and children were screaming, asking me what was happening. We have lost our home but have escaped with our lives, thankfully."

EDUARDO MOVEAMIO, Lima, Peru

STOP AND THINK

1. How did the 2007 earthquake compare to earlier ones these people had experienced?
2. How do you think people felt about sharing their stories on a website?

Selection 4

UNDERWATER

FOCUS: What happens when an earthquake happens underwater?

On December 26, 2004, a powerful earthquake shook the ocean floor 150 miles northwest of the island of Sumatra. Waves spread across the Indian Ocean from the earthquake's epicenter.

The Tsunami

The earthquake was the result of the collision of two of Earth's **tectonic** plates. Although the earthquake, with a **magnitude** of 9.1 on the Richter Scale, was one of the strongest ever recorded, most of the 200,000 deaths were caused by the **tsunami** that followed it.

Tsunamis are waves that can travel 500 miles per hour across the open ocean—as fast as a jet plane. In the deep ocean, the waves are only about one or two feet high. Closer to shore, the waves slow down but grow much taller. When they slam into a coastline, they can be as high as 100 feet—as tall as a ten-story building.

Banda Aceh before the tsunami

Banda Aceh after the tsunami

EARTHQUAKE

Waves as high as 80 feet hit the coast of Sumatra just 15 minutes after the quake. After two hours, the tsunami had smashed into the coasts of Sri Lanka, India, and Thailand. It took seven hours for the waves to reach Somalia, a country in East Africa about 3,000 miles from the epicenter of the earthquake.

The tsunami was **observed** all over the world, from Australia to Antarctica. It was even recorded along both coasts of North and South America.

What Do Animals Know?

There have been reports about the strange behavior of animals before the waves hit: elephants running for high ground, dogs refusing to go outside, birds and bats leaving low-lying areas. Had these animals **sensed** the coming disaster?

Can animals sense earthquakes and tsunamis before people do?

Some people believe animals have a "sixth sense" that warns them of danger. More likely, their ability to feel **distant** vibrations makes them able to pick up warning signs before they are **discernible** to humans. But there is no **proof** that using animals to predict earthquakes is **reliable**. The stories about animals' sixth sense remain just that—stories.

STOP AND THINK

1. What is the relationship between tsunamis and earthquakes?
2. If you had a pet that behaved strangely, would you predict an earthquake?

CULTURAL CONNECTION

EARTHQUAKE SAFETY:

ADVICE FROM THE EXPERTS

FOCUS: How can people be prepared for earthquakes?

Earthquakes. How can we be safe when there is no way to prevent earthquakes, and even geologists cannot **reliably** predict when they will strike? Earthquake safety boils down to knowing what to do when the earth won't stand still—and being prepared. We asked kids in three earthquake-**prone** cities about earthquake safety.

TOKYO, JAPAN Ask any child in Ms. Yuki Kuwosawa's class what to do when the ground starts shaking and you get the same answer. It translates to: "Drop, cover, and hold." I asked student Misaki Saito to explain.

"When we feel tremors, we *drop* to the ground and get *cover* under a desk or table. We *hold* onto the desk as the earth moves."

Great. But why?

"This way," she said, "we stay safe from anything that falls down during the earthquake."

That's right, Misaki. Many injuries during an earthquake come from falling objects such as books, pictures on the walls, and tall furniture like shelves and cabinets. Crouching underneath a heavy desk or table can also protect you from broken glass from windows. If there is no desk or table nearby, stand in a doorway, away from windows and tall furniture.

LOS ANGELES, CALIFORNIA

Kids in L.A. also have advice about earthquake safety. I asked Hector Vargas about ways to stay safe.

"One thing you can do is earthquake-proof your home," he said. "You try to think what bad things might happen in an earthquake, and then make sure they won't happen. So, make sure your heavy **possessions** aren't in places where they could fall on you. Move your bed so you don't sleep too close to windows, or underneath glass picture frames or heavy bookshelves. You don't want broken glass and stuff falling on you when you're sleeping."

"And don't keep liquids that can catch fire, like paint thinner and alcohol, near the stove," added Hector's buddy, Trang.

"Yeah, and speaking of fire, said Hector," you should know where to shut off the gas to your whole house, and the electricity, too. You will need to do that quickly if the lines get broken in a quake. You don't want to be searching around for the shutoffs when your house is all upside down."

"Basically," said Trang, "you want to be prepared for the next quake, because you never know when it might come."

JUNEAU, ALASKA "One way to stay safe after an earthquake is to make sure that your house has an emergency kit," explained Annette Hamilton, a student at Glacier School. Annette and her friends Sasha and Mary Grace have put together a sample kit for the school's Readiness Day demonstration.

"Here's a battery-operated radio," said Sasha. "You need one so you can find out what's going on. Don't forget extra batteries. And you need a flashlight or two, and batteries for them as well. Also pack a penknife, matches, candles, a hand-operated can opener, plenty of bottled water, and blankets."

"Here's what's for dinner!" said Mary Grace, showing us a carton loaded with cans and packets of dried food. "Your emergency kit should include enough food for each person in your family for a week—well, at least for three days. Make sure you only include things that will keep for a long time."

"Last but not least," said Annette, "don't forget your first-aid kit. Let's hope you don't need it, but after an earthquake, you might. It should have bandages and gauze, **antiseptic** and antibiotic cream, plus the medicines anyone in the family needs to take."

"It might seem like a lot of trouble to get this stuff together," Sasha said, "but it's worth it. Your kit could save a life."

These are some of the things you would need in an earthquake emergency kit.

Earthquake preparation and safety procedures can make the difference between life and death. If you live in an area where earthquakes often occur, you may already be familiar with some of these ideas. If you aren't familiar with them, we **recommend** that you organize an Earthquake Awareness Week at your school.

Make an Emergency Contact Card

It's a good idea to carry a card with you so that if a disaster happens, you are prepared. Be sure to have on your card:

1. Your name
2. Your home address
3. Contact information for members of your household: include work or school numbers and cell phone numbers
4. An out-of-town contact
5. A family meeting place outside of your neighborhood
6. Your family doctor

STOP AND THINK

1. Why is it important to think about earthquakes before they happen?
2. What items would you include in an emergency kit?

Reading Longer Words

In this unit you learned more about how to read longer words.

Step 1: Divide the word into parts.

Compound word?
Divide between the words.

Prefix?
Divide after the prefix.

Suffix?
Divide before the suffix.

VCCV letter pattern?
Divide between the consonants.

VCV letter pattern?
Divide before the consonant.
or
Divide after the consonant.

Step 2: Read each word part.

Step 3: Read the whole word. Sound right? If not, try an alternative.

Ends in a consonant?
Try a short vowel sound.

Ends in a vowel?
Try a long vowel sound.

Has a VCe pattern?
Try a long vowel sound.

Ends in *-le, -al,* or *-el*?
Try dividing before the consonant preceding the *l.*

Has a syllable with vowel + *r*?
May change the sound of the vowel.

Has a vowel pair?
Pair stays together.

Divide the Words

dis/count	ex/claim
four/teen	view/point
un/a/fraid	en/chant/ment
mer/chan/dise	no/where
mush/room	pa/ren/the/ses

Read Word Parts	Read Whole Words
dis count →	discount
dis count →	discount
ex claim →	exclaim
four teen →	fourteen
view point →	viewpoint
un a fraid →	unafraid
en chant ment →	enchantment
mer chan dise →	merchandise
no where →	nowhere
mush room →	mushroom
pa ren the ses →	parentheses

Read More Words

Use what you learned in Units 1–5 to read these words from the unit.

stationary	facilities	bureaucrat	survived	certificates
possessions	antiseptics	revitalized	epicenter	discernable

Vocabulary

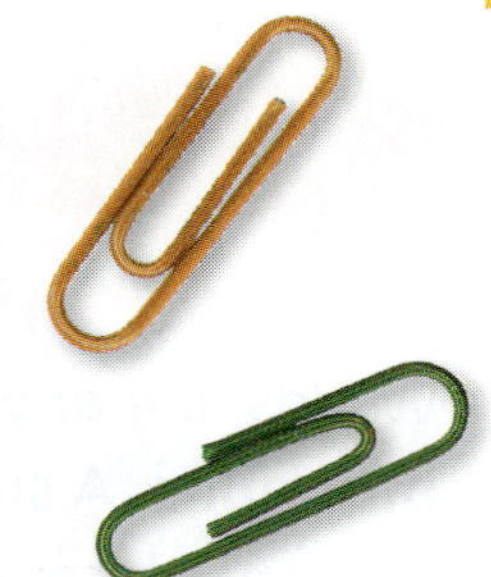

Multiple-Meaning Words

Some words have more than one meaning. These are multiple-meaning words. To decide which definition is being used in a sentence, look for context clues.

Magnitude is a multiple-meaning word. You will find more than one definition in the dictionary

magnitude

A. the measure of the amount of energy released by an earthquake as indicated on the Richter Scale

B. greatness of extent, importance, or size

Try substituting the different definitions of a multiple-meaning word in a sentence to determine which definition is being used.

Look at the word *magnitude* in the sentences:

Sentence 1: The large number of patients indicated the magnitude of the problem.

Sentence 2: The scientists reported that the disaster was a magnitude-six earthquake.

Definition A is about the amount of energy released in an earthquake. That makes sense for Sentence 2, but not Sentence 1. Sentence 2 is about an earthquake.

Definition B makes sense for Sentence 1. The sentence is about the size of a problem.

Indefinite Pronouns & Personal Pronouns

Singular Indefinite Pronouns

Words like *anybody*, *everything*, and *someone* are **indefinite pronouns**. A singular indefinite pronoun refers to a nonspecific person, place, or thing.

Some Singular Indefinite Pronouns

- anybody, anything, anyone
- everybody, everything, everyone
- somebody, something, someone
- either, neither
- no one, none, nothing, nobody
- each

Indefinite pronouns can function in a sentence in all the ways that a regular pronoun functions.

Sentence	Indefinite Pronoun	Function
Someone needs to turn off the light.	someone	subject
I heard something in the next room.	something	direct object
For the holiday grab bag, I had to buy someone a gift.	someone	indirect object
There are enough chairs for everybody.	everybody	object of the preposition (*for*)

Personal Pronouns

A **personal pronoun** is used in place of a specific noun that is named. The noun that a personal pronoun refers to is called the **antecedent**. Indefinite pronouns do not have antecedents.

Sentence	Personal Pronoun	Antecedent	Indefinite Pronoun
Terry can't find anyone to help her sew costumes.	her	Terry	anyone
The firefighters ordered the family to take nothing with them.	them	family	nothing

Plural Indefinite Pronouns

Some pronouns are **plural indefinite pronouns**. A plural indefinite pronoun refers to several nonspecific people, places, or things.

Plural Indefinite Pronouns
few, both, others, many, several

Subject/Verb Agreement with Indefinite Pronouns

Singular indefinite pronouns function as third-person singular subjects. They take verbs that add *-s* or *-es* in the present tense. Plural indefinite pronouns function as third-person plural subjects. They do not agree with verbs ending in *-s* or *-es* in the present tense.

Sentence	Singular or Plural Indefinite Pronoun?	Verb
Is everyone all right?	singular	is
Nobody has the correct answer for this question.	singular	has
In this scene, **something jumps** out from behind the door.	singular	jumps
There are millions of women in the city. **Many work** full-time.	plural	work
Do you want to listen to Mozart or Beethoven? **Both sound** great!	plural	sound
Everyone knows that Washington, D.C., is not located in any state.	singular	knows
Neither works well as an official class song.	singular	works
I tried on all the raincoats, and **several look** good with these boots.	plural	look
Everybody rushes too quickly down that hill.	singular	rushes

Write an Expository Essay

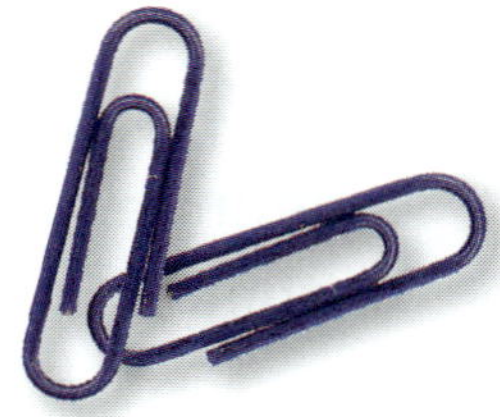

Sentence fluency is the rhythm and flow of the sentences that make up a story. An essay should be enjoyable to read, and good sentence fluency really stands out when a piece of writing is read aloud. Sentences should sound "natural" to the reader, rather than mechanical or choppy.

First Draft

You've read the final draft of "An Ancient Fish." Read the first draft.

Just as dinosaurs once ruled the earth, Prehistoric fish once swam the seas. One of these fish is still around. It is called the coelacanth (seel-AH-canth). It thrives in the world's oceans. Studying this creature can teach us, lessons about life on the planet in the past. The coelacanth first appeared more than a million years before the dinosaurs.

For a long time scientists thought the coelacanth was extinct. Only fossilized specimens had been found. But in 1938 South African fishermen caught one in their nets. A marine biologist was walking through the local fish market. She noticed the fish's odd shape. Four fins stick out of its belly. This is where it's nickname Old Four-Legs comes from. More than a decade after the first specimen was found other discoveries followed. Researchers have found other coelacanth colonies. The colonies are everywhere from the Indian Ocean to the islands of South East Asia.

Since its discovery scientists have learned a lot about the coelacanth. But there is still a great deal that remains a mystery. The more scientists study this fish, the more we learn about it and about our own past a million years before the dinosaurs.

Writing Traits Checklist

- **Ideas**
  Is the subject of the essay clearly introduced?
- **Organization**
  Is the information presented in a logical order?
- **Sentence Fluency**
  Are the sentence beginnings varied?
- **Voice**
  Are specific facts and details provided about the subject?
- **Word Choice**
  Does the writer choose clear, interesting words?
- **Conventions**
  Are there any errors?

Final Draft The writer made many revisions to complete this final draft.

Just as dinosaurs once ruled the earth, prehistoric fish once swam the seas. Amazingly, one of these fish is still around. Called the coelacanth (seel-AH-canth), this odd fish thrives in the world's oceans. Studying this creature can teach us important lessons about life on the planet in the distant past. Just think: the coelacanth first appeared more than a million years before the dinosaurs!

For a long time scientists thought the coelacanth was extinct, because only fossilized specimens had been found. But in 1938, South African fishermen caught one in their nets. An alert marine biologist had made a habit of walking through the local fish market. Right away she noticed the fish's odd shape. Four stout fins stick out of its stocky belly, leading to the fish's nickname, "Old Four-Legs." More than a decade after the first specimen was found, other discoveries followed. Now researchers have found coelacanth colonies from the Indian Ocean to the islands of Southeast Asia.

Since its discovery, scientists have learned a lot about the coelacanth, but there is still a great deal that remains a mystery. The more scientists study this ancient fish, the more we learn about it and about our own deep past, a million years before the dinosaurs.

UNIT 6 BEYOND BOUNDARIES

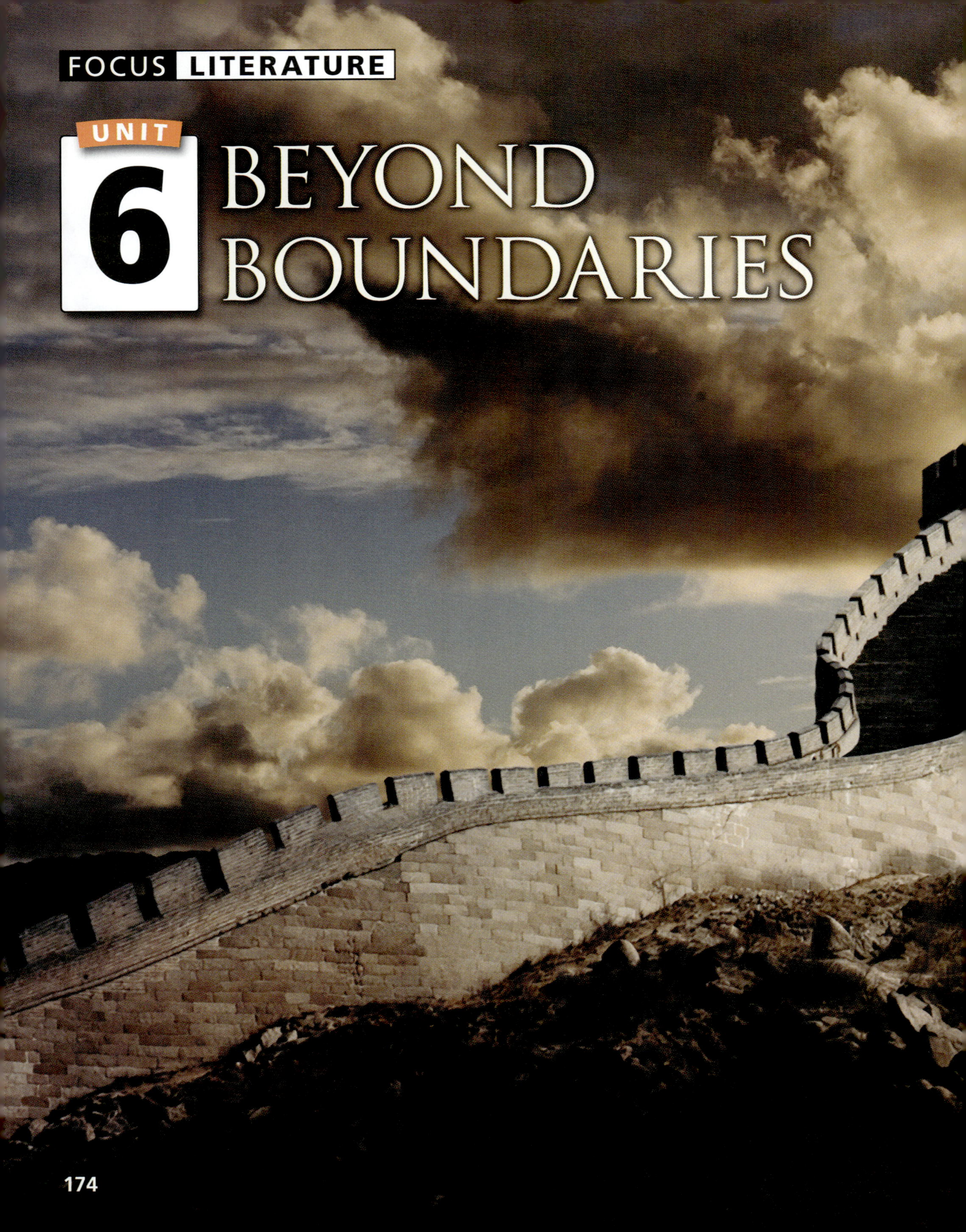

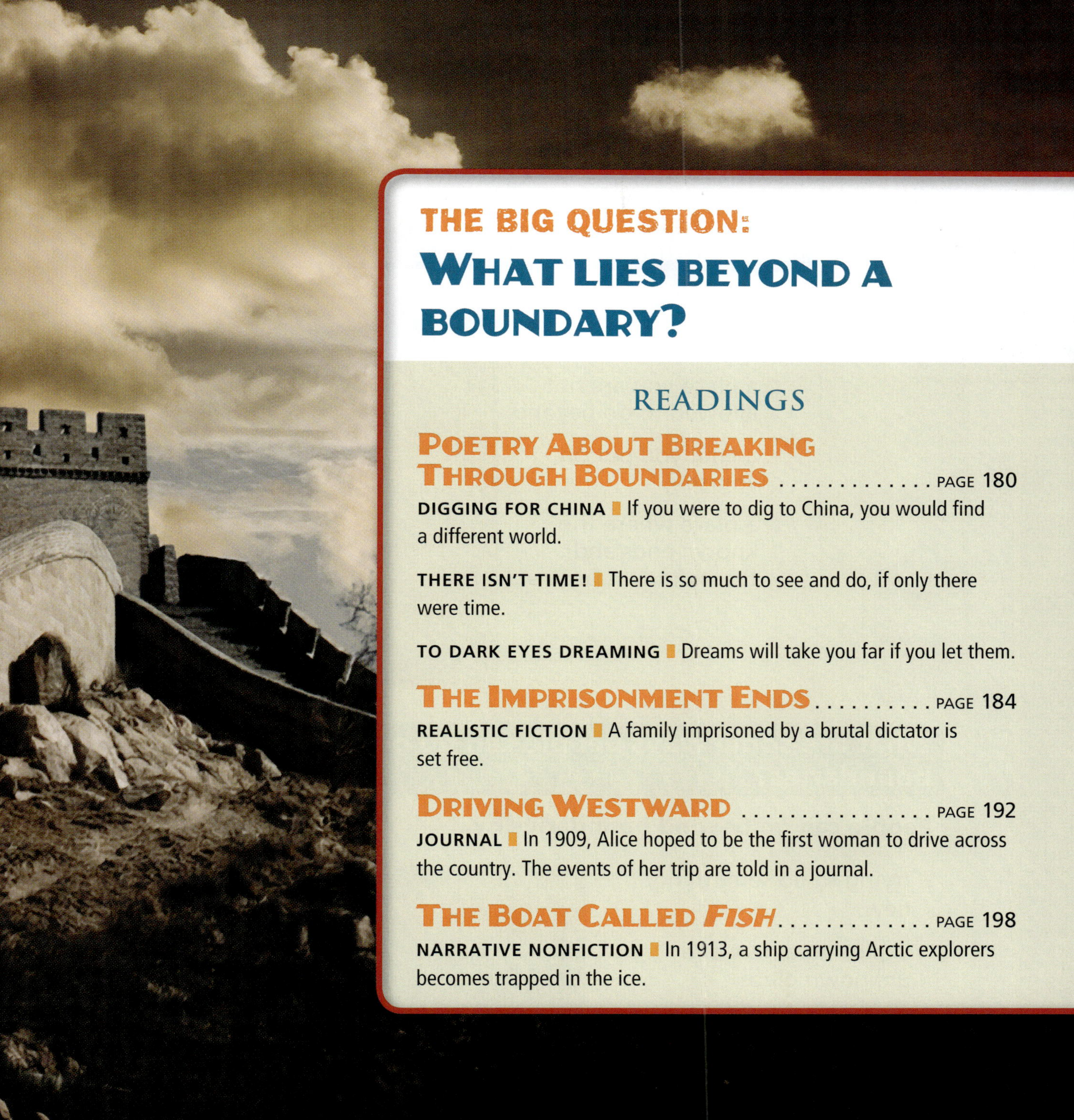

THE BIG QUESTION:

WHAT LIES BEYOND A BOUNDARY?

READINGS

Looking Beyond Boundaries

Think about a boundary. What can a boundary be?

A boundary can be...

- ☐ a fence.
- ☐ a place you are not allowed to go beyond.
- ☐ a limit you put on yourself.
- ☐ a place where the known ends and the unknown begins.

What are some ways people can go beyond boundaries?

People can go beyond boundaries by...

- ☐ trying to do something new.
- ☐ exploring a new and unknown place.
- ☐ finding strength to change their lives.
- ☐ doing something no one has done before.

What happens when a dictator rules a country?

When a dictator rules a country...

- there are no free elections.
- there is no free speech.
- people can be arrested without cause.
- people must follow the dictator's rules.

In 1909, what problems did people have driving cross-country?

In 1909, people driving cross-country...

- had no road maps.
- had to travel on bad roads.
- had to repair their cars themselves.
- had few gas stations where they could buy gasoline.

What would people need to survive in a very cold place like the Arctic?

To survive in the Arctic, people would need...

- very warm clothing.
- a lot of food.
- some sort of shelter.
- fuel for stoves and lamps.

Literary Words

accustom
aggravate
array
burrow
dictator
editorial
fatigue
neglect
plod
thrust

accustom

Accustom means to familiarize by use, habit, or constant practice.

"John tried to accustom himself to the cold weather."

aggravate

Aggravate means to make worse or more severe.

"If you scratch a mosquito bite, you'll only aggravate the itch."

editorial

An **editorial** is a newspaper article that presents the opinion of the publisher, an editor, or a journalist.

"The editorial criticized the city's plan to build a stadium."

fatigue

Fatigue means bodily or mental tiredness.

"After hiking for many hours, the group felt great fatigue."

array

Array means a grouping or organization of items.

"The dessert table had a large array of cakes and pies."

burrow

Burrow means to make a hole or tunnel in, into, or under something.

"A worm burrows its way underground."

dictator

A **dictator** is a person with absolute power.

"The dictator ruled the country with an iron fist."

neglect

Neglect means to pay little or no attention to.

"Children often neglect their chores."

plod

Plod means to trudge or walk heavily and slowly.

"The old mule plodded along the dusty trail."

thrust

Thrust means to push or shove with force.

"She had to thrust her way through the crowd."

from Digging for China
by Richard Wilbur

"Far enough down is China," somebody said.
"Dig deep enough and you might see the sky
As clear as at the bottom of a well.
Except it would be real—a different sky.
Then you could **burrow** down until you came
To China! Oh, it's nothing like New Jersey.
There's people, trees, and houses, and all that,
But much, much different. Nothing looks the same."

There Isn't Time!
by Eleanor Farjeon

There isn't time, there isn't time
To do the things I want to do,
With all the mountain-tops to climb,
And all the woods to wander through,
And all the seas to sail upon,
And everywhere there is to go,
And all the people, every one
Who lives upon the earth to know.
There's only time, there's only time
To know a few, and do a few,
And then sit down and make a rhyme
About the rest I want to do.

To Dark Eyes Dreaming

by Zilpha Keatley Snyder

Dreams go fast and far
these days,
They go by rocket **thrust**,
They go **arrayed**
in lights
or in the dust of stars.
Dreams, these days,
go fast and far.
Dreams are young, these days,
or very old,
They can be black
or blue or gold.
They need no special charts,
nor any fuel.
It seems, only one rule applies,
to all our dreams—
They will not fly except in open sky.
A fenced-in dream
will die.

Comprehension

TARGET SKILL **Author's Purpose** One purpose an author has for writing a story is to share a message about life. This message is known as the **theme**. Often, a story's theme is not directly stated, but it may be repeated throughout the story in a variety of story elements, including the descriptions, feelings, thoughts, and actions of characters.

The following paragraphs taken from the selection "The Imprisonment Ends" contain clues about the theme and the author's purpose for writing this story. In this story, Marta and her family have been imprisoned by the cruel dictator of their country. They have endured experiences most people would not understand. At last the government has been overthrown. Marta's relatives come to bring them home.

The description of Lucia gives clues about the theme because it shows a healthy, beautiful, and wealthy girl who did not suffer as much as her cousin did during a terrible time in her country.

The author uses dialogue to show the theme. In this case, Lucia shows her selfishness during a horrible time in her country.

My cousin Lucia was behind them, one arm around Ricardo. With her clear pink complexion, her shiny hair falling to her shoulders, Lucia looked healthy and beautiful. She was wearing a bright red woolen dress and gold jewelry.

"Was it awful, Marta?" Lucia asked.

The answers I had so often rehearsed did not come.

"It was terrible for us, Marta! you can't imagine how awful it got to be at the end. So many were killed, and there were bombs and burnings everywhere. We had to send the help to do the shopping. We didn't dare go out. Why, not even to the post office, you know. The only safe place was the country club. Mama and I and our friends spent most of our days there, and Papa would pick us up before the curfew."

The author uses a character's thoughts to show the theme. Clearly, Marta has thought a lot about all that she has suffered, but she cannot talk about it to her own cousin, because she feels the other girl could not understand.

The top box shows how the theme is related to the author's purpose for writing the story. The bottom three boxes show clues from the text that give examples of the theme.

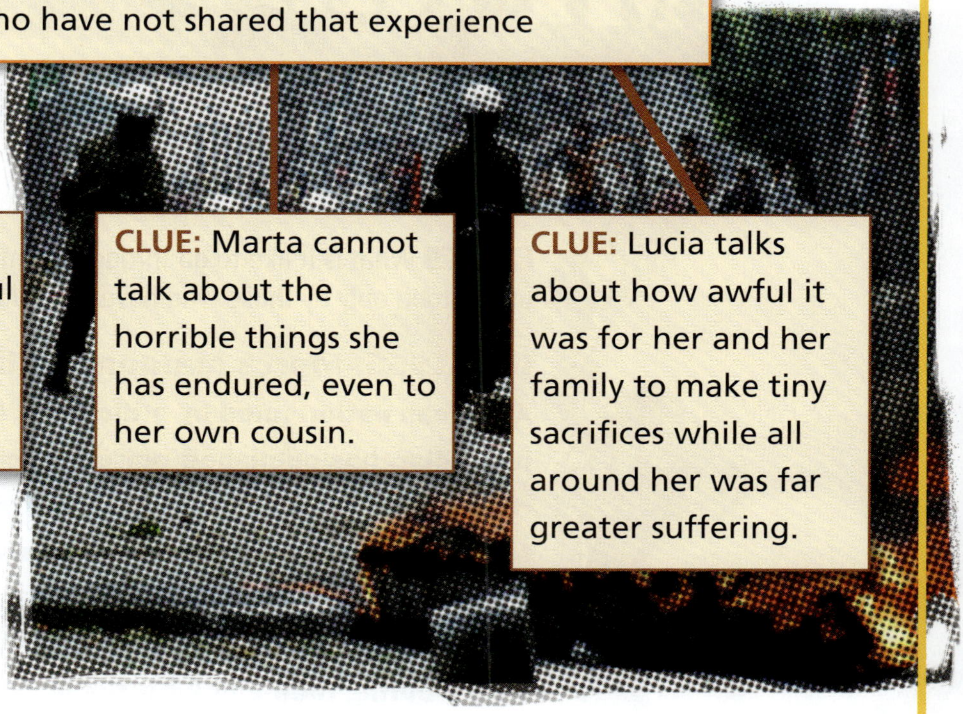

AUTHOR'S PURPOSE/THEME: To show how hard it can be for people who have endured hardship to be understood by people who have not shared that experience

CLUE: Lucia looks healthy and beautiful and wears bright clothing and gold jewelry.

CLUE: Marta cannot talk about the horrible things she has endured, even to her own cousin.

CLUE: Lucia talks about how awful it was for her and her family to make tiny sacrifices while all around her was far greater suffering.

TARGET STRATEGY **Infer/Predict** Ask yourself questions about the theme and author's purpose.

- How did reading the description of Lucia help you infer the theme?
- How did Marta's response to Lucia help you infer the theme?
- How do you predict the author will continue to use Marta to show the theme?

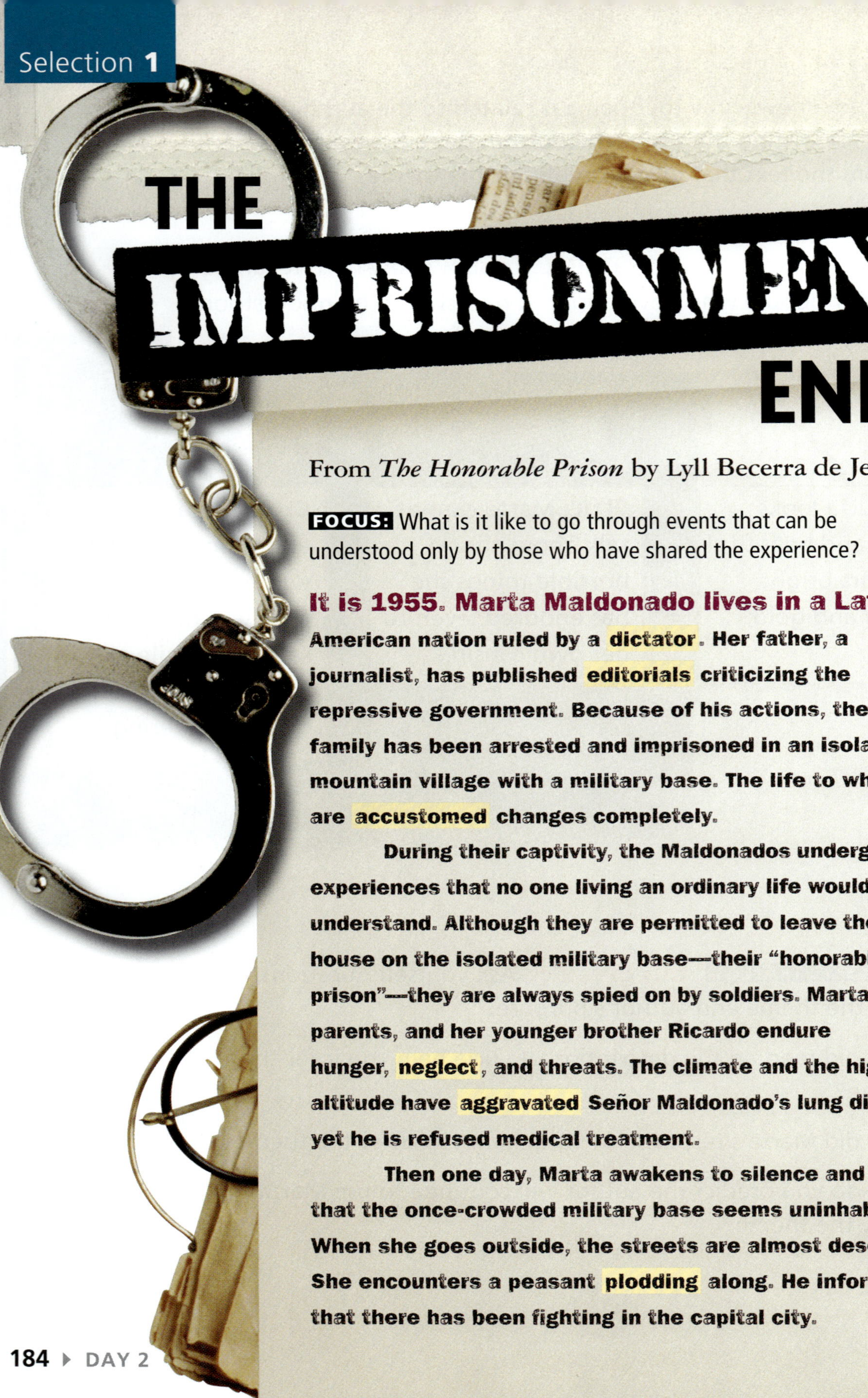

THE IMPRISONMENT ENDS

From *The Honorable Prison* by Lyll Becerra de Jenkins

FOCUS: What is it like to go through events that can be understood only by those who have shared the experience?

It is 1955. Marta Maldonado lives in a Latin American nation ruled by a dictator. Her father, a journalist, has published editorials criticizing the repressive government. Because of his actions, the entire family has been arrested and imprisoned in an isolated mountain village with a military base. The life to which they are accustomed changes completely.

During their captivity, the Maldonados undergo experiences that no one living an ordinary life would understand. Although they are permitted to leave the shabby house on the isolated military base—their "honorable prison"—they are always spied on by soldiers. Marta, her parents, and her younger brother Ricardo endure hunger, neglect, and threats. The climate and the high altitude have aggravated Señor Maldonado's lung disease, yet he is refused medical treatment.

Then one day, Marta awakens to silence and sees that the once-crowded military base seems uninhabited. When she goes outside, the streets are almost deserted. She encounters a peasant plodding along. He informs her that there has been fighting in the capital city.

And then clearly I hear the horses' hooves beating against the pavement of the main road, resounding like a thousand castanets. I stop midway up the hill. Horsemen are waving their hats, yelling "*¡Al fin!*" and that scream, "At last!" seems to erupt from every corner of the earth.

"*¡Viva la libertad!*"

"*¡Vivaaaa!*"

Overcome by **fatigue** and exhilaration, I sit by the door of the house, but only for an instant. The pounding of my heart repeats at last, at last, at last!

Marta realizes that the government has probably been overthrown, and she and her brother rush to Mama, who is sitting by Papa's bedside. Mama receives the news by crying in exhaustion, but Papa remains unconscious and does not respond.

The mayor, who has never displayed any courage by helping the Maldonados before, now visits the family. He calls Señor Maldonado a "powerful voice in the event the country is celebrating today." Since the mayor has a telephone, Mrs. Maldonado demands that he phone for a doctor and an ambulance, and Ricardo supplies the phone numbers of relatives.

They came, as my father had predicted, our relatives and his friends.

At noon, when we were around his cot, we heard car doors slamming and a tumult of voices, some of which we recognized. Mama and Ricardo leaped to their feet and rushed out of the room. I stood by the door, hiding.

How many times had I dreamed of the moment they would come and my father would say, "See, we are going home at last!" Now that the moment had arrived, I did not want to see any of them.

"Margarita, is it you, my dear, my dear!" Uncle Alberto was exclaiming in the entrance hall. There were sniffles. "Ricardito, let me embrace you!"

Uncle Alberto and Aunt Lila were the first to come into the house. I saw them through the half-open doorway. Tall, well-dressed, they looked handsomer than I remembered. Their presence lit the corridor in spite of their solemn faces and dark clothes. I was startled by the contrast with my mother's cadaverous appearance, to which I had grown accustomed. Now, close to her older brother, my mother was an old woman. He and Aunt Lila held Mama by the arms, guiding her cautiously, as though she were disabled.

My cousin Lucía was behind them, one arm around Ricardo. With her clear pink complexion, her shiny hair falling to her shoulders, Lucia looked healthy and beautiful. She was wearing a bright red woolen dress and gold jewelry.

"Was it awful, Marta?" Lucia asked.

The answers I had so often rehearsed did not come.

"It was terrible for us, Marta! You can't imagine how awful it got to be at the end. So many were killed, and there were bombs and burnings everywhere. We had to send the help to do the shopping. We didn't dare go out. Why, not even to the post office, you know. The only safe place was the country club. Mama and I and our friends spent most of our days there, and Papa would pick us up before the curfew."

My father's name was on everybody's lips. "Miguel was the first who alerted the country to the **torture** of political prisoners" and "We are **indebted** to Miguel!" and "A journalist obsessed by justice and truth, that's who he is, Miguel Maldonado." Someone called him a hero.

I recalled something my father said one evening in our home in the city, after discovering that he was losing friends because of his editorials against the dictator. He said, "Many are calling me a **traitor**. You see, one is either a hero or a traitor. Nothing in between pleases my countrymen."

The hammock was swaying with the comings and goings of the visitors. Suddenly, the ugly house was becoming dear. It was filled with my father's presence, the echo of his words. "They will come, my friends…and who knows, maybe Uncle Alberto will also be here to drive us to the city. Everyone will say his short speech. It will be a little ridiculous and tiresome…but we'll survive our small glory."

Risking nothing, they had come at last, indeed. They are here, I thought with bitterness, to **partake** in the momentary glory of "my brother-in-law," "my uncle," "my friend." They know how to play the national sport. How many of them, I wondered, like the mayor, are perennial members of the winning team?

My father was in a **coma**, yet I felt he was more alive than the ones moving about, patting each other's backs, repeating their empty phrases. I leaned against the hammock. How strange that, of all the emotions overwhelming me all at that moment, I was not feeling my father's absence. His presence was powerful, and I knew at that instant that it would always be with me.

This novel is partly autobiographical: the author, Lyll Becerra de Jenkins, grew up in Latin America, and her father was a prominent judge and an outspoken journalist who publicly criticized his country's repressive government.

STOP AND THINK

1. Why was Marta unimpressed by the people who were praising her father?
2. What emotions besides fear might be felt by someone who endures a difficult experience?

LEARN THE WORDS

Your Turn

Use Your Words:

accompany
amusing
axle
canvas
coma
emerge
ensure
entries
floe
galley
indebted
parka
partake
puncture
ripple
stall
talcum
terrain
torture
traitor

- Read the words on the list.
- Read the dialogue. Find the words.

MORE ACTIVITIES

1. Take a Survey

Graphic Organizer

If you could enter a race, what kind of race would it be? Ask 12 of your classmates to vote on which race they would enter: running, swimming, or biking. Tally their responses. Make a graph showing your results. Share your results with the rest of the class.

Which Race Would You Enter?

Race	Votes
Running	
Swimming	
Biking	

2. Make a Drawing

Listening and Speaking

Have you ever entered a race and won? Draw a picture of yourself winning a race. Show the picture to your partner. Talk about it with your partner. Describe how you won.

3. Write a Letter

Writing

Suppose you and a parent were in a car race. The car breaks down and you have to walk the rest of the way. Write a letter to a friend telling about your experience. Share your letter with your class.

4. It's Amusing!

Vocabulary

Amusing means "entertaining or funny." With a partner, think of other words that mean the same or almost the same as *amusing*. Make a list of the words and share them with your class.

5. You Are the Poet

Writing

Think of all the words that rhyme with *race*. Write them down. Write a short poem about a race. Share the poem with your partner. Talk about ways the poem can be improved.

6. Make a List

Vocabulary

Think about all the words that have to do with races. The words can relate to running races, bike races, swimming races, or any other race you can think of. With a partner make a list of the words. Share the list with your class.

Running race	Bike race	Swimming race	(other)	(other)

Driving Westward

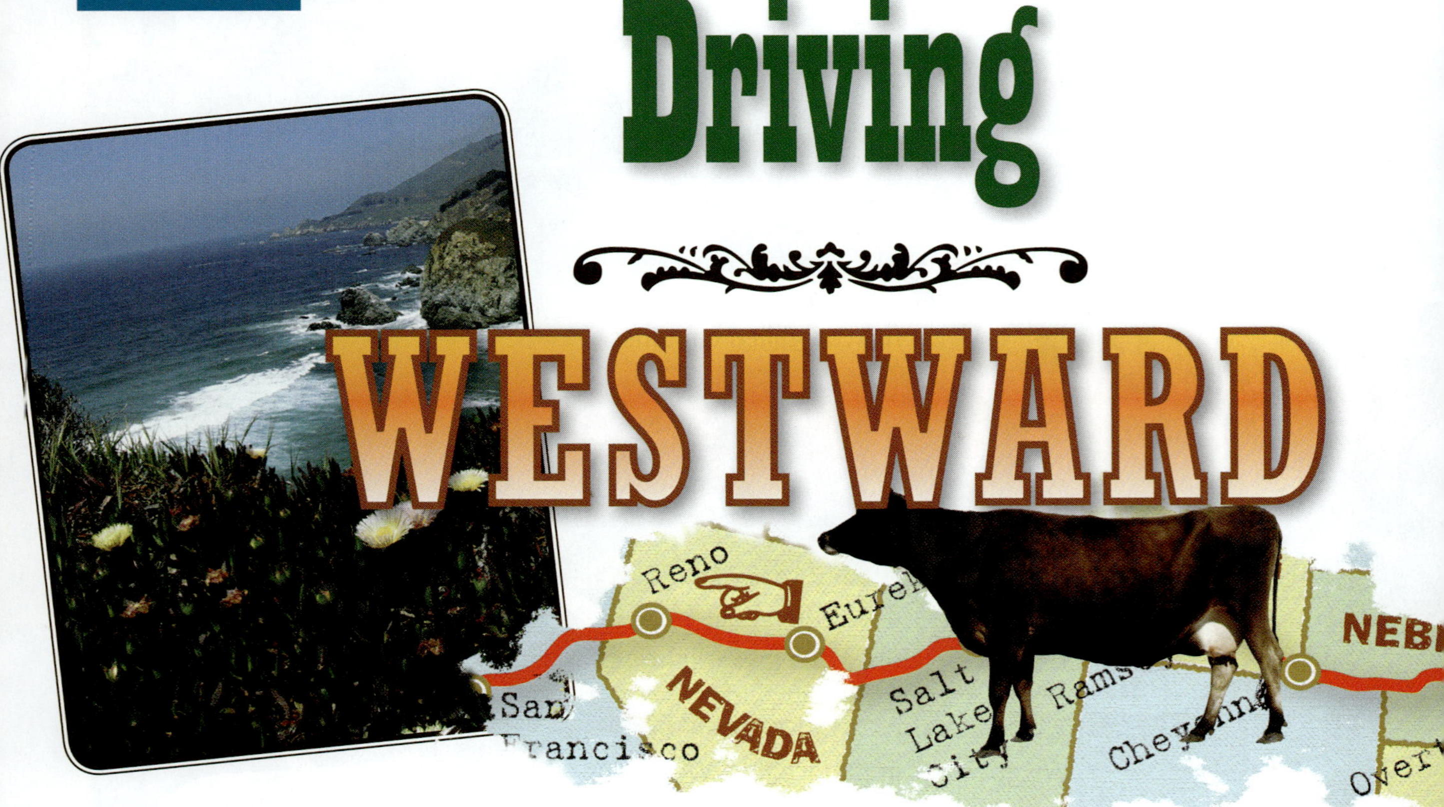

From *Coast to Coast with Alice* by Patricia Rusch Hyatt

FOCUS: How would it feel to be one of the first people to do something entirely new?

In 1909, cars were still a new invention. It was still rare to see one on the road. The United States had no real highways yet. Road maps didn't even exist. That's when 21-year-old Alice Ramsey got into her Maxwell and set out from New Jersey. She hoped to be the first woman to drive all the way across the country. Alice was accompanied by her friend Minna Jahns, age 16. Her older sisters-in-law, Nettie and Maggie, were also along for the ride. This selection uses historical details. It imagines what Minna's journal might have said. J. D. Murphy, mentioned in the entries, was a reporter following the story.

June 9, 1909

The Trip Starts New York State

Our Maxwell touring car is a shiny beauty, and Alice has it perfectly fixed up for the trip. Most Maxwells are painted Speedster Red. But this one is a DR model, so it is painted bright green. DR stands for doctor. It must cost much more than the standard red auto, which I know is $550, because the DR is a more powerful machine, built to drive over hilly country and sandy roads that a doctor must travel to reach sick people. Alice says the steering is a bit stiff, but that's good for starting out.

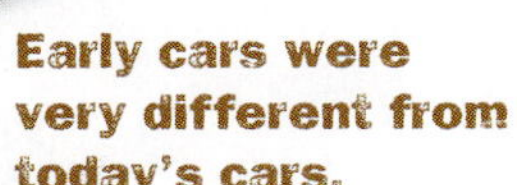

Early cars were very different from today's cars.

The Maxwell people have exchanged the regular 14-gallon gas tank for one that holds 20 gallons. We have a rack for two extra tires on the right side of the car. And, of course, we have a tire repair kit. There's also a picnic hamper full of food like cornflakes and canned tomatoes, and a box camera. Last week Alice showed all three of us how to take pictures.

The Maxwell's gas tank is just under my seat, and one of my jobs is to keep track of our fuel level with a ruled stick. Someone should invent a device that tells you when the tank is getting empty. Nettie's been asking me to measure almost every hour. I feel like talking back, but I don't want to spoil everything the first day out. Alice whispered to me that Nettie gets nervous, and in a while I'll be able to prove to her that the fuel goes down slowly and doesn't vanish in a poof like a magician's rabbit.

On the auto's left running board is a carbide generator to make the gas fumes that power our headlamps. Yes, we are going to be able to drive after sunset! That's something Lewis and Clark couldn't do when they explored the West about a hundred years ago. To turn on our headlamps, I drop special carbide pellets into the generator; then Alice and I jump down, and I open the front glass over the two headlamps. Alice strikes the match and holds it to each gas escape tube until the flame is steady. Then I snap the glass partway shut, and we're ready to go. We will have to drive somewhat slower at night, but our top speed in the daytime should hit 40 miles an hour!

June 23, 1909

Fixing a Flat — Rochelle, Illinois

To cross Illinois, we've been joined by J. D. Murphy again and three motorcars full of photographers and car salesmen. Everybody wants to be a part of our trip. The driving has been pretty tame so far, except for the rain, but the locals keep telling us the roads get worse as we move farther west.

Alice and I went shopping this morning for strong towing rope, a block and tackle (to hook and lift the car out of ditches if we need to), and short shovels. Then the four of us climbed aboard and led the parade of news people west over farm roads that crossed cornfields divided by small creeks. I counted 12 scarecrows, and then the Maxwell started to wobble. It was a flat tire!

Maggie asked Alice if she wanted to use the tank of compressed air. But Alice said no because we may need to save that air for flat tires in the desert or in the rain. So I brought Alice the tire repair kit from the spare tire drum, and Nettie brought the pliers and tire irons from the toolbox. The reporters stood around and watched.

Alice cranked our little jack to raise the wheel off the ground. She loosened the tire rings with the irons, pulled out the flat tube, and declared, "This is just like Mother takes the insides out of a turkey before stuffing it for Thanksgiving dinner."

She showed how to feel the inside of the tube for the hole that caused the flat. Then I roughed up the rubber so the cement would stick. Once the cement was tacky on both the tire and the patch, Alice held them together until the patch was set firm.

Of course, I already knew how to fix a flat. Alice was giving the lesson for the reporters, who were scribbling on their notepads.

Before she replaced the tube in its **canvas** tire, Alice felt carefully all around the inside of the tire to make sure there were no nails or tacks to cause another **puncture**. She dusted the tube with **talcum** powder, carefully stuffed it back in place, and replaced the tire rings.

Then Alice turned to the press boys and told them the tire was ready for a pump. And they all took a turn.

The car crosses several more states. In Iowa, the other three women get out and prepare to continue to Omaha, Nebraska, by train. The car needs to be as light as possible for its drive up Danger Hill. Only J. D. Murphy will accompany Alice in the car, to act as her witness. His news story will prove that Alice made it up the hill.

June 29, 1909

Still Waiting in Omaha

Omaha, Nebraska

More News—Alice and J. D. arrived this very afternoon. While Alice left to wash her hair, J. D. told us about climbing Danger Hill. He said after they turned the corner and started up, smooth as you please, they saw another motorcar in trouble about two-thirds of the way up. That car's motor was coughing and spitting. The driver got out several times with a shovel to knock mud off the wheels. His car **stalled** again and again, but luckily his brakes held.

Alice shouted up the hill to the other driver that she had a rope and could pull him up.... The driver said yes, please help, so Alice pressed her pedal hard and drove up until she was just past the stalled car.

Alice told the other driver to put his motor in low gear so her engine wouldn't be pulling dead weight. She tied her rear **axle** to the front hook of the other motorcar. It was slippery going, but tire chains kept both cars on Danger Hill road all the way to the top.

I'm sorry I missed watching that tow.

When the car's axle breaks, Alice orders a new one by telephone. Amusingly, it has to be sent from the manufacturer by train.

July 11, 1909

Ranchland Fences — **Overton, Nebraska**

Alice and a local mechanic had our axle installed by 9 P.M. last night. Today we've been bumping along cattle and horse trails, following the telegraph wires west, since there are no real roads and we have no map. "After all," Alice says, "these poles and wires MUST lead us to the next town."

The grass out here **ripples** like an ocean blowing around us. We have been crossing miles and miles of sheep and cattle ranches. This was the old Overland stage route of years ago.

I have a new job: opening and closing the fence gates as we drive through the fields.

Alice and her friends arrive safely in California on August 6. Alice and the car return east by train. Her former passengers remain in San Francisco for a few days to see the sights. Then they also take the train home. Alice, the first woman to drive coast to coast, has made her mark on history.

STOP AND THINK

1. What does Alice do that shows that she is the right person to be on this adventure?
2. What might a person like Alice look forward to doing nowadays?

THE BOAT CALLED FISH

From *The Lamp, the Ice, and the Boat Called Fish*
by Jacqueline Briggs Martin; pictures by Beth Krommes

In the early decades of the twentieth century, there were still unexplored territories in the world—mostly areas that were hard to reach because of terrain or extreme climate. This selection is based on accounts of a 1913 Arctic expedition.

FOCUS: In an extreme environment, what skills might be the most important ones to ensure survival?

Names you need to know

Aleutian a language of the Arctic region

Iñupiaq a native people of Alaska

How to say the words

Qiruk (KEE-rook)	the mother
Kurraluk (KOO-ra-look)	the father
Kataktovik (KUT-uk-tow-vik)	his friend
Pagnasuk (PAG-na-sook)	the older daughter
Makpii (MUK-bee)	the younger daughter
ugruk (OOG-rook)	bearded seal
ulu (OO-loo)	a knife with many uses

The boat was built in the 1880s to carry salmon and was named *Karluk,* Aleutian for "fish." After a while it carried crews to hunt bowhead whales. Then the hunting stopped, and the *Karluk* had no work—until the summer of 1913, when it sailed north from British Columbia toward the Arctic Circle.

There were no fishing crews and no whalers on board, but scientists of the Canadian Arctic Expedition, traveling up the coast of Alaska to study the plants and people in the high north. The leader of the group was an explorer named Stefansson. He wanted to find new islands in the icy ocean. There were also a cook, a captain, a crew, one black cat, and forty sled dogs.

When the boat reached Point Barrow, Stefansson invited an Iñupiaq family to join the expedition. Stefansson knew the group would need fur clothes and boots of caribou and sealskin to survive the Arctic cold. They would need fresh meat from seals and *ugruk*—bearded seal. Qiruk, the mother, could look at a man, cut a fur skin with her round-bladed *ulu*, and sew a pair of pants that would fit him exactly. She could make boots that would keep his feet from freezing. Kurraluk, the father, and his friend Kataktovik were good hunters. They had the patience to wait by seal holes for hours. Qiruk and Kurraluk brought their two daughters. Pagnasuk was eight years old and little Makpii was two.

The crew built a place on the deck for the family to live. Inside their small room they had a seal oil lamp that gave warmth and light. Perhaps the two girls had a ball, made of sealskin and filled with caribou hair, to toss and catch. The crew never heard them cry. They played while the forty dogs howled and fought and the black cat ran in the **galley**.

Winter came early in 1913, and soon the captain was steering the ship between huge chunks of ice—some as big as houses.

In mid-August the boat was stopped by a large sheet of ice, up to a foot thick and dotted with water holes. As the weather grew colder the water thickened with gray needles of new ice.

While Pagnasuk and Makpii tossed their sealskin ball, while the carpenter taught tricks to the black cat, while the sled dogs scrapped, and while they all slept, the ice around the boat froze solid.

Then the boat and the ice were one, and the boat could go only where the ice went. That was when the leader, Stefansson, and five others left the boat with sleds and dogs to hunt caribou. They were on land when a storm blew the ice-locked boat out to sea. Stefansson sent a report to the government in Ottawa that the *Karluk* would probably be sunk by ice but he was sure its passengers would survive. Then Stefansson was off to look for new land.

That was when the boat's captain, Robert Bartlett, became the leader. That was when Qiruk sewed every day. No one could tell what would happen. Would the boat sink? Would they have enough food? Would they be able to stay warm in the cold, dark winter? As long as the ice was solid the boat was safe. If the ice should crack, then wind or water would be strong enough to push a piece of ice through its wooden sides and the boat would sink.

During that time, Qiruk, whom the crew now called "Auntie," sewed boots, pants, and parkas for the people on the boat. Kurraluk and Kataktovik went seal-hunting out on the ice. These preparations would help the crew to survive.

For three months the boat continued to drift in its icy trap—wherever the wind and water took it. The crew and the scientists used boxes and barrels to build the walls of a house on a large ice **floe** not far from the ship. That ice was thirty feet thick and half as big as a football field—"able to stand a good deal of knocking," the captain wrote later.

In December, while the ice shifted, groaned, and scraped around him, Kurraluk worked in the Arctic twilight and built a house of snow next to the box house. Mr. Hadley, the ship's carpenter, made three long sledges, or sleds. They all knew that if the ship did sink, they would have to haul their clothes and food supplies to land.

They kept themselves busy and even had holidays. When Christmas came, the captain, the Iñupiat, the scientists, and the crew feasted on oysters and bear steak, cake and biscuits. The captain gave Auntie a comb, a looking glass, and a new dress. He gave Makpii and Pagnasuk new dresses, too. And he gave Kurraluk and Kataktovik new hunting knives. They ran races and had a tug of war, and everyone was jolly. No one talked about when the boat might sink.

On New Year's Day they went out on the ice to play soccer. Qiruk was goaltender.

The air was so cold the captain could not blow his whistle.

Nine days later, at the end of the day, when Pagnasuk and her sister may have been sitting by the seal oil lamp, listening to their father tell stories of a ten-legged polar bear, they heard a loud splitting sound. A large, sharp point of ice was breaking through the side of their boat!

"All hands abandon ship!" the captain called. He sent Qiruk and the two girls to the box house to start a fire in the stove so all would have a warm shelter. The others carried supplies off the ship and onto the ice floe. The carpenter took the black cat to the box house in a basket. They could not see where they were going in the dark night and blowing snow. The ship's doctor fell into the sea and had to be pulled to safety.

Everyone stood outside to watch the *Karluk* as it disappeared underwater. By the next morning the ice was solid. The *Karluk* was locked under the sea. The thirteen crew members, the captain, the six scientists, the Iñupiaq family, their friend Kataktovik, the dogs, and the cat were left on an island of blue ice in the cold, dark Arctic.

The members of the expedition were stranded for months in the Arctic, with the greatest threats to survival being starvation and exposure to the icy weather. The hunting and food preservation skills of the Iñupiaq family helped ensure that many members of the expedition lived. During that time, Kataktovik and Captain Bartlett separated from the others and journeyed hundreds of miles on foot to find help. Through their courageous efforts, a ship finally picked up the survivors. Without Qiruk, Kurraluk, Kataktovik, and Bartlett, no one from the boat called "Fish" would have emerged from the Arctic alive.

STOP AND THINK

1. Why were the clothes made by Qiruk more useful than the sailors' original clothes?
2. If you knew you were going into an environment of extreme cold, how would you prepare?

Reading Longer Words

In this unit you learned more about how to read longer words.

Step 1: Divide the word into parts.

Compound word?
Divide between the words.

Prefix?
Divide after the prefix.

Suffix?
Divide before the suffix.

VCCV letter pattern?
Divide between the consonants.

VCV letter pattern?
Divide before the consonant.
or
Divide after the consonant.

Step 2: Read each word part.

Step 3: Read the whole word. Sound right? If not, try an alternative.

Ends in a consonant?
Try a short vowel sound.

Ends in a vowel?
Try a long vowel sound.

Has a VCe pattern?
Try a long vowel sound.

Ends in *-le, -al,* or *-el*?
Try dividing before the consonant preceding the *l*.

Has a syllable with vowel + *r*?
May change the sound of the vowel.

Has a vowel pair?
Pair stays together.

Divide the Words

de/ment/ed	at/tempt/ed
de/fend/ed	re/mand/ed
dis/rupt/ed	il/lu/sion
con/fir/ma/tion	sus/pen/sion
com/pre/hen/sion	pro/nun/ci/a/tion

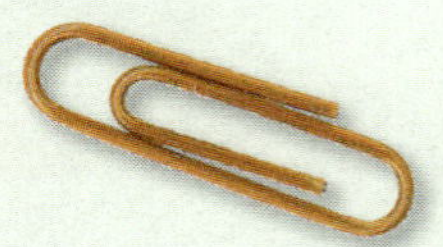

Read Word Parts	Read Whole Words
de ment ed →	demented
at tempt ed →	attempted
de fend ed →	defended
re mand ed →	remanded
dis rupt ed →	disrupted
il lu sion →	illusion
con fir ma tion →	confirmation
sus pen sion →	suspension
com pre hen sion →	comprehension
pro nun ci a tion →	pronunciation

Read More Words

Use what you learned in Units 1–7 to read these words from the unit.

complexion	accustomed	unconscious	cadaverous	ridiculous
tomatoes	headlamps	ripples	carpenter	preservation

Vocabulary

Word Origins

Words evolved over time from different languages. You can find information about the origin of a word in some dictionaries. The Library Media Center in your school is a good place to look for different dictionaries.

ed·i·tor (ĕdĭtər) noun. person who writes editorials; person who prepares writings for publication by correcting errors and checking facts. [Late Latin, *editor*, from Latin *editus*, publish, give out.]

The red type tells you that the word *editor* comes from the Latin word *editus*. There are words in Italian and French that come from the same Latin root.

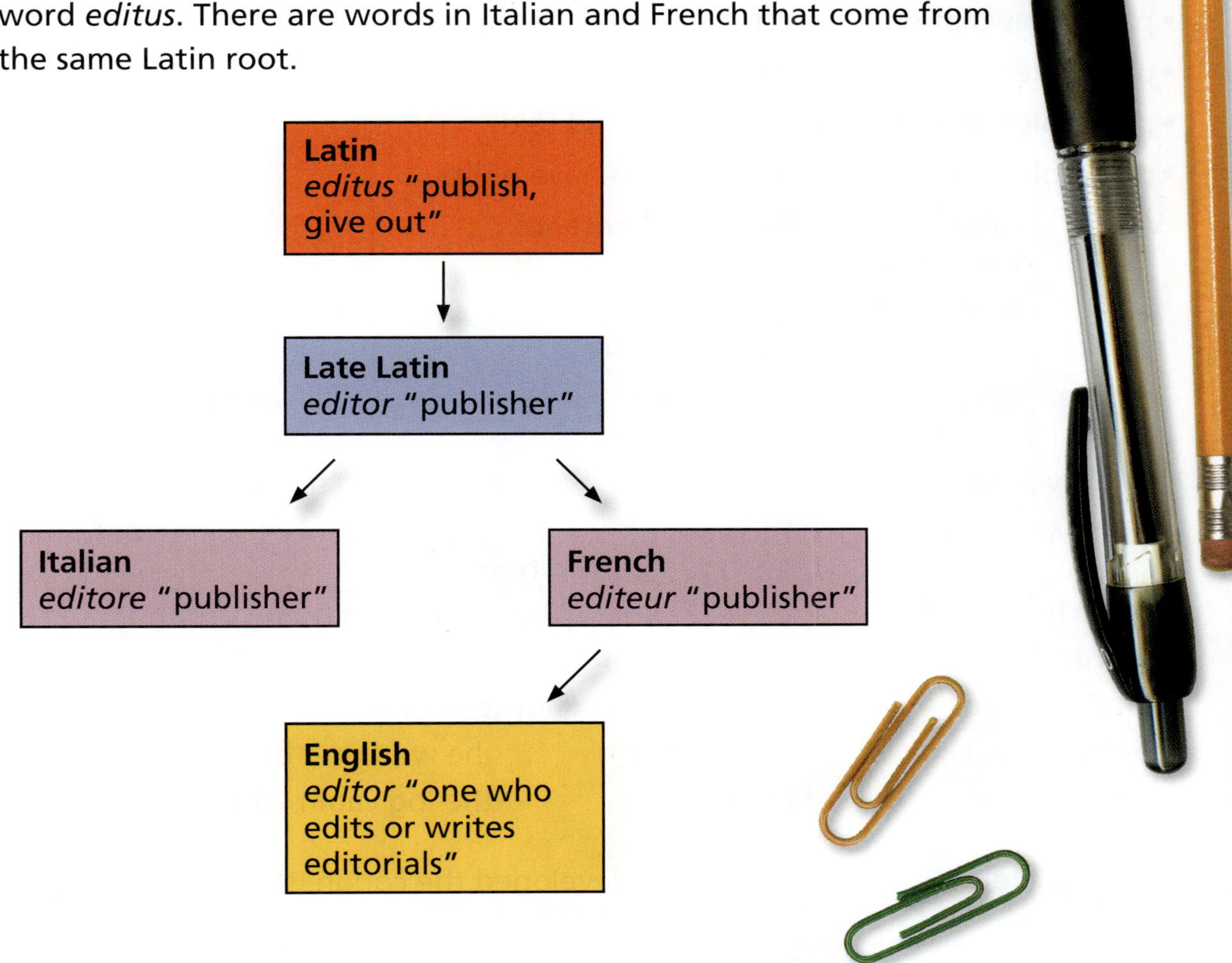

Irregular Present Perfect and Past Perfect Verbs

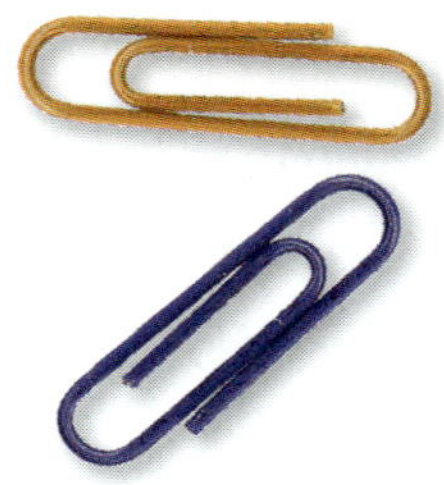

Recall that you create the future perfect tense by combining the future form of the helping verb *to have* with the past participle of a main verb.

Present Perfect	*has* or *have* + past participle
Past Perfect	*had* + past participle

The past participle of an **irregular verb** does not end in *-ed*.

There are many different irregular past participles, which need to be memorized. However, there are some patterns to look for:

- participles that end in *-n* (to show ⟶ have shown)
- participles that end in *-en* (to speak ⟶ had spoken)
- participles that end in *-ght* (to think ⟶ have thought)
- participles that end in *-d* (to say ⟶ had said)
- participles that end in *-t* (to build ⟶ have built)

Verb	Irregular Past Participle	Used in a Sentence
to speak	spoken	My parents **have spoken** with my teacher more than once this term.
to take	taken	My brother **had taken** all his final exams before he got sick.
to grow	grown	That boy **has grown** three inches since last spring!
to show	shown	The agent **had shown** us six homes before we found the one we liked best.
to catch	caught	She **has caught** the cold that is going around.
to bring	brought	We **had brought** our suitcases to the train station.
to tell	told	I **have told** you not to do that.
to say	said	The worker **had said** he wouldn't be in today.
to build	built	The family **has built** the log cabin with their bare hands.
to feel	felt	Before she developed the cough, she **had felt** soreness in her throat.
to do	done	They **have done** everything they could to help him.
to have	had	Mr. Lanford **had had** that old car for many years.

Spelled the Same: Past Tense Forms and Past Participles

For some verbs, the simple past tense is spelled the same as the past participle.

Verb	Past Tense	Past Participle
to find	found	found
to have	had	had
to fight	fought	fought
to buy	bought	bought
to feel	felt	felt
to hold	held	held
to make	made	made
to think	thought	thought

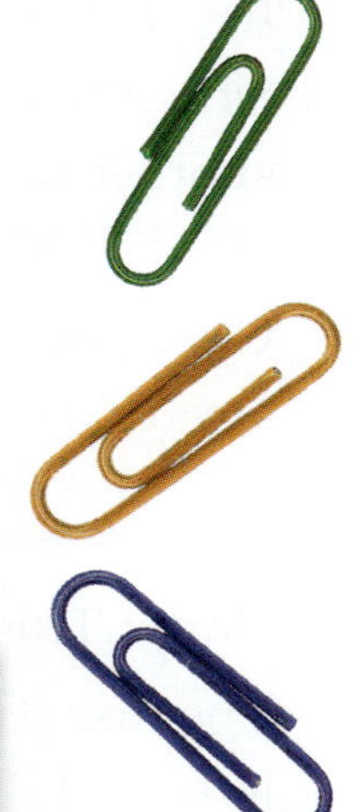

The Past Perfect Tense: Sequence of Actions

The past perfect tense is used to show that one event happened before another event.

Sentence	Past Perfect Verb Phrase	Other Verb	Which Happened First?
I had thought I would learn to play the tuba, but the trombone interested me more.	had thought	interested	thought
Joanne had said she would go on the hike until she saw the size of the mountain.	had said	saw	said
Paco's dad had spoken to the coach about his son's injury before the game began.	had spoken	began	spoken

Business Letters

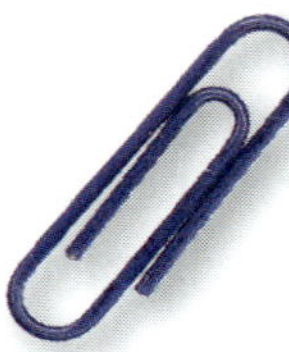

A **business letter** is more formal than a personal letter.

A business letter has six parts.

Heading: This contains your return address with the date.

Inside Address: This is always on the left margin, and includes the address you are sending your letter to. It should include the name of the recipient as well.

Skip a line after the heading before the inside address. Skip another line after the inside address before the greeting.

Greeting: The greeting in a business letter is always formal. It always includes the person's title and last name. The greeting in a business letter always ends in a colon.

Body: This is the main part of the letter.

The first paragraph should clearly state the main point of the letter, while the second paragraph often includes supporting details to explain or justify your purpose. In the final paragraph, you should briefly restate your main point and why it is important. It is usually polite to close the letter by thanking the reader for his or her time.

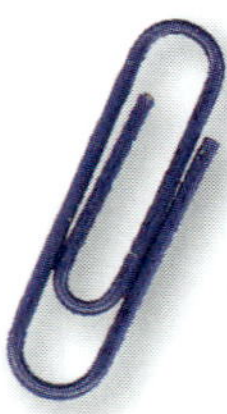

Skip a line between the greeting and the body, and between each paragraph in the body. Skip a line between the body and the closing.

Closing: The closing always ends with a comma, and should be aligned with the left margin.

Signature: Skip two lines and then sign your name.

Here is a good example of a business letter.

heading

Ms. Ciara Walters
12187 Destiny Way
Fleming, CA 99030

May 26, 2008

inside address

Mr. Wayne Jennings
Rain City Cameras
15456 Pyramid Way
Bournemouth, WA 73133

greeting

Dear Mr. Jennings:

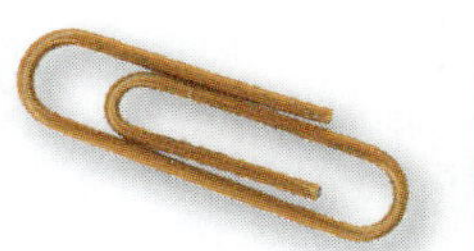

body

I recently purchased one of your cameras while on vacation in Washington. Unfortunately, when I returned home to California, I discovered that several of the camera's parts were missing. The instructions were also missing. As a result, I have been unable to use it.

I am writing to request replacements for the missing parts, as well as a copy of the instructions. If that is not possible, I would like a full refund. Enclosed please find my receipt of purchase, as well as a list of the missing parts.

I sincerely hope that you will address this situation as soon as possible. I thank you for your time and attention.

closing

Sincerely,

signature

Ciara Walters
Ciara Walters

FOCUS LITERATURE

UNIT 7

THE BIRTH OF JUSTICE

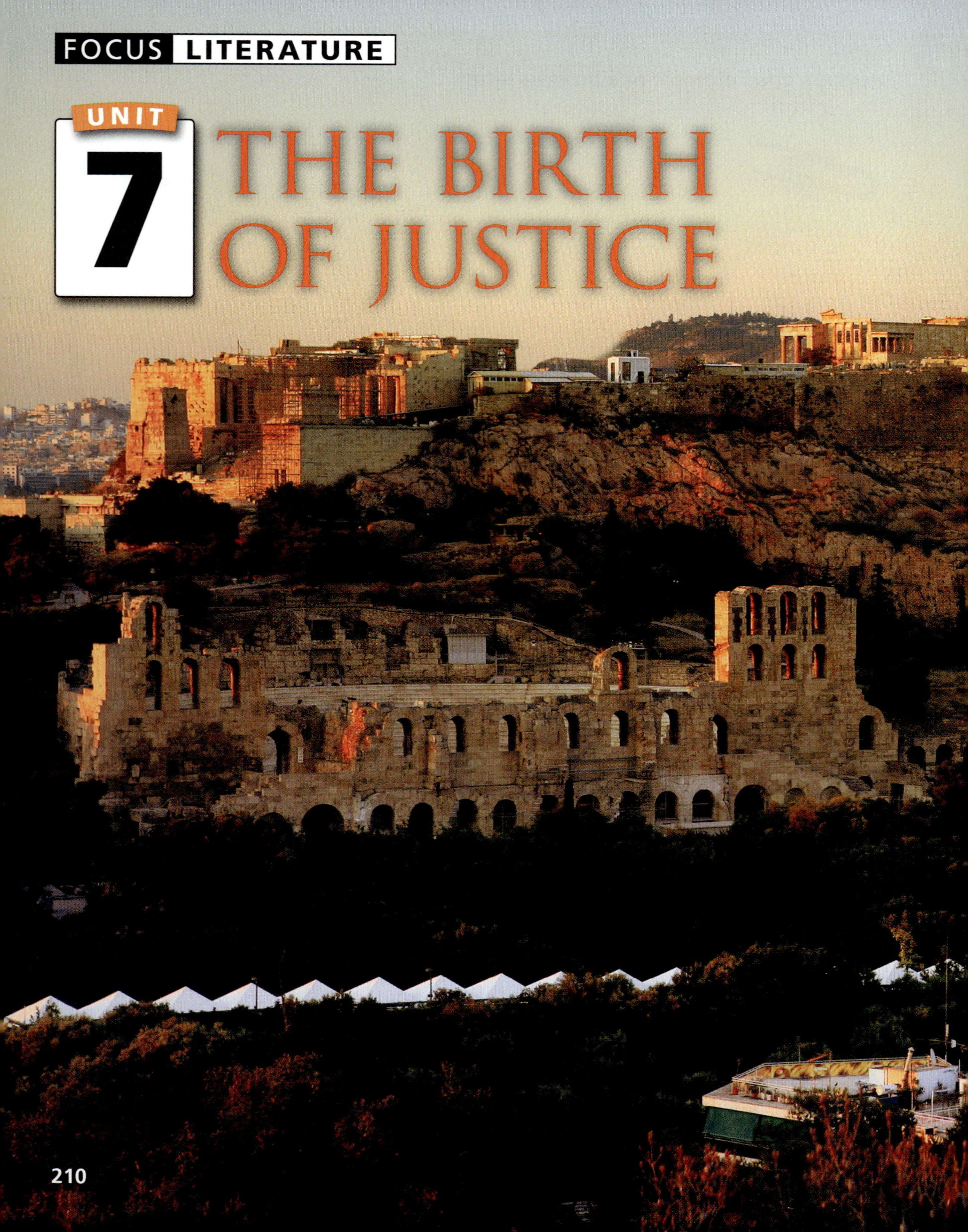

THE BIG QUESTION:

HOW DID OUR IDEAS OF JUSTICE DEVELOP?

READINGS

Looking at Justice

What is a republic?

A republic is...

- ☐ a country.
- ☐ a place where leaders are elected.
- ☐ a place where leaders make the laws.
- ☐ a place where a group of leaders rule.

How did ancient Greek philosophers help advance the concept of justice?

Ancient Greek philosophers...

- ☐ asked questions that caused people to think.
- ☐ wrote explanations of their reasoning.
- ☐ debated ideas with students.
- ☐ opened schools to teach others.

What was a city-state?

A city-state...

- was bigger than a city but smaller than a state.
- had its own laws, customs, money, and army.
- had citizens who could vote.
- might battle other city-states.

What do we know about the ancient Jews?

The ancient Jews...

- had a written language.
- were said to be descended from Abraham.
- worshipped one God.
- created a system of laws to govern themselves.

What ancient ideas or writings still influence many people today?

Many people today are still influenced by...

- the Bible.
- Plato's writings about Socrates' ideas.
- Plato's *Republic*.
- the ideas of Aristotle.

Literature Words

confirm

consist

distinct

identity

inherit

justice

mournful

nomad

sacrifice

underlying

confirm

Confirm means to establish the truth or validity of something.

"John's teacher confirmed that the math test was canceled."

consist

Consist means to be made up of, or composed of.

"The lunch consisted of sandwiches, salad, and lemonade."

justice

Justice means the administration of a deserved punishment or reward.

"The thief received justice when he was sent to jail."

mournful

Mournful means feeling or expressing sorrow or grief.

"The family was mournful when their pet hamster died."

distinct

Distinct means to be different in nature or quality from all others.

"You can tell the twins apart because they have distinct features."

identity

Identity is the condition of being oneself and not another person.

"Who I am and what I like are all part of my identity."

inherit

Inherit means to receive property from a relative.

"When his aunt died, John inherited her car."

nomad

A **nomad** is a person who belongs to a group that has no permanent home, but travels from place to place.

"The nomads traveled across the desert, setting up tents when night fell."

sacrifice

A **sacrifice** is the offering of something, such as an animal or a human life, to a god.

"In ancient times, a lamb was sacrificed to the gods."

underlying

Underlying means the foundation of something.

"The freedom to vote is an underlying principle of democracy."

READ TOGETHER

ABRAHAM'S JOURNEY

The origins of many of the world's religions are recorded in ancient texts. For Christians and Jews, the Bible tells of their religious faith, laws, and practices. The Jewish Bible **consists** of the parts that Christians call the Old Testament. The first book of the Old Testament includes the story of Abraham, one of the patriarchs, or founding fathers, of Judaism. Archaeological discoveries in the twentieth century have **confirmed** the likely locations of some of the places mentioned in this biblical tale of faith.

UR Abraham lives in this Sumerian city in southern Mesopotamia around 2000 B.C.E. He is the leader of a large clan, or tribe, that has a **seminomadic** culture.

HARAN Here Abraham receives a message from God, telling him to lead his clan to a new homeland. God also makes a promise to Abraham, "I will make of thee a great nation." Abraham's faith is tested. Not only is he an old man, but God doesn't tell him where he is supposed to go. Abraham leads his clan on a long and difficult journey.

SHECHEM Abraham reaches this settlement in Canaan and is told by God that this is the promised land. Today the area is called Israel.

EGYPT A famine drives Abraham and his wife Sarah to Egypt, where they are treated well. Wealthy with cattle, silver, and gold, they travel back to Canaan.

BETHEL Here Abraham receives another message from God. Abraham will have many descendants and the land will belong to them for all time to come. Abraham is surprised, since he and Sarah are over 100 years old and have no children. So Abraham has a son with his wife's servant, Hagar. Then Sarah also gives birth to a son, Isaac.

MT. MORIAH Abraham gets a difficult order from God. He must take Isaac to this mountain and **sacrifice** him. Abraham's faith is tested again. He decides that he must obey God. Just as he is about to kill Isaac, God stops him. A ram is killed instead.

CAVE OF MACHPELAH Sarah convinces Abraham to buy this cave near Hebron as the family burying ground. When she dies at the age of 127, she is buried here. Abraham marries another woman and has many more children. But only Isaac—and his descendants—**inherit** the promised land. At the age of 175, Abraham dies and is buried next to Sarah.

GET READY TO READ

Comprehension

TARGET SKILL **Classify and Categorize** Sorting information into categories helps you remember and understand what you read. A **category** is a group of items that are alike in some way.

When you read, you **classify and categorize**. That means you put text details into categories. Each item in a category is alike in some way. Sometimes authors classify and categorize information as a text structure.

Clue words and sentences help you know how the author categorizes and classifies information in the text.

The following paragraph is taken from the selection "A Landmark Book of Early Thought: The Bible." It contains clue words and sentences that help you recognize categories.

The clue word *some* tells that not all text details will belong in this category.

This sentence helps us understand what items belong in the second category.

How do we know today what ancient people were like? Some cultures have left behind objects such as pottery, ruined buildings, and carvings. These remains can tell a lot about how people lived. However, they can't tell what people thought or believed. Other cultures have left behind inscriptions and documents. These tell about people's ideas. A written language allows a culture to speak to us from thousands of years in the past.

This sentence describes items in the first category.

The words *however* and *other* signal a different category.

You can use a chart to help you categorize and classify. The number of columns depends on the number of categories.

Artifacts	Written Records
Tell how people lived	Tell about people's ideas

The first category tells what we know about cultures that left behind only artifacts, such as pottery, ruined buildings, and carvings, but no written documents. The second category tells what we know about cultures that also left behind a written record.

TARGET STRATEGY **Question** As you read, ask yourself these questions to help you categorize and classify text details:

- How are these things alike?
- How are they different?
- In which groups do these things belong?

Selection 1

A Landmark Book of Early Thought:

The Bible

FOCUS: How has the Bible influenced modern beliefs?

How do we know today what ancient people were like? Some cultures have left behind objects such as pottery, ruined buildings, and carvings. These remains can tell a lot about how people lived. However, they can't tell what people thought or believed. Other cultures have left behind inscriptions and documents. These tell about people's ideas. A written language allows a culture to speak to us from thousands of years in the past.

The Hebrews, or Jews, are one of the earliest people to have a written language that can still be read today. Most of their written records make up the book we call the Bible. The Bible is more than a religious book. It is also a a record of the history, laws, and ideas of the Hebrews, the people of Israel. Later parts of the Bible give an account of the origin and ideas of the Christian religion, which also began in Israel. The ideas found in the Bible are important because they still guide the thinking of many people today.

Moses gave the Ten Commandments to the Hebrews.

THE HISTORY OF THE JEWS

The Bible begins the history of the Jews by telling when they became a **distinct** people. It gives an account of Abraham, who lived sometime between 2000 and 1700 B.C.E. Through his son, Isaac, he is said to be the father of the people of Israel. The Bible tells that Abraham made a pledge to believe in just one God instead of many gods. The belief in one God is the way Jews have identified themselves throughout their history. Muslims believe that Abraham is also the father of the Arab people, through his son Ishmael. So three of the world's most important religions—Judaism, Christianity, and Islam—date their beginnings back to Abraham.

THE JEWISH LAW BOOK

At the beginnings of many cultures, wrongdoing is often what the rulers say it is. If a king, chief, or high priest wants to punish a person, the person will be punished. It's hard for ordinary people to know how to act when they don't know what a ruler will decide from one day to the next!

A great moment of change in a culture comes when its people establish laws. Clearly established laws tell people what they can and cannot do. Laws can also give people a way to ask for **justice** when someone else does something wrong to them.

In the Bible, the establishment of laws came during the time of Moses, probably around 1400 B.C.E. The Jews had been enslaved for years in the land of Egypt. After gaining their freedom, they wandered in the desert for years. This was the first time they were able to govern themselves. They wrote down a detailed system of laws. According to Jewish and Christian belief, God gave these laws to Moses.

The laws in the Bible deal with many aspects of behavior and daily life. The most famous laws are the Ten Commandments. Some of the commandments are basic laws that make it possible for people to live as a group. They tell that it is wrong to do things such as kill, steal, and tell lies about other people. Other laws in the Bible instruct when to observe holy days. Another section tells the people of Israel to set up a court system. This part of the Bible is the foundation of all Jewish law.

OTHER THINGS WE LEARN FROM THE BIBLE

The Bible later tells about the years when Israel was a kingdom, ruled by kings such as Saul, David, and Solomon. These kings lived between 1100 and 900 B.C.E. After their reigns, Israel was defeated several times by powerful kingdoms. Through the hard times, the Bible records that Jews continued to identify themselves as a distinct people who followed certain laws and worshiped just one God. They preserved their **identity** even when they were ruled by civilizations in which people worshiped many gods.

Other books of the Bible record prayers, poems, songs, and sayings of the Jewish people. Some are happy and some are **mournful**. Some are statements of belief. Others are emotional reactions to events in the history of Israel.

Beautiful stained glass windows showing scenes from the Bible can be found in many churches and synagogues.

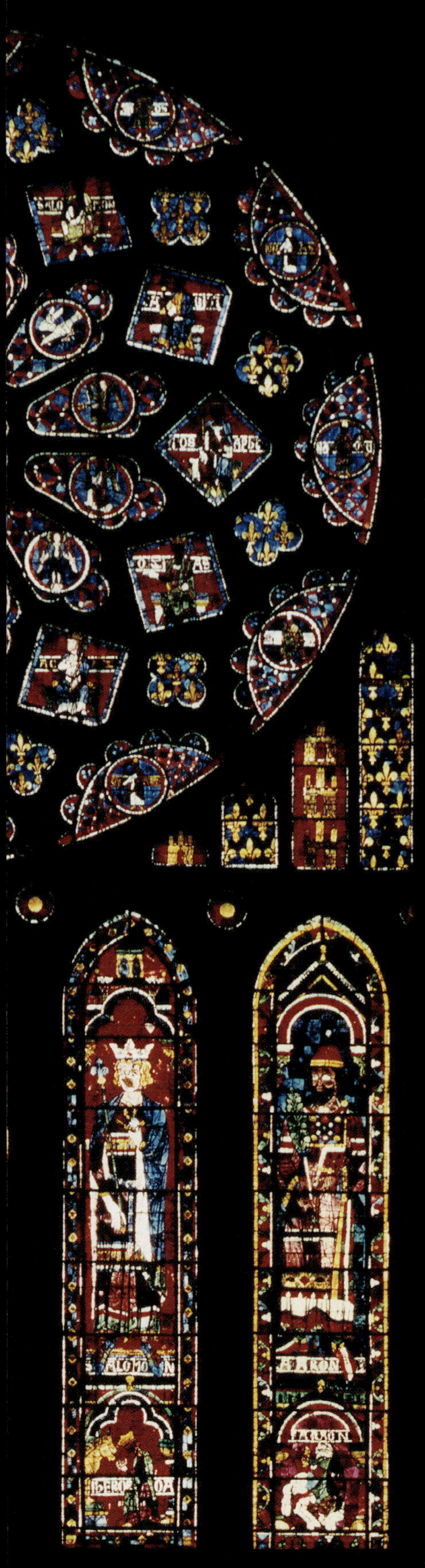

These sections show that ancient people had the same feelings, joys, and fears as people today. In fact, many people today find comfort and insight in these parts of the Bible.

For Christians, the Bible has an added section: the books of the New Testament. These tell of the life of Jesus and document the beliefs that Christians hold. This section is also important as history. It describes the land of Israel in the first century C.E., when it was part of the Roman Empire.

THE BIBLE AS A BASIS FOR LATER THOUGHT

Taken together, the Jewish and Christian sections of the Bible form one of the foundations of Western thought. Many scholars say that the Bible stresses two ideas: behaving respectfully toward God, and behaving justly toward other human beings. **Underlying** both ideas is a belief that each individual, whether a king or a poor farmer, has worth and responsibilities.

STOP AND THINK

1. According to the Bible, who was Abraham?
2. Why do you think the rules and laws found in the Bible are still important today?

Your Turn

Use Your Words:

abandon	**plumage**
aristocrat	**portray**
ascend	**proclaim**
barbaric	**prosper**
bold	**quarrel**
core	**quote**
devote	**refugee**
disembark	**republic**
myth	**revere**
perceive	**tribute**

- Read the words on the list.
- Read the dialogue. Find the words.

MORE ACTIVITIES

1. Venn Diagram

Graphic Organizer

In ancient Greece, aristocrats were rich nobles. Refugees were people who came to Greece seeking freedom. How were the lives of these two groups different? How were they alike? Write about aristocrats. Write about refugees. Write about things both groups shared in the center circle. Share your diagram with your class.

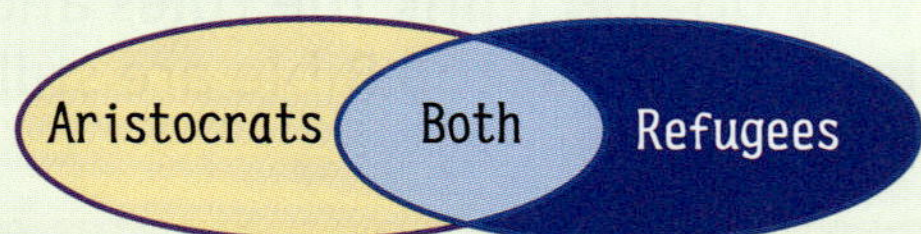

2. Make a Drawing

Speaking and Listening

Suppose you lived in ancient Greece. How would you dress? Draw a picture of yourself dressed as an ancient Greek. Show the picture to your partner. Talk about it.

3. Write a Postcard

Writing

Imagine you could travel back in time to visit this city in ancient Greece. Write a postcard to a friend back home describing your adventure.

4. Let's Quarrel!

Vocabulary

Quarrel means "to argue." With a partner, think of other words that mean the same or almost the same as *quarrel*. Make a list of the words and share them with your class.

5. Tell Me About It

Speaking and Listening

Write down five questions you would like to ask a person in ancient Greece. Have your partner play the role of an ancient Greek. Ask your partner the questions. Then switch.

6. Make a List

Vocabulary

Embark means "to get on a plane or ship." *Disembark* means "to get off a plane or ship." *Dis-* is a prefix that means "to do the opposite of." Think of all the words you know that have the prefix *dis-*. Make a list. Share the list with your class. Talk about the words' meanings.

Word	Word with *dis-*

THE THREE WISE MEN OF GREECE

FOCUS: What key ideas were most important to ancient Greek philosophers?

A young man is walking through the ancient Greek city of Athens. An older man comes up to him and looks him in the eye. The older man is a rather odd-looking character wearing threadbare clothes. "What is beauty?" he wants to know. "What is wisdom?" What kind of answer does he expect? How would you answer him?

PHILOSOPHERS AND THE SECRETS OF LIFE

This odd man was the great philosopher Socrates. In about 400 B.C.E., Socrates constantly asked questions such as these and pressed people to explain their answers.

The word *philosophy* means "the love of wisdom." A philosopher is a seeker of truth. Socrates wasn't the first Greek philospher. For centuries, Greece had been a land where ideas were greatly respected. Many philosophers before Socrates were interested in the external world and how it worked. They used observation and logic to figure out truths about matter, change, and other aspects of the physical world. You could really call some of their discoveries scientific or mathematical. For example, Pythagoras and his followers believed that reality was based on numerical relationships, so they explored many mathematical ideas.

REREAD

Classify + Categorize

What do Socrates and Pythagoras have in common?

Socrates and the Sophists

By the time of Socrates, a group of philosophers called Sophists existed. These people were philosophers for hire. They earned money by teaching practical wisdom. For example, Sophists specialized in teaching rhetoric, the art of speaking convincingly. Rhetoric and the Sophists' other teachings were designed to help people **prosper** in the world of that time. Being successful in Athens meant understanding how to manage property, appreciating the arts, and knowing how to take part in the government. Being a leading citizen also meant knowing how to conduct oneself well toward one's fellow citizens. So Sophists were very interested in the idea of examining what made a good and just life. This branch of philosophy is called ethics.

Like the Sophists, Socrates was interested in ethics and in self-knowledge. However, he disagreed with them because he wanted to search for truth, not just to be able to argue convincingly on all sides of an issue. In this search, he questioned people's beliefs about ideas such as government, religion, and human nature.

Many Athenians were fascinated by Socrates' question-based approach. They loved talking and arguing with him, and groups often gathered around him for hours. One of his favorite pastimes was exposing the flimsy arguments of Sophists and politicians. It's no surprise that many important Athenians didn't appreciate Socrates' questioning. In 399 B.C.E., a group of them accused Socrates of corrupting the minds of young people. He was brought to trial and sentenced to death.

Socrates

Plato and Aristotle

THE NEXT GREAT ATHENIAN PHILOSOPHER

Socrates didn't write down any of his ideas. Fortunately, one of his students, Plato, did. Born in 429 B.C.E., Plato came from a wealthy, **aristocratic** family and could afford to **devote** his life to philosophy. He was one of the citizens who followed Socrates through the streets, listening and debating. Plato later wrote how Socrates discussed ideas.

Plato agreed with his teacher's **core** beliefs that argument and common sense were needed to understand the world. One of Plato's most famous ideas was about how we **perceive** reality. He argued that humans are like people chained in a cave who can only see the shadows of what is going on outside. We can't help but think that the shadows are reality. But are they? Are we observing reality or only the shadows of reality?

The most famous of Plato's writings is called *The Republic*. This work investigates what it means to live a good life. Plato considers two aspects of this issue: how an individual can be a just person, and what a just political system would be. In the course of thinking about these matters, Plato brings up topics such as how citizens should be educated, what role the arts should play in an ideal state, and what an ideal government would be like. *The Republic* has influenced thinkers from Plato's time to ours.

From Plato to Aristotle

Plato opened a school to impart his ideas to other young philosophers. One of his students was Aristotle. This young man excelled, and soon Plato was calling him the "mind of the school." Aristotle would continue at Plato's school for twenty years, until his teacher's death around 347 B.C.E.

Aristotle was deeply interested in the natural world. He wanted to understand how nature worked. He tried to sort out plants and animals, classifying them according to their characteristics. To do this, he studied organisms directly, collecting data and making observations. He felt that things in nature should be observed in their own settings—a belief that many wildlife scientists hold today.

REREAD

Classify + Categorize

What classification of study interested Aristotle?

Perhaps Aristotle's greatest influence on later thinkers was the idea that "the fate of empires depends on the education of youth." Thousands of years later, we still believe that young people must be educated in order for our country to do well.

STOP AND THINK

1. How were Socrates, Plato, and Aristotle connected?
2. Which of these ancient philosphers' questions would you still want to find the answers for? Why?

Letters from Two City-States

FOCUS: What were the political differences between ancient Athens and Sparta?

ATHENS *From Apollo, Son of Nestor the Oil Trader, to his sister Arianna.*

Dearest Arianna,

Father and I arrived safely at the port of Athens. What a fascinating place! As we **disembarked** from the ship, I saw a bustling marketplace where the finest goods are displayed—everything from honey and figs to rare birds with shining **plumage**.

Citizens stride around as if they own the world—and I suppose in Athens they do. Here, each citizen is granted the right to vote in important state decisions. Of course no women or enslaved people can become citizens, so they can't vote. I find Athenians to be a **quarrelsome** people who love to settle their arguments in the courts of law. Seeing Athens makes me wonder if there might be a form of government that takes the best of Greek democracy but leaves behind the worst.

Many Athenians seem suspicious of Father and me. Our dear island of Aegina was united successfully with Athens in the Persian wars, but now Athenians are demanding a **tribute** from us, though they would disguise the tax by calling it a "contribution." Fortunately, our pure, delicious olive oil still commands a cordial reception at each establishment we visit.

I miss you, dear twin, and hope this postcard finds you in excellent health.

Your loving brother,
Apollo

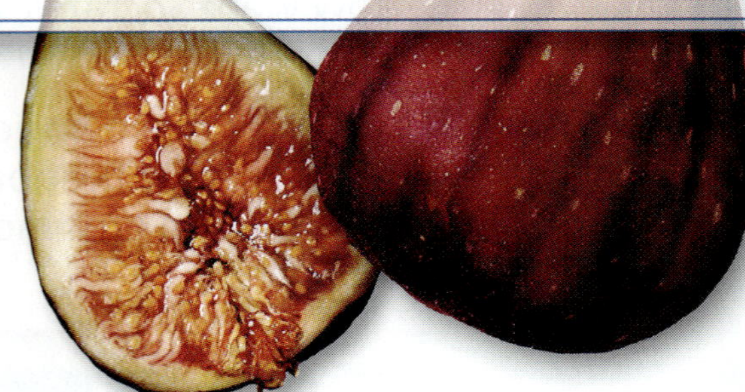

SPARTA *From Arianna, Daughter of Nestor the Oil Trader, to her brother Apollo.*

Dearest Apollo,

I write to you after a rough sea journey to Sparta. I find it a very strange place—so different from your description of Athens. Here it is the soldiers who stride about **boldly**, and I am sure that I have seen ten enslaved people for every citizen. The state's policies are different, too. While there is a senate, elected by an assembly of citizens, only landowners can take part in the assembly.

ANCIENT SPARTA MARKETPLACE

I saw few children as Uncle and I visited the oil merchants, because Spartans send their children off to military training camps. From what I can tell, the purpose of the camps is to teach boys and girls that there is no greater glory than fighting for one's state. It isn't hard to foretell more wars in the future of Sparta.

There is one Spartan idea that I appreciate: women have certain rights, and sometimes women even supervise family businesses. The Spartans are not surprised to see me helping manage Uncle's accounts. I suppose that even the Spartan form of government might have some good ideas to impart to the rest of Greece.

Hoping to see you soon, dear twin,

Arianna

STOP AND THINK

1. Who could vote in ancient Athens?
2. Would you rather live in ancient Athens or Sparta? Why?

Selection **4**

Interview with Pericles

FOCUS: What were Pericles' contributions to the progress of ancient Greece?

Our intrepid reporter from the *Athens Times* finally caught up with Pericles in 431 B.C.E. Here's the interview with the great man himself.

Athens Times: Hail, most glorious Pericles!

PERICLES: There is no need for formality. I am no tyrant, but an elected leader who has served his beloved Athens for many years.

PERICLES RULED ATHENS FROM 443 B.C.E. UNTIL HIS DEATH IN 429 B.C.E.

Athens Times: We appreciate that, sir. People say that your policies are determined by two complementary goals: promoting democracy and preserving the empire of Athens. Would you agree with this **portrayal**?

PERICLES: Yes, that is an accurate description of my goals. Our state is called a democracy precisely because it puts power in the hands of the *demos*, or common people. Any citizen can speak to the assembly, and all can vote. When it is a question of settling private disputes, all citizens are equal before the law. When it is a question of choosing a person for a position of public responsibility, what counts is a person's ability, not his family background. Poverty should not keep anyone from serving the state.

Athens Times: Ah, you are referring to the policy of paying Athens's poorest citizens so that they too can serve as jurors in the court system. A fine idea, sir. Regarding our empire, nobody will deny that the works of your master builders can now be found all over Athens. We have new gymnasiums, temples, theaters, and your crowning achievement, the Parthenon. Yet, people say we cannot feel complacent. The Peloponnesian War continues to loom over us. When will it end? How can we afford it?

PERICLES: We must stop Sparta and make sure we don't lose democracy because of that **barbaric** land. Before anyone calls for an end to our war expenditures, he should remember that the military program also employs metalworkers, shipbuilders, and many other Athenian craftsmen. We need to keep Athens safe.

Athens Times: But people are **abandoning** their farms and taking refuge inside Athens's fortifications for protection. They live in squalor. Can we possibly control the diseases that these refugees carry?

PERICLES: Plague has not struck us. We are making room for the refugees. The Athenian empire will be admired now and long into the future.

Athens Times: May those words **ascend** from your lips to Athena's own ears.

BUILT IN THE FIFTH CENTURY B.C.E., THE PARTHENON IS A TEMPLE OF THE GODDESS ATHENA.

Two years after this interview might have taken place, Pericles died of the plague, which was brought into Athens by war **refugees**. A few years later, Athens surrendered to Sparta. But many of Pericles' ideas—especially the belief that a person's lack of wealth should not prevent him from enjoying the rights of citizenship—continue to influence governments to this day.

STOP AND THINK

1. What did Pericles think about democracy?
2. Do you think Pericles' goals of promoting democracy and preserving the Athenian empire were complementary or contradictory? Explain your answer.

THE BIRTH OF A REPUBLIC

*"Go, **proclaim** to the Romans it is heaven's will that my Rome shall be the capital of the world."*

–Romulus, as **quoted** by the Roman historian Livy

FOCUS: Can parts of a myth be true?

In January 2007, workers were busy at an archaeological dig on the Palatine Hill in Rome, Italy. This hill, one of the oldest parts of Rome, was home to some of Rome's greatest emperors. And here, legend says, Rome began.

Ancient Romans **revered** this site. They believed it was the place where a mother wolf nursed orphaned twin boys as if they were her own cubs. According to legend, the boys, named Romulus and Remus, were the sons of Mars, the god of war. When they grew up, they argued over where to build a settlement. Remus chose the Aventine Hill; Romulus chose the Palatine Hill. Romulus ended up killing Remus and thus became the first king of Rome. He promised that the city would one day be great.

Stone carving of Romulus and Remus

As archaeological workers took dirt samples from the hill, they suddenly broke through layers of earth. They had uncovered an underground grotto, or cave. About 52 feet deep, it was decorated with wall paintings and seashells. Could it be the same cave where ancient Romans had worshiped their city's founders?

Vaulted grotto thought to be the home of Romulus and Remus

Andrea Carandini, a historian at the University of Rome, believes that it is. Earlier, he had found remains of a wall in the Palatine Hill that dated to about 750 B.C.E., about the time of Romulus and Remus's legendary fight. Carandini believes the cave and wall show that Rome began as it does in the **myth**. "There was no gradual expansion of an old core," he stated. Instead, a city that "was great and remains great" grew up quickly.

Rome went from a group of farm villages by way of a monarchy to a new form of government called a **republic** by 509 B.C.E. In a republic, elected leaders make government decisions. Rome continued to grow, conquering new lands. In time, it became a powerful empire. By about 117 C.E., under Emperor Trajan, the empire extended from Britain to Africa. It seemed that Romulus's promise had been fulfilled.

BEWARE THE IDES OF MARCH

By the first century B.C.E., Rome had been a republic for hundreds of years, and leaders called consuls headed the army and Senate. The consul Julius Caesar had other ideas. He made himself king of Rome in 44 B.C.E., naming himself "Dictator for Life." The senators of Rome soon grew tired of Caesar's rule. A group of them stabbed him to death on March 15, the "ides" or middle of the month.

STOP AND THINK

1. What does Carandini believe the grotto proves?
2. How could you find out about archaeological digs near your city?

Selection 6

CULTURAL CONNECTION

Through the Colosseum's Arch

The Colosseum today

FOCUS: Do the spectacles in the Roman Colosseum remind you of any spectacles today? Explain.

Marisol and Annie were in the library looking at a book about the Roman Empire. It had a bookmark in it. Curious, Marisol opened the book to the marked page and saw an illustration of two gladiators fighting in the Roman Colosseum. The colors in the picture glowed strangely, and Marisol felt a bit sick. "Inaugurated in 80 C.E., the Colosseum was the site of spectacles ranging from gladiator fights to mock naval battles," she read. "It could seat up to 50,000 people and was a way for the emperors to entertain the people."

"It looks so real," Annie said, peering over her shoulder. "You can almost hear the crowd shouting."

"Yeah, I thought I heard something, too," Marisol said.

"Hey, there's writing on this bookmark," said Annie. She read, "'Those who love freedom may enter through the arch.'"

Suddenly the girls heard a roar of voices. The library ceiling melted away, replaced by a cloudless sky, and bookshelves turned into an enormous stone arch curving over their heads. People in togas streamed past. One man in a fancy purple toga gave the girls a strange look and then hurried through the arch.

Who was that?" asked Marisol.

"He's a senator," said a boy standing nearby. "He's accustomed to people making way for him." Marisol and Annie stared at the boy, who had a friendly smile and wore a tunic hitched above his knees.

"I **perceive** that you're out-of-towners," he said, looking them up and down. "I was about to show you to your seats, but I suppose I'd better get you dressed properly first." The boy took off, zigzagging through people in a corridor. The girls looked at each other and hurried to catch up with him.

"Here's the lost and found," said the boy as he led them into a room piled with cloaks and walking sticks. "Fortunately, someone forgot a bundle of laundry here last week. I'll give you the **identity** of married ladies so nobody will question why you're here unescorted. Here are a couple of tunics."

"Married ladies?" Marisol said. But the boy seemed to know what he was doing, so she and Annie slipped the garments over their jeans and T-shirts.

"Now, we'd best start up to the ladies' seats. You're all the way at the top." The boy started off again, calling over his shoulder, "My name is Lucius, by the way."

They followed Lucius up a flight of broad stone steps. He paused at the top. "We'll never get you to your seats in time. Come on, we'll just stand in this entrance; nobody will notice us once the spectacle starts."

When they emerged into dazzling sunlight, the girls gasped. The Colosseum of Rome lay before them, like the picture in the library book but a thousand times louder—and smellier. A vendor pushed past them. "Get your cold drinks here!" he yelled. "I've got sausages in buns; just a few coins!"

Gladiator mosaic

"Cheap meat," sniffed Lucius. "I can make better sausages than that."

In the arena, two gladiators approached a boxed seating area. A man wearing a wreath on his head nodded slightly to the warriors. "Hail, Emperor," said the fighters in unison. "We who are about to die salute you!"

"Which emperor is that?" asked Marisol.

"It's Emperor Trajan, of course," Lucius answered. "And see the box next to him? The man dressed in a fine green toga is my master, and he permits me to keep a small portion of the gratuities I earn here. If I continue saving at the present rate, I'll be able to buy my freedom when I'm twenty-five." He shook his head. "How I look forward to having the rights of a citizen!"

The gladiators were now circling each other as the crowd shouted their names. One man threw his net, entangling the second fighter, who quickly slashed through the net with his sword and then parried a dagger blow with his shield. The crowd roared.

Annie nudged Marisol. "We must be here for a reason," she whispered. "We were granted this trip because we love freedom, right?"

"I was just thinking about that," Marisol said. "Do you think we're supposed to free the gladiators?"

Lucius overheard the girls. "Free them?" he asked. "They're both criminals, sentenced to die, and thanks to the kindness of the emperor, one will live. You don't want to free their kind!"

"Then who—" Marisol began. She looked at Lucius. "You're enslaved, but your master will let you buy your freedom?" He nodded.

She removed her earrings and held them out. "Take these. I hope they're enough."

Lucius's jaw dropped. As he stammered his thanks, the girls heard a deafening roar from the Colosseum crowd. Colors blurred, and then they were sitting back in the library.

"Hey, my earrings are gone," said Marisol.

Annie began reading from the open book. "Enslaved people in the Roman Empire could be freed by paying the same amount they had cost their masters. Many rose to respectable positions. One of the most famous of the freed slaves became a renowned cook. An anonymous Roman historian wrote about him, 'No sausages could rival those of Lucius.' "

STOP AND THINK

1. How did Lucius gain his freedom?
2. How do you know this story is a fantasy?

Reading Longer Words

In this unit you learned more about how to read longer words.

Step 1: Divide the word into parts.

Compound word?
Divide between the words.

Prefix?
Divide after the prefix.

Suffix?
Divide before the suffix.

VCCV letter pattern?
Divide between the consonants.

VCV letter pattern?
Divide before the consonant.
or
Divide after the consonant.

Step 2: Read each word part.

Step 3: Read the whole word. Sound right? If not, try an alternative.

Ends in a consonant?
Try a short vowel sound.

Ends in a vowel?
Try a long vowel sound.

Has a VCe pattern?
Try a long vowel sound.

Ends in *-le, -al,* or *-el*?
Try dividing before the consonant preceding the *l*.

Has a syllable with vowel + *r*?
May change the sound of the vowel.

Has a vowel pair?
Pair stays together.

Divide the Words

civ/il/ized
com/plain/ing
nar/row/ly
in/struc/tion/al/ly
qual/i/fi/ca/tion
sac/ri/ficed
sum/mar/y
won/der/ful
ret/ri/bu/tion
po/lit/i/cal

Read Word Parts		Read Whole Words
civ il ized	→	civilized
sac ri ficed	→	sacrificed
com plain ing	→	complaining
sum mar y	→	summary
nar row ly	→	narrowly
won der ful	→	wonderful
in struc tion al ly	→	instructionally
ret ri bu tion	→	retribution
qual i fi ca tion	→	qualification
po lit i cal	→	political

Read More Words

Use what you learned in Units 1–7 to read these words from the unit.

identity sacrifice underlying inscription plumage
disembark philosophers aristocratic perceive complementary

Vocabulary

Using Word Parts and Context Clues to Infer Meaning

Many prefixes and suffixes come from Greek or Latin. Context clues are words, phrases, and sentences that surround an unfamiliar word and give hints or clues to a word's meaning. The meanings of prefixes and suffixes, along with context clues, can be used to determine the meaning of an unfamiliar word.

Word Strategies: Using Word Parts and Context Clues
1. Look for context clues. Find words, phrases, and sentences surrounding the familiar word.
2. Look for word parts. Look for familiar words "inside" unfamiliar words: • Break the word into parts. • Find the root word. What does it mean? • Find a prefix or suffix? What does it mean? • Put the word parts together? What is the meaning of the word?
3. Use context clues and word parts to guess meaning.
4. Use your meaning in the original sentence. Does your meaning make sense in the sentence?
5. Check the dictionary. Use a dictionary to check your meaning. Does your meaning match the definition in the dictionary?

Irregular Future Perfect Verbs & Compound Subject/Verb Agreement

Irregular Future Perfect Verbs

Recall that you can create the future perfect tense by combining the future form of *to have* with the past participle of a main verb.

Future Perfect	*will have* + past participle

Remember that the past participle for some verbs is **irregular**. This means that they do not end in *-ed*.

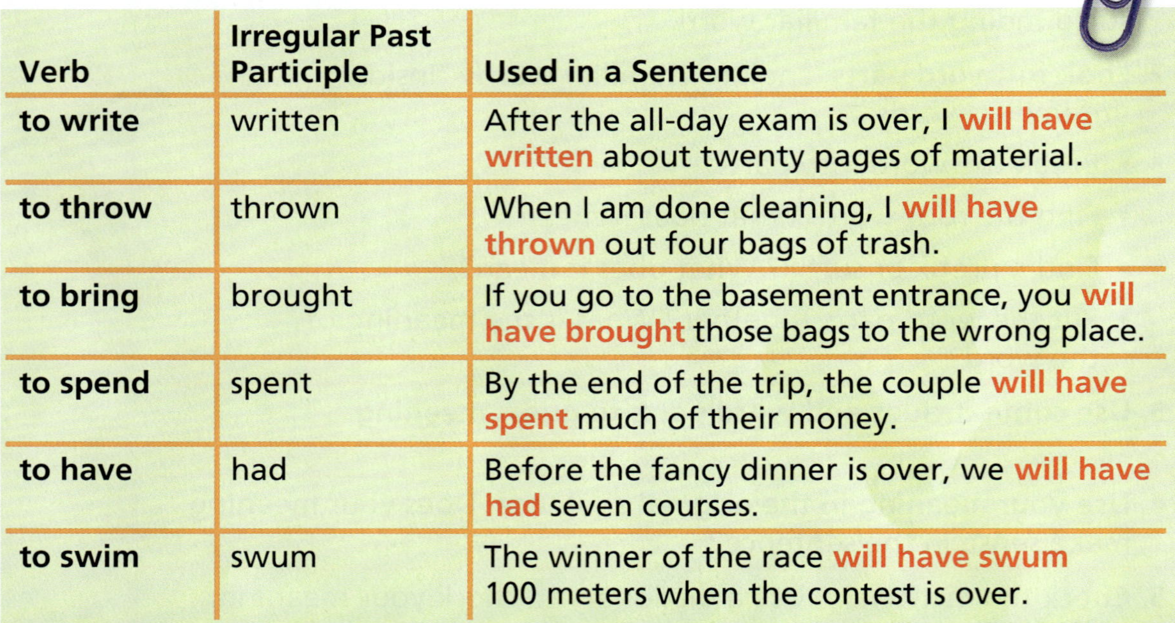

Verb	Irregular Past Participle	Used in a Sentence
to write	written	After the all-day exam is over, I **will have written** about twenty pages of material.
to throw	thrown	When I am done cleaning, I **will have thrown** out four bags of trash.
to bring	brought	If you go to the basement entrance, you **will have brought** those bags to the wrong place.
to spend	spent	By the end of the trip, the couple **will have spent** much of their money.
to have	had	Before the fancy dinner is over, we **will have had** seven courses.
to swim	swum	The winner of the race **will have swum** 100 meters when the contest is over.

The Future Perfect Tense: Sequence of Actions

The future perfect is used to describe an event that will happen before another event happens.

Sentence	Future Perfect Verb Phrase	Other Verb	Which Will Happen First?
Wendy will have done the dishes by the time her mother comes home.	will have done	comes	done
We will have bought all the supplies before we cook.	will have bought	cook	bought

Compound Subject / Verb Agreement

Sentences with **compound subjects** have more than one subject. A **conjunction** (such as *and* or *or*) links them.

Conjunction	Singular or Plural Verb	Why
and	plural	Both subjects perform the action.
or	singular	Either subject—not both—performs the action.

The subject and verb of a sentence have to agree. In the case of compound subjects, the conjunction determines what form of the verb should be used.

Sentence	Subject	Conjunction	Subject Functions As a...	Correct Verb
Suzie **and** Lara **jump** rope.	Suzie and Lara	and	plural (both girls jump rope)	third-person plural (jump)
My brother **or** sister **does** the dishes.	brother or sister	or	singular (either person does the dishes)	third-person singular (does)

When two sentences are combined using a compound subject, the verb can change, depending on which conjunction you use.

First Sentence	Second Sentence	Add a Logical Conjunction	New Sentence	Correct Verb
Paula **plays** in the orchestra.	Kevin **plays** in the orchestra.	and	Paula and Kevin **play** in the orchestra.	third-person plural (**play**)
My aunt **takes** care of my mail.	My neighbor **takes** care of my mail.	or	My aunt or my neighbor **takes** care of my mail.	third-person singular (**takes**)

REVISING A FIRST DRAFT

Write a Persuasive Essay

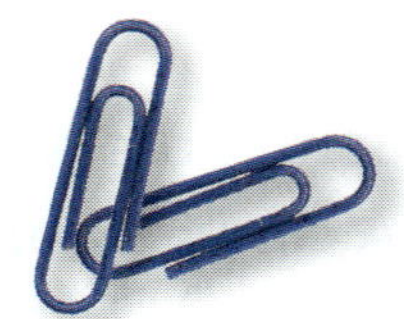

Organization is the road map that directs the reader through your writing. It gives an essay a sense of structure. A persuasive essay should begin with a clear statement of the writer's position on the issue. Supporting facts and details should be presented in a logical, orderly fashion.

First Draft

You've read the final draft of "Staying Connected." Read the first draft.

Writing Traits Checklist

- **Ideas** Does the writer state the issue clearly?
- **Organization** Is the writer's position stated clearly? Is the opposing position clearly stated?
- **Sentence Fluency** Are the sentence beginnings varied?
- **Voice** Do facts and details support the position?
- **Word Choice** Does the writer choose clear, persuasive language?
- **Conventions** Are there any errors?

Cell phones are an essential part of daily life. Students and their families have come to rely on cell phones for their convenience, and for the safety they offer. But the recent ban on cell phones at Chambers middle school has made life difficult for students, including me. ^[I believe this policy needs to be changed.]

Staying connected is important for students. Cell phones make it possible to keep in touch—whether at lunch or during breaks. Then there's the safety issue. For most students, having a cell phone handy in an emergency is a necesity. Our parents agree. With so many parents working and their kids involved in different activities and at different schools ^ their schedules often change. Students at our school can no longer call their parents because of the ban. Sadly, the majority of students have always used their cell phones responsibly. ^ Only a minority of students in the country cause the kind of problems that lead to school bans. ^[Some students used their phones during class to talk or to cheat on a test.] Kids should be disiplined on a case-by-case basis as problems arise.

Cell phones allow students to stay connected. If the ban were lifted, the vast majority of us would resume using our cell phones responsibly.

Final Draft The writer made many revisions to complete this final draft.

Cell phones are an essential part of daily life. Students and their families have come to rely on cell phones for their convenience, and the safety they offer. But the recent ban on cell phones at Chambers Middle School has made life difficult for students, including me. I believe this policy needs to be changed.

Staying connected is important for students. With so many parents working and their kids involved in different activities and at different schools, their schedules often change. Cell phones make it possible to keep in touch—whether at lunch or during breaks. Then there's the safety issue. For most students, having a cell phone handy in an emergency is a necessity. Our parents agree.

The majority of students have always used their cell phones responsibly. In fact, only a minority of students nationwide cause the sort of problems that lead to school bans. Why punish so many students because a few used their phones during class to talk or try to cheat on a test? Why not just discipline kids on a case-by-case basis as problems arise?

Cell phones allow students to stay connected. If the ban were lifted, the vast majority of us would resume using our cell phones responsibly.

UNIT 8

A JOB WELL DONE

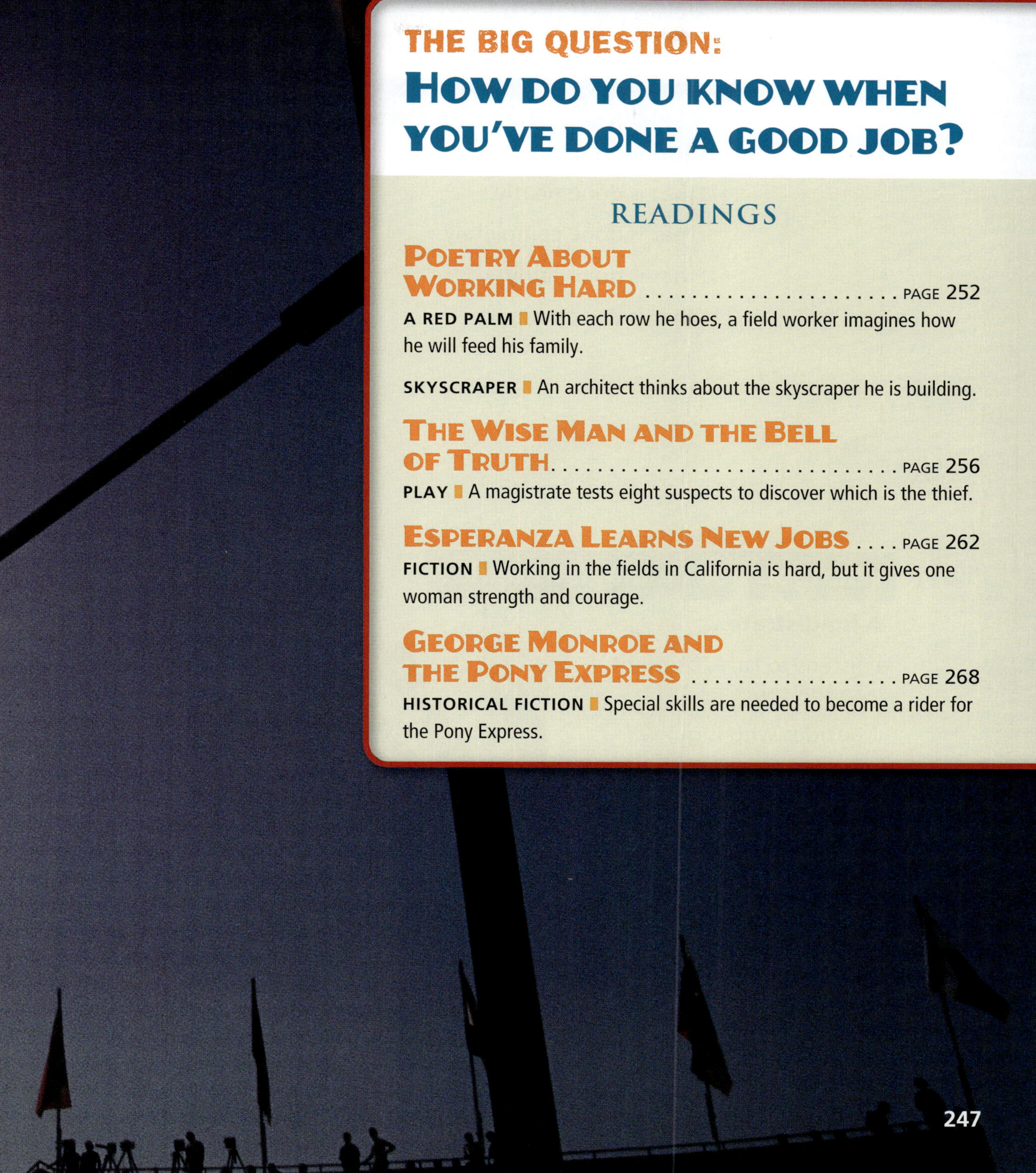

THE BIG QUESTION:

HOW DO YOU KNOW WHEN YOU'VE DONE A GOOD JOB?

READINGS

A Job Well Done

What is a job well done?

A job well done is a job...

- that is done neatly.
- that is done completely.
- that is done fairly.
- that is done on time.

What job does a magistrate do?

A magistrate...

- listens to cases brought to the court.
- decides who is guilty.
- decides who is innocent.
- punishes the guilty person.

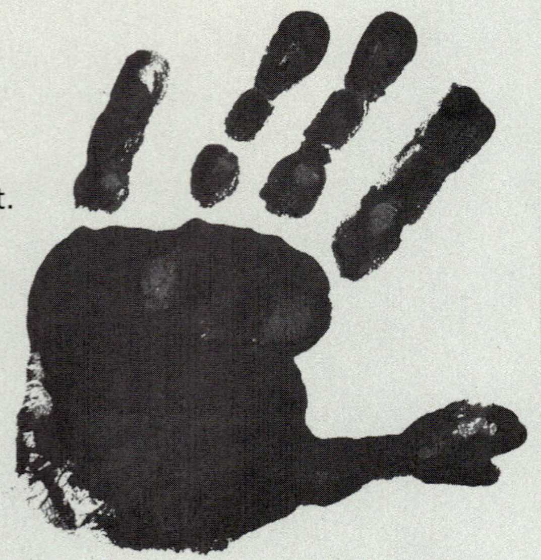

What kinds of work does a farm worker do?

A farm worker...

- ☐ picks fruit and vegetables.
- ☐ packs fruit and vegetables.
- ☐ pulls weeds.
- ☐ plants seeds.

What was the Pony Express?

The Pony Express was...

- ☐ a place that sold ponies.
- ☐ a place to get a pony ride.
- ☐ a show with ponies that did tricks.
- ☐ a company that carried mail quickly from one place to another using riders on horses.

What did Pony Express riders have to do?

Pony Express riders had to...

- ☐ ride a horse well.
- ☐ ride day and night.
- ☐ deliver the mail, no matter what.
- ☐ face danger from weather and attackers.

Literature Words

- administer
- blister
- bronze
- district
- enforce
- innocent
- magistrate
- peal
- sigh
- specify

administer

Administer means to manage or be in charge of things such as law or government.

"In a court, a judge or magistrate administers justice."

blister

A **blister** is a swelling on the skin containing watery matter.

"Tom got blisters on his hands from rowing all day."

innocent

Innocent means free from wrongdoing; not guilty.

"The judge said the man was innocent and set him free."

magistrate

A **magistrate** is a civil officer with the power to administer and enforce the law.

"The magistrate ordered the robber to go to jail."

bronze

Bronze is a metal consisting of copper and tin.

"A bronze statue was erected in the plaza."

district

A **district** is a region that is marked off for election or other government purposes.

"Five hundred people from our district voted against the new hotel."

enforce

Enforce means to ensure that people obey rules and laws.

"A police officer enforces the law."

peal

Peal refers to a loud, prolonged ringing of bells.

"The bells pealed loudly when the victory was announced."

sigh

To **sigh** is to let out one's breath as from sorrow, weariness, or relief.

"Jenna sighed when she broke her favorite cup."

specify

Specify means to mention or name specifically; to state in detail.

"The owner specified the kind of worker he needed for the job."

READ TOGETHER Poetry About Working Hard

from

A Red Palm

by Gary Soto

You're in this dream of cotton plants.
You raise a hoe swing, and the first weeds
Fall with a sigh. You take another step,
Chop, and the sigh comes again,
Until you yourself are breathing that way
With each step, a sigh that will follow you into town.

That's hours later. The sun is a red blister
Coming up in your palm. Your back is strong,
Young, not yet the broken chair
In an abandoned school of dry spiders.
Dust settles on your forehead, dirt
Smiles under each fingernail.
You chop, step, and by the end of the first row,
You can buy one splendid fish for wife
And three sons. Ten hours and the cupboards creak.
You can rest in the backyard under a tree.

SKYSCRAPER

BY
BOBBI KATZ
(to honor
WILLIAM VAN ALEN,
skyscraper
architect)

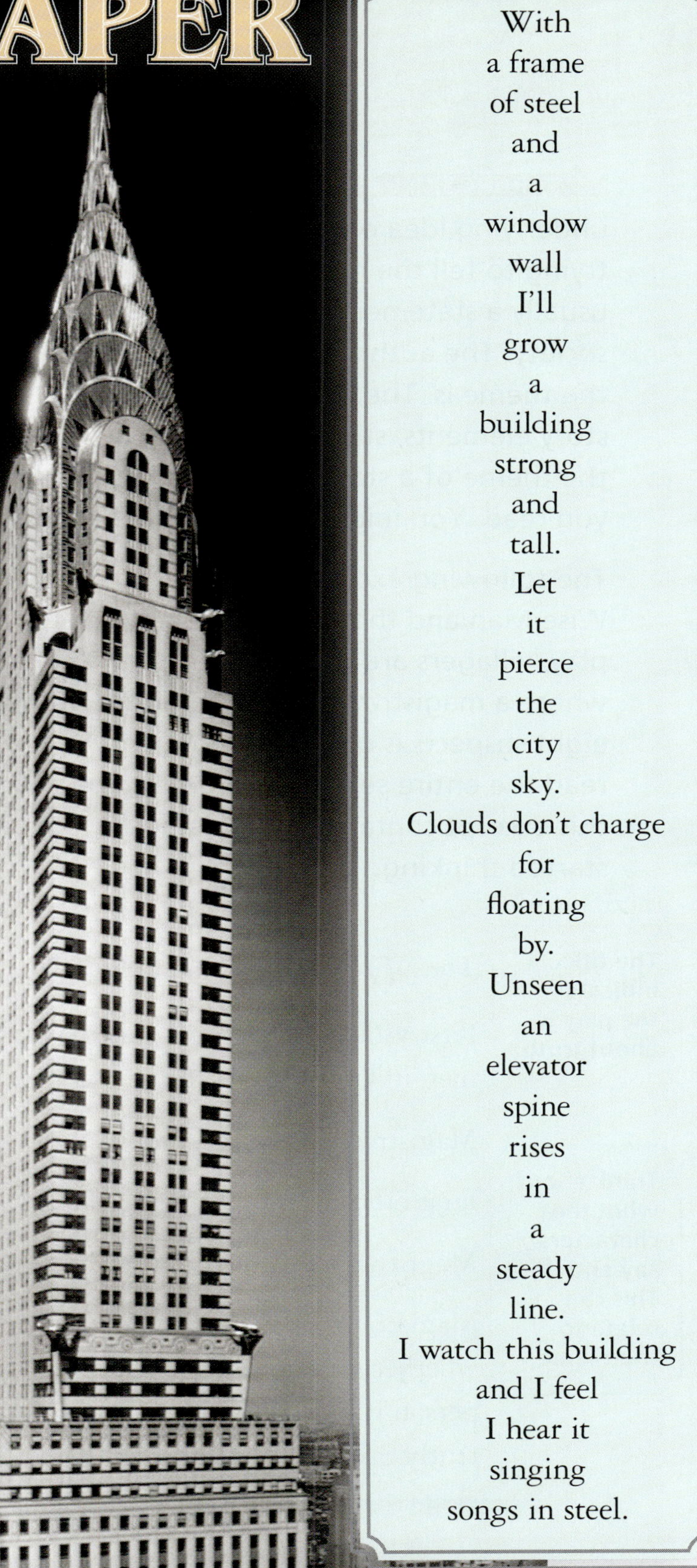

With
a frame
of steel
and
a
window
wall
I'll
grow
a
building
strong
and
tall.
Let
it
pierce
the
city
sky.
Clouds don't charge
for
floating
by.
Unseen
an
elevator
spine
rises
in
a
steady
line.
I watch this building
and I feel
I hear it
singing
songs in steel.

Comprehension

TARGET SKILL **Author's Purpose** Most stories express an underlying idea or **theme**. The theme is a message the author is trying to tell the reader about the **subject** or plot of the story. It is usually a statement made by the author about human nature or society. The author does not usually tell the reader directly what the theme is. The reader has to infer the theme through other story elements, such as character, action, and image. To identify the theme of a story, you should think about these elements as you read. You might also consider the title of the story.

The following excerpt is taken from the play "The Wise Man and the Bell of Truth." At the start of the play, villagers are on their way to the courthouse, where a magistrate will try to figure out which of eight suspects is guilty of a robbery. You will need to read the entire selection to determine the theme, but this excerpt contains some elements that will get you started thinking.

The title indicates the play is about truth.

The Wise Man and the Bell of Truth

First villager: I've heard this magistrate is one of the wisest men in China. He'll figure out who the robber is…

Magistrate: Have you prepared the bell as I asked?

First official: In every detail, Honorable Magistrate…

Magistrate: Excellent. I'm ready to see the suspects now...

Magistrate: I have here a bell with great powers. It can tell whether anyone who rubs it is guilty or innocent. If a guilty person rubs it, it will peal loudly, and we will all know the truth. Suspects, I want each of you to go to the bell and rub it.

The subject is how the magistrate investigates who the robber is.

Think about what the characters say and do. This can relate to the theme.

Story Element	Question to Ask	Possible Answer
Title	What, if anything, does the title tell about the selection?	The play has something to do with truth.
Subject/Plot	What is the selection about?	how the magistrate investigates who is guilty of the robbery
Characters and Actions	How does the magistrate say that he will find out who is guilty?	He tells all the suspects to rub a bell because the bell will ring when the guilty suspect rubs it.
Characters and Actions	Why does the magistrate want to find the guilty suspect?	so that this suspect can be punished and the others set free
Possible Theme	What does the author want you to think about guilt and innocence?	The truth will come out in the end.

The first column lists some story elements that may reflect the theme.

The second column lists questions a reader might ask himself or herself while reading to help clarify the theme.

The third column lists possible answers to those questions that will help the reader identify the theme.

TARGET STRATEGY **Summary** As you read, look beyond the words that describe the actual events. Think about things that are not explicitly stated in the story. Predict why things are happening. Ask yourself, "What message is the author trying to tell me?"

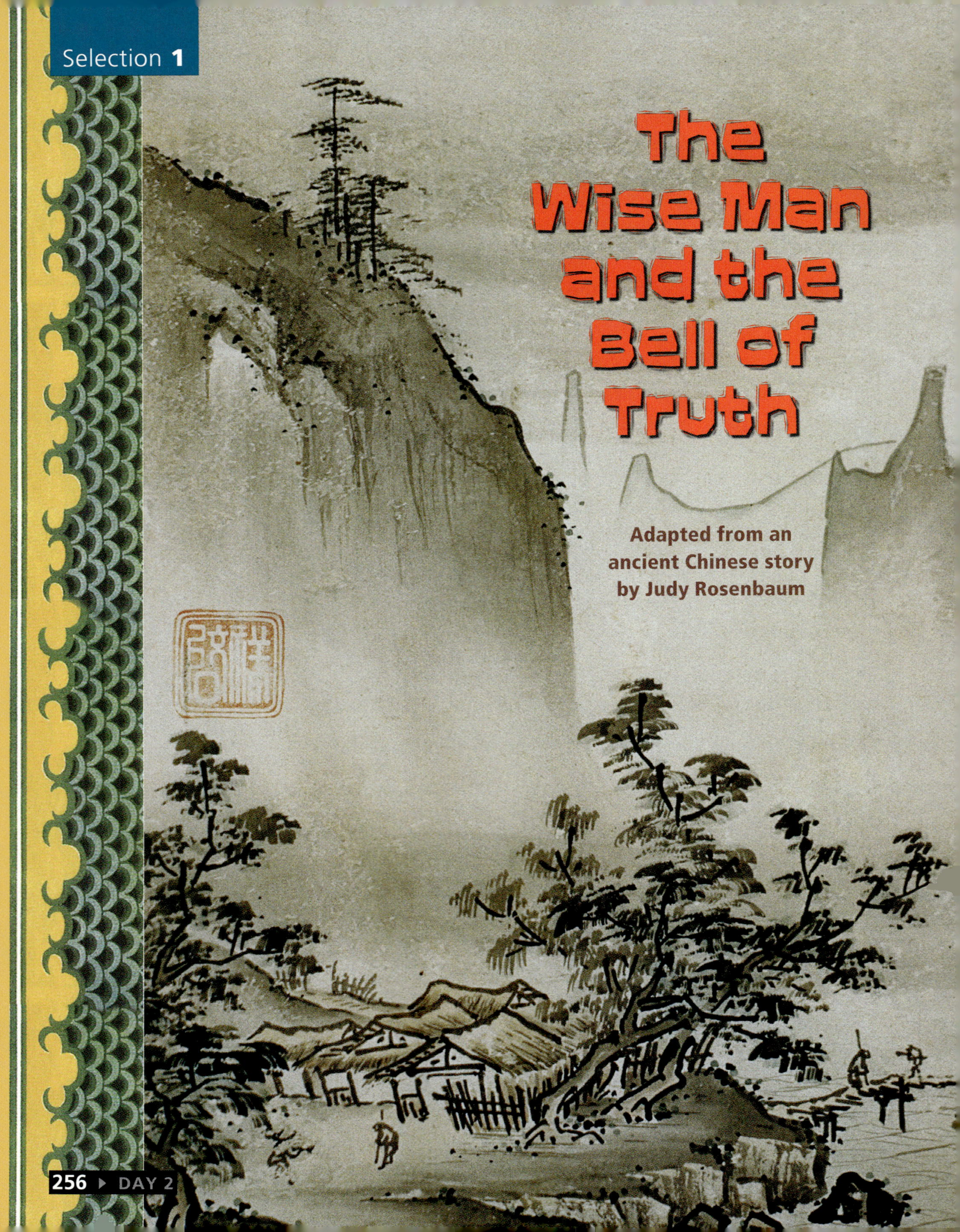

The Wise Man and the Bell of Truth

Adapted from an ancient Chinese story by Judy Rosenbaum

FOCUS: How can finding out the truth lead to justice?

Stories from many countries tell about wise people who solve problems around them. This ancient Chinese story features a ***magistrate*** *—an official with the power to* ***administer*** *and* ***enforce*** *the law. He knows that the most important thing about his job is to punish the guilty, not the* ***innocent****.*

(Two villagers walk in from opposite directions and meet onstage.)

First villager: Are you on your way to the courthouse? I'll walk with you.

Second villager: I am. They say that the magistrate has arrived from the **district** capital. He's to question all the suspects in the robbery.

First villager: I hear they arrested a dozen people.

Second villager: I hear they arrested a hundred people!

(The village woodcutter joins them.)

Woodcutter: It was only eight people. I delivered firewood to the courthouse yesterday. Of course, the suspects all claim they didn't do it.

First villager: I've heard that this magistrate is one of the wisest men in China. He'll figure out who the robber is.

(The curtain falls. It rises again to show the courtroom. The magistrate is standing with two local officials. In the center of the room is a huge ***bronze*** *bell, completely covered with a cloth. The bell is suspended from a wooden frame.)*

Magistrate: Have you prepared the bell as I asked?

First official: In every detail, Honorable Magistrate. We burned the logs, as you **specified**. Now we have covered the bell as you directed us.

Magistrate (*going over to the bell and lifting the cloth so that he can see the bell, but the audience can't*)**:** Excellent. I'm ready to see the suspects now.

(About a dozen people, including the two villagers and the woodcutter, gather with their backs to the audience, facing the magistrate and the bell. The two court officials bring in eight suspects.)

Magistrate: I have here a bell with great powers. It can tell whether anyone who rubs it is guilty or innocent. If a guilty person rubs it, it will **peal** loudly, and we will all know the truth. Suspects, I want each of you to go to the bell and rub it. Say not a word until all of you are finished.

*(The eight suspects line up. One by one, they reach under the cloth and seem to be rubbing the bell. They move to stage right as they finish and stand looking down **anxiously** until all eight are done.)*

Woodcutter: The bell hasn't made a sound. Maybe it doesn't work!

First villager: Or maybe the real thief isn't in this group.

*(All the villagers **murmur** and comment to one another. The Magistrate walks over to the group of suspects.)*

Magistrate *(loudly enough to be heard over the crowd)***:** If I may have your attention! *(Everyone quiets down.)* Thank you. *(He addresses the suspects.)* All of you, please show me the palms of your hands.

(The suspects all hold out their hands. Seven of them have ***grimy*** *palms, as though they have rubbed their hands in* ***soot****. The eighth one has clean hands.)*

Magistrate *(pointing to the man with clean hands)*: Arrest this man. Set the rest free.

(The relieved former suspects run to join the other villagers amid murmurs and cheers from the crowd.)

Guilty man *(as he is being led away)*: How did you know? I didn't touch that miserable bell!

Magistrate: That's the first true thing this man has said. He didn't lay a hand on the bell, because he thought that his touch would make the bell ring. What he didn't know was that I had the bell's surface covered with soot. Anyone who rubbed the bell would get soot on his hands. The innocent men had nothing to fear from touching the bell, so they all rubbed it. The only one who didn't was the real thief, who knew his own guilt and feared that the bell would **reveal** it. Which it did, though not the way he expected.

First villager: You are indeed a wise man, Honorable Magistrate.

Woodcutter *(to Second villager)*: How about that? I helped administer justice. Without my firewood, they never would have been able to tell clean hands from dirty.

Second villager: I'm not sure that makes you wise, but you certainly were useful.

First villager: Isn't it funny that by keeping his hands clean, that thief showed how dirty he really was.

STOP AND THINK

1. What did the magistrate do that showed how clever he was?
2. What are some important traits that a magistrate or a judge should have?

Your Turn

Use Your Words:

anxious	instance
assure	labor
cavernous	murmur
crochet	penetrate
devise	regal
ease	relay
execute	reveal
experience	smudge
frigid	soot
grime	threat

- Read the words on the list.
- Read the dialogue. Find the words.

MORE ACTIVITIES

1. Take a Survey

Graphic Organizer

Where would your classmates like to go on a class trip? Ask 12 classmates which of the following places they would want to visit most. Fill in one box for each answer. What are your results? Talk about them with your class.

2. Dialogue

Listening and Speaking

There are shadows on the wall of the cave. Have you seen shadows? What unusual figures did you see or imagine them to be? Draw a picture of one and talk about it with your partner.

place	1	2	3	4	5	6	7	8	9	10	11	12
Zoo												
Art Museum												
Circus												
Aquarium												

3. You Are the Author

Writing

Imagine that you and a friend have found a cave. Write a paragraph telling about what you find in the cave.

4. Make Sentences

Vocabulary

Play this game with a partner. Take turns making up sentences that contain two of the following words: *soot, grime, smudge*. Is your sentence the best it can be? If not, work with your partner to make it better. Write down your sentences and share them with your class.

5. Class Trip to a Cave

Writing

Would you like to go on a class trip to a cave? Why or why not? Write down two reasons why you would or would not want to go. Share your reasons with your partner.

6. Make a List

Vocabulary

A miner works in a mine digging for things such as gold, diamonds, and coal. What other of Earth's resources do miners dig for? Make a list and share the list with your class. How many things did you find?

Esperanza Learns New Jobs

FROM

Esperanza Rising

by Pam Muñoz Ryan

FOCUS: How can hard times make someone become stronger?

In 1930, Esperanza Ortega is the happy, rather spoiled daughter of a ranch owner in Mexico. When Papa is killed by bandits, his powerful stepbrother, Tío Luis, is eager to seize the property. Tío Luis ***threatens*** *trouble if Mama doesn't marry him. Mama and Esperanza flee to California, along with their former servants, Alfonso and Hortensia, who have arranged for jobs as fieldworkers for themselves and for Mama. Esperanza's life has changed completely. Once wealthy, she now lives in poverty in a work camp. She herself works, taking care of fellow workers' children while Mama* ***labors*** *in the fields. Then Mama gets sick. To earn money to bring her grandmother, Abuelita, to California, Esperanza realizes that it is her turn to become a fieldworker. Her first job is cutting the eyes out of potatoes.*

SOME OF THE PEOPLE IN THE STORY:

Alfonso and **Hortensia**—*the Ortegas' friends and former servants*
Miguel—*Alfonso and Hortensia's son*
Juan and **Josefina**—*Alfonso's brother and sister-in-law*
Isabel—*Juan and Josefina's daughter*
Abuelita—*Mama's mother, Esperanza's grandmother*

Esperanza huddled with Josefina, Hortensia, and a small group of women waiting for the morning truck to take them to the sheds. A thick ground fog that hugged the earth settled in the valley, surrounding them, as if they stood within a deep gray cloud. There was no wind, only silence and **penetrating** cold.

Esperanza bundled in all the clothing that she could put on, old wool pants, a sweater, a ragged jacket, a wool cap, and thick gloves over thin gloves, all borrowed from friends in the camp. Hortensia had shown her how to heat a brick in the oven and bundle it in newspaper, and she hugged it to her body to keep warm as they rode on the truck.

Since the driver could only see a few yards ahead, the truck rumbled slowly on the dirt roads. They passed miles of naked grapevines, stripped of their harvest and bereft of their leaves. Fading into the mist, the brown and twisted trunks looked **frigid** and lonely.

The truck stopped at the big packing shed. It was really one long building with different open-air sections, as long as six train cars. The railroad tracks ran along one side, and docks for trucks ran along the other. Esperanza had heard Mama and the others talk about the sheds. How they were busy with people; women standing at long tables, packing the fruit; trucks coming and going with their loads fresh from the fields; and workers stocking the train cars that would later be hooked to a locomotive to take the fruit all over the United States.

But cutting potato eyes was different. Since nothing was being packed, there wasn't the usual activity. Only twenty or so women gathered in the **cavernous** shed, sitting in a circle on upturned crates, protected from the wind by only a few stacks of empty boxes.

The Mexican supervisor took their names. With all the clothing they were wearing, he barely looked at their faces. Josefina had told Esperanza that if she was a good worker, the bosses would not concern themselves with her age, so she knew she would have to work hard.

Esperanza copied everything that Hortensia and Josefina did. When the women put the hot bricks between their feet to keep them warm while they worked, so did she. When they took off their outer gloves and worked in thin cotton ones, she did the same. Everyone had a metal bin sitting behind them. The fieldworkers brought cold potatoes and filled up their bins. Hortensia took a potato and then, with a sharp knife, she cut it into chunks around the dimples. She tapped her knife on one of the dimples. "That is an eye," she whispered to Esperanza. "Leave two eyes in every piece so there will be two chances for it to take root." Then she dropped the chunks into a burlap sack. When the sack was full, the fieldworkers took it away.

"Where do they take them?" she asked Hortensia.

"To the fields. They plant the eye pieces and then the potatoes grow."

Esperanza picked up a knife. Now she knew where potatoes came from.

Time passes, Esperanza gains strength and ***experience****. One night, as she sits with her sleeping mother in the hospital, she tells Mama, "Don't worry. I will take care of everything. I will be* la patrona *for the family now."*

Esperanza's breath made smoky vapors in front of her face as she waited for the truck to take her to tie grapevines. She shifted from foot to foot and clapped her gloved hands together and wondered what was so new about the New Year. It already seemed old, with the same routines. She worked during the week. She helped Hortensia cook dinner in the late afternoons. In the evenings she helped Josefina with the babies and Isabel with her homework. She went to see Mama on Saturdays and Sundays.

She huddled in the field near a **smudge** pot to keep warm and mentally counted the money she would need to bring Abuelita here. Every other week, with the small amounts she saved, she bought a money order from the market and put it in her valise. She figured that if she kept working until peaches, she would have enough for Abuelita's travel. Her problem then would be how to reach Abuelita.

The men went down the rows first, pruning the thick grapevines and leaving a few long branches or "canes" on each trunk. She followed, along with the others, and tied the canes on the taut wire that was stretched post to post. She ached from the cold and had to keep moving all day long to stay warm.

That night, as she soaked her hands in warm water, she realized that she no longer recognized them as her own. Cut and scarred, swollen and stiff, they looked like the hands of a very old man.

"Are you sure this will work?" asked Esperanza, as she watched Hortensia cut a ripe avocado in half.

"Of course," said Hortensia, removing the big pit and leaving a hole in the heart of the fruit. She scooped out the pulp, mashed it on a plate, and added some glycerin. "You have seen me make this for your mother many times. We are lucky to have the avocados this time of year. Some friends of Josefina brought them from Los Angeles."

Hortensia rubbed the avocado mixture into Esperanza's hands. "You must keep it on for twenty minutes so your hands will soak up the oils."

Esperanza looked at her hands covered in the greasy green lotion and remembered when Mama used to sit like this, after a long day of gardening or after horseback rides with Papa through the dry mesquite grasslands. When she was a little girl, she had laughed at Mama's hands covered in what looked like *guacamole.* But she had loved her to rinse them because afterward, Esperanza would take Mama's hands and put the palms on her own face so she could feel the suppleness and breathe in the fresh smell.

Esperanza was surprised at the simple things she missed about Mama. She missed her way of walking into a room, graceful and **regal**. She missed watching her hands **crocheting**, her fingers moving nimbly. And most of all, she longed for the sound of Mama's strong and **assured** laughter.

She put her hands under the faucet, rinsed off the avocado, and patted them dry. They felt better, but still looked red and weathered. She took another avocado, cut it in half, swung the knife into the pit and pulled it from the flesh. She repeated Hortensia's recipe and as she sat for the second time with her hands smothered, she realized that it wouldn't matter how much avocado and glycerin she put on them, they would never look like the hands of a wealthy woman from El Rancho de las Rosas. Because they were the hands of a poor *campesina*.

When things in Esperanza's life begin to improve, she has the satisfaction of realizing that her actions have helped bring about the change. Her experience has taught her to dream new dreams about the future, and it has given her the confidence to make those dreams come true.

STOP AND THINK

1. How does using the avocados remind Esperanza of her old life?
2. When have you felt proud of how well you did a difficult task?

GEORGE MONROE AND THE PONY EXPRESS

~ from *Reflections of a Black Cowboy: Pioneers*
by Robert Miller

FOCUS: What would it be like to find the job you were born to do?

In this selection, a narrator called Old Cowboy tells how George Monroe, a young African American, was in the right place at exactly the right time. Though the Pony Express is well known in legend, it actually lasted less than two years. So George was one of only a few lucky people who got to take part in this thrilling adventure—the extreme sport of its day! The Pony Express was a mail delivery service to California, founded by William Russell, William Waddell, and Alexander Majors. The letter carriers were brave young men on very fast horses.

The plan they **devised** to move the mail was simple, yet depended on clockwork **execution**. Mail traveled from New York to St. Joseph, Missouri, by railroad. From there it was placed on a steamboat and crossed the Missouri River. At this point, the Pony Express, covering a route of over two thousand miles of wild and untamed country, took over. A fresh rider picked up the mail and took off cross country toward California. Each rider rode a sixty-to-seventy-mile run, stopping at **relay** stations long enough to change horses. When the rider completed his run, a fresh rider would take the mail from him and continue for another seventy miles or so, then pass the mail to yet another rider until the mail reached California. The Pony Express worked the same way going from California to Missouri.

Choosing Pony Express riders was no easy job. The men had to know how to ride, shoot, speak several Indian tongues, but most of all, they had to be slender in body type and strong as a bull. Few men could fit the bill, but a handful made the cut. The one who stands out the most in my mind was a black man named George Monroe.

Monroe was the son of a gold miner during the heyday of California's gold rush. He was perfectly made for the role of a Pony Express rider. Not only did he have the body type for that job, but George could handle a horse like he was born on it.

One of the men doing the hiring for the Pony Express was Bolivar Roberts, manager of the western half of the business. One day early in 1860, he rode into Carson City, Nevada, looking for men to hire. When word leaked out that Roberts was in town, young men grabbed their fastest ponies and headed there quicker than a squirrel can blink. Among them was George Monroe.

"I hear they're payin' pretty good wages for this new job," said one would-be rider to another.

"Anything's better than what I got right now, which is a pocketful of nothing," laughed another. All the men had gathered over at the livery stable waiting for Mr. Roberts to show up. George rode up in a cloud of dust and dismounted with the **ease** and style of a showman. The other men took notice of how George handled his horse with so much confidence and skill.

Around ten in the morning, Mr. Roberts finally made his way over to the livery stable to check out what kind of men answered his newspaper ad. As he got closer to the livery stable he saw old men, fat men, young boys, and young men, all of them as anxious as a bunch of corralled mustangs. He knew from a glance that he'd turn down most of them. He wasted no time in sorting out the men he thought had a chance at being hired. "You, you, and you stand over there. I'm sorry, son, you're too young. I can't use you either, sir," said Mr. Roberts as he picked his way through the crowd like a cowboy looking for the right saddle horse.

"You, mister, over there," Roberts said to George Monroe. The big foreman pointed toward the small cluster of men who had been chosen in the first round.

Once his first cut was selected, Roberts had to determine which of the chosen could ride and handle a horse. Now you got to understand, most men back in them days could ride a horse. If you couldn't you didn't get around much, but there were a few men that had a gift for riding and could make a horse do anything. Mr. Roberts knew the kind of territory these men would be riding through. Horsemanship would be key to their survival, especially in hostile Indian country.

Approaching the chosen few, Roberts said, "Men, as you know, you have been selected to compete for the jobs as riders with the Pony Express, but before you're hired you've got to show me you can handle a horse." By now the back of the livery was cleared out except for a few half-wild mustangs. Mr. Roberts had seen to it that these horses would be made ready just for this occasion. Once the men had gathered around back, each one was given a number. "All right men, listen up. When your number is called, I want you to grab a saddle over there on the fence, run over and saddle one of those mustangs, and ride him around those three barrels and back to this finish line. You all got that?"

All the men mumbled they understood. George was the third man in line. He knew if he got the job it meant money in his empty pockets. He liked that, and he also liked the danger and prestige of being a Pony Express rider.

"I'm gonna nail this job down tighter than an undertaker's coffin," smiled a young cowboy to George.

George just smiled back. "Good luck fella," he said.

The cowboy's number was called, and he took off like a mule stung by a yellow jacket. He wasn't bad either. Fact was, he did a better than average job. Half out of breath, he charged across the finish line.

"Top that!" he said to George.

George just winked at the young fellow and when his number was called he was off to the races. He ran to his horse and just got the saddle on when the mustang bolted and took off in a quick gallop. George had always been known to be quick and nimble as a deer and his speed served him well in this **instance**. Running alongside that stallion, he caught up with him and in one motion leaped up onto him, grabbing the horn of the saddle with one hand as his foot fit perfectly in the stirrup. Fast as greased lightning, he was on that stallion's back spinning him around like a tornado, heading him straight for the barrels. George moved past those barrels with such speed and ease, it was like watching a child play with his favorite toy. He turned a possible embarrassment into a skilled ride, and he did it in record time.

When he finished, Mr. Roberts was anxious to see what the others could do, and he wasn't disappointed. Seems like George's little incident challenged the other cowboys' skills, and some of them started showing off. By the end of the day he had seen enough. He was pleased with his choices, and it was time to tell the men what they were hired for. "I'm pleased to say, all sixty of you men have been hired as riders for the Pony Express. What I'm about to tell you now may change your mind about working for us. Your pay will be $120 to $125 a month. You'll have to ride both day and night, in rain, snow, sleet. Nothing gentlemen, I mean nothing, will stop you from reaching your destination short of death. You'll encounter desperadoes, hostile Indians, and sometimes you'll have to ride double duty. Whatever is expected of you, you'll do. Your main objective is to get the letters through. Is that understood? Now how many still want the job?"

Not a single man backed away.

"Welcome aboard, gentlemen. In the morning you'll be leaving for your first assignment."

That was the beginning of man and a fast horse racing across this country to carry mail.

STOP AND THINK

1. What are some things that made George Monroe a good choice to be a Pony Express rider?
2. What job would you most like to try out for? Why?

Reading Longer Words

In this unit you learned more about how to read longer words.

Step 1: Divide the word into parts.

Compound word?
Divide between the words.

Prefix?
Divide after the prefix.

Suffix?
Divide before the suffix.

VCCV letter pattern?
Divide between the consonants.

VCV letter pattern?
Divide before the consonant.
or
Divide after the consonant.

Step 2: Read each word part.

Step 3: Read the whole word. Sound right? If not, try an alternative.

Ends in a consonant?
Try a short vowel sound.

Ends in a vowel?
Try a long vowel sound.

Has a VCe pattern?
Try a long vowel sound.

Ends in *-le, -al,* or *-el*?
Try dividing before the consonant preceding the *l.*

Has a syllable with vowel + *r*?
May change the sound of the vowel.

Has a vowel pair?
Pair stays together.

Divide the Words

pul/ver/ized	chas/tised
ob/struct/ing	gi/gan/ti/cal/ly
de/bat/ed	du/ti/ful
rad/i/cal	per/mu/ta/tion
in/sti/tu/tion	fab/ri/cat/ed

Read Word Parts	Read Whole Words
pul ver ized →	pulverized
chas tised →	chastised
ob struct ing →	obstructing
gi gan ti cal ly →	gigantically
de bat ed →	debated
du ti ful →	dutiful
rad i cal →	radical
per mu ta tion →	permutation
in sti tu tion →	institution
fab ri cat ed →	fabrication

Read More Words

Use what you learned in Units 1–7 to read these words from the unit.

administer	magistrate	miserable	penetrating	experience
cavernous	supervisor	fieldworker	stirrup	assignment

Vocabulary

Antonyms

Antonyms are words that are opposite or nearly opposite in meaning.

There are two types of antonyms. The first type is the complementary antonym. Complementary antonyms are words like *on* and *off*. They express an either/or relationship. A light switch is either on or off; there is nothing else it can be.

The second type of antonym is the gradable antonym. Gradable antonyms are those that form opposite ends of a continuous scale. An example of gradable antonyms is *wet* and *dry*. We can name a number of other conditions between *wet* and *dry*, such as *soggy* and *damp*.

Laugh and *cry* are gradable antonyms, because they form opposite ends of a continuous scale. A number of words can fit between *laugh* and *cry* on the scale.

laugh
giggle
chuckle
smile
frown
sniffle
sob
cry

GRAMMAR REVIEW

Complex Sentences & Compound/Complex Sentences

Simple, Compound, and Complex Sentences

- A **simple sentence** is made up of just one independent clause.
- A **compound sentence** has two or more independent clauses joined by a coordinating conjunction (*and, but, or*).
- A **complex sentence** has one independent clause and one or more dependent clauses.

Sentence	Simple, Compound, or Complex?	Why?
Leigh took the train, and Amira traveled by bus.	compound	two independent clauses joined by a conjunction *(and)*
My best friend and I are in the same classes.	simple	two subjects but just one verb
I would have bought a ticket if I had known about the concert.	complex	one independent clause and one dependent clause (using the conjunction *if*)

Kinds of Complex Sentences

Two kinds of complex sentences are those containing an **adverbial clause** and those containing an **adjectival clause**.

An **adverbial dependent clause**—
- usually starts with a subordinating conjunction *(while, because, if)*
- tells how, when, where, or why

An **adjectival dependent clause**—
- usually starts with a relative pronoun *(who, whom, that, which)*
- modifies a noun or pronoun in the independent clause

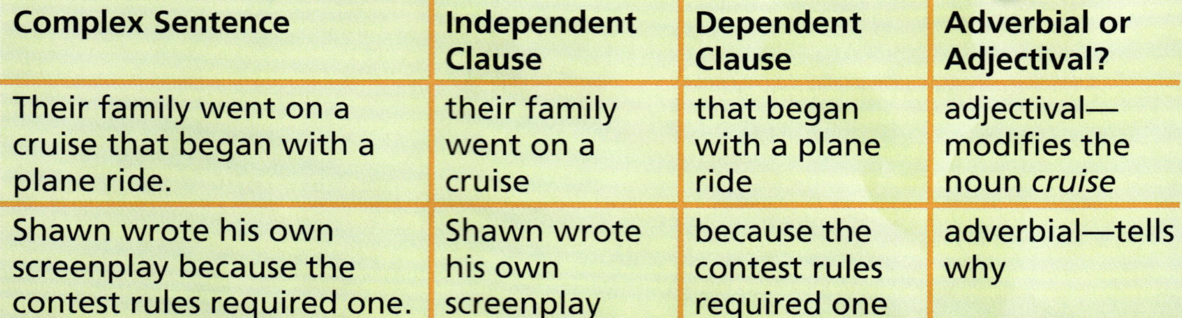

Complex Sentence	Independent Clause	Dependent Clause	Adverbial or Adjectival?
Their family went on a cruise that began with a plane ride.	their family went on a cruise	that began with a plane ride	adjectival—modifies the noun *cruise*
Shawn wrote his own screenplay because the contest rules required one.	Shawn wrote his own screenplay	because the contest rules required one	adverbial—tells why

Compound/Complex Sentences

A **compound/complex sentence** has two or more independent clauses and one or more dependent clauses. The dependent clauses can be adverbial or adjectival.

Compound/Complex Sentence	Independent Clauses		Dependent Clause(s)	Adjectival or Adverbial?
The critic loved the film, **which** she saw twice, **and** she wrote a positive review.	the critic loved the film	she wrote a positive review	which she saw twice	adjectival
I usually avoid riding on that street **because** it is bumpy, **but** sometimes I have no choice.	I usually avoid riding on that street	sometimes I have no choice	because it is bumpy	adverbial

Identifying Sentence Types

Sentence	Compound, Complex, or Compound/Complex?	Why?
The President might give a speech, **or** he might hold a press conference.	compound	two independent clauses joined by a conjunction *(or)*
My computer, **which** I took to the repair shop, runs much better now.	complex	one independent clause and one dependent clause (adjectival)
Miguel often sings **while** he works, **but** sometimes he whistles.	compound/complex	two independent clauses and one dependent clause (adverbial)

Diagramming a Compound-Complex Sentence

The critic loved the film, which she saw twice, and she wrote a positive review.

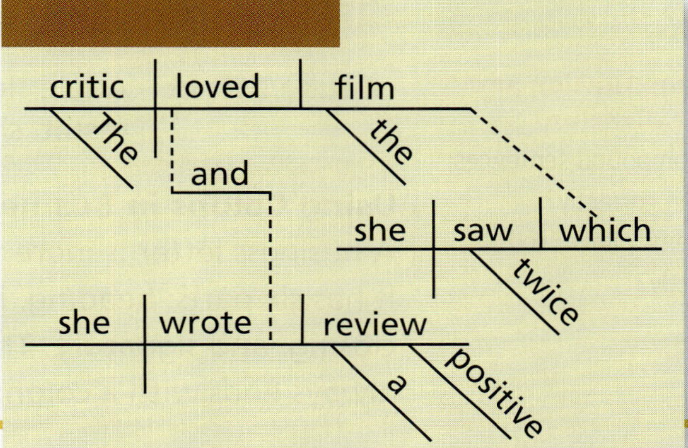

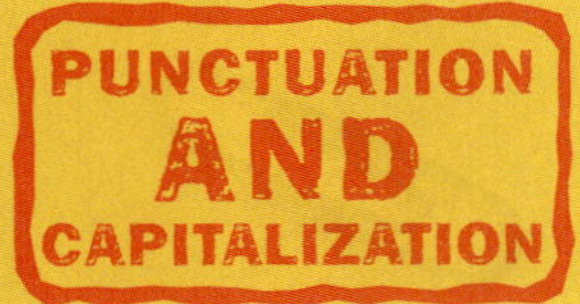

Using Commas in Compound Sentences

When two independent clauses are linked together, they make a compound sentence.

When the two clauses are linked with a conjunction (*and, but, for, or, so*), place a comma after the first independent clause, right before the conjunction.

I caught a trout, but Suzanne caught two hammerhead sharks.

If the two clauses do not have a separate subject, a comma is usually unnecessary.

I walked for a while and then ran.

Using Semicolons

Semicolons are used to connect independent clauses when there is no conjunction (for example, *and*).

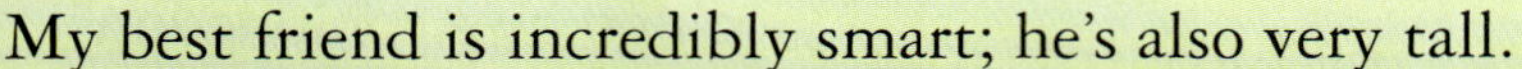

My best friend is incredibly smart; he's also very tall.

When we use a semicolon, we're suggesting that there is a relationship between the two clauses. Usually, you can tell the relationship from the context.

Cause	I'm afraid of cows; **therefore**, I could never live on a farm.
Contrast	You should get your tires fixed; **otherwise**, you might have an accident.
Cause/Effect	Adele slept through her Spanish test; **as a result**, she flunked the class.

Writing Traits Checklist

✔ **Punctuation and Capitalization**
Are compound sentences written correctly?
Are semicolons used correctly?

Using Colons in Business Letters

A business letter is more formal than a personal letter. It has six parts: heading, inside address, greeting, body, closing, and signature. The greeting in a business letter always ends with a colon.

Only one sentence of each pair is written correctly.

1. a. Renee has a great voice and loves to sing.
   b. Renee has a great voice, and loves to sing.
2. a. I'm definitely going to graduate this year; I have only one course left to take.
   b. I'm definitely going to graduate this year, I have only one course left to take.
3. a. Both Ann and Dana tried out for the play, however, only Ann got the part.
   b. Both Ann and Dana tried out for the play; however, only Ann got the part.
4. a. We gave him a map, and yet he still got lost.
   b. We gave him a map and yet he still got lost.
5. a. I have a hard time falling asleep at night; as a result, I'm often tired.
   b. I have a hard time falling asleep at night, as a result, I'm often tired.
6. a. Jackie gets paint all over the furniture; it makes her mother furious.
   b. Jackie gets paint all over the furniture, it makes her mother furious.
7. a. I do like to tango; on the other hand, I love to waltz.
   b. I do like to tango, on the other hand, I love to waltz.
8. a. Tim is good at making people laugh, and Jay makes them feel at home.
   b. Tim is good at making people laugh; and Jay makes them feel at home.
9. a. Dave is a good actor, but his sister is a movie star.
   b. Dave is a good actor but his sister is a movie star.
10. a. You don't remember me, but I remember you.
    b. You don't remember me; but I remember you.

GLOSSARY

abandon (ə băn′dən) – to go away from or leave something with no intention of returning

access (ăk′sĕs) – the ability or means to approach, enter, or make use of

accompany (ə kŭm′pə nē) – to go with, be present with, or travel with

account (ə kount′) – an oral or written description or report of events

accustom (ə kŭs′təm) – to make or become used to

acquaintance (ə kwān′təns) – a person one knows slightly

administer (ăd mĭn′ĭ stər) – to manage or have charge of

aggravate (ăg′rə vāt) – to make worse or more serious

amber (ăm′bər) – a hardened, clear, yellowish brown substance that oozed from trees, became buried, and was fossilized, often trapping ancient seeds and insects

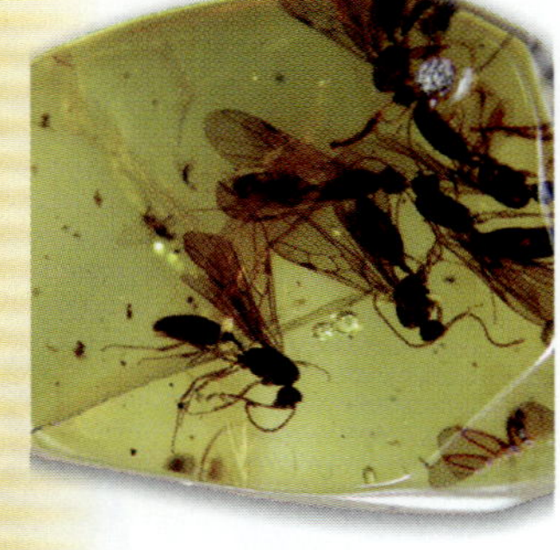

amber

amusing (ə myōō′zĭng) – causing to laugh or smile

angle (ăng′gəl) – the figure or space formed by the coming together in a point of two lines or surfaces

antiseptic (ăn′tĭ sĕp′tĭk) – a substance that kills, or prevents the growth of, microorganisms that produce infection

anxious (ăngk′shəs) – troubled, worried; uneasy of mind

aquatic (ə kwăt′ĭk) – living, growing, or taking place in, on, or near water

archaeology (är′kē ŏl′ə jē) – the scientific study of past human life and culture through remains such as graves, tools, and pottery

aristocrat (ə rĭs′tə krăt′) – a member of the ruling classes or of the nobility

array (ə rā′) – an orderly arrangement or display

artifact (är′tə făkt) – any object made or shaped by people, especially things of archaeological or historical interest

ascend (ə sĕnd′) – to go or move upward; to rise

assured (ə shŏŏrd′) – confident and sure

attest (ə tĕst′) – to provide clear proof of, or to declare to be true or genuine

axle (ăk′səl) – the bar or rod on which a wheel or wheels turn

axle

balance (băl′əns) – a steady and stable state

barbaric (bär băr′ĭk) – uncivilized and rough; wild

base (bās) – the supporting part, bottom, or foundation on which something rests

blister (blĭs′tər) – a bubble-like swelling on the skin that contains watery liquid and is caused by burning or irritation

bold (bōld) – fearless and confident

bronze (brŏnz) – a brown metal formed from a mixture of copper and tin

ă pat / ā pay / âr care / ä father / ĕ pet / ē bee / ĭ pit / ī pie / îr pier / ŏ pot / ō toe / ô paw / oi noise / ŏŏ took / ōō boot / ou out / ŭ cut /

bureaucrat (byŏŏr′ə krăt) – a government official with particular functions and authority

burrow (bûr′ō) – to dig a hole or tunnel

canal (kə năl′) – an artificial waterway cut through land and used for irrigation or navigation

canvas (kăn′vəs) – a strong, coarse cloth of cotton, hemp, or flax, used for making things like sails or tents

capital (kăp′ĭ tl) – the city that is the official seat of government in a country or state

cavernous (kăv′ər nəs) – resembling a large cave or cavern in vastness or effect

certificate (sər tĭf′ĭ kĭt) – an official document that provides evidence of the truth of something, such as a birth, marriage, or completion of a course of study

collapse (kə lăps′) – to fall, cave in, or crumble suddenly

collectively (kə lĕk′tĭv lē) – taken as a whole; combined

coma (kō′mə) – a state of deep unconsciousness, often caused by injury or disease

common (kŏm′ən) – belonging to, or shared equally, by two or more people or things

communicate (kə myōō′nĭ kāt′) – to convey information about something

compete (kəm pēt′) – to strive against another or others to attain a goal or advantage

confirm (kən fûrm′) – to support or prove the truth of

consequence (kŏn′sĭ kwĕns) – something that is the effect or result of an earlier occurrence

consist (kən sĭst′) – to be made up or composed (of)

convince (kən vĭns′) – to make a person feel certain that something is true

core (kôr) – the central or most important part of something

corrupt (kə rŭpt′) – guilty of dishonest and immoral practices, such as bribery

courage (kûr′ĭj) – the ability to control fear when facing danger or pain; bravery

crochet (krō shā′) – to make a piece of needlework by using a hooked needle to loop thread into a pattern

cylinder (sĭl′ən dər) – an object or shape with straight sides and round ends, such as a can

decade (dĕk′ād) – a period of ten years

decipher (dĭ sī′fər) – to decode or make out the meaning of

decline (dĭ klīn′) – a gradual decrease or downward slope

decompose (dē kəm pōz′) – to rot, decay, or disintegrate into basic parts

delicate (dĕl′ĭ kĭt) – pleasing, exquisite, fine, or dainty

density (dĕn′sĭ tē) – the quantity of something in a given area of measurement

deplete (dĭ plēt′) – to use up or empty out

despite (dĭ spīt′) – although; nevertheless; in spite of

devise (dĭ vīz′) – to design, plan, form, or invent

certificate

cylinder

dusk

edible

devote (dĭ vōt′) – to give or apply something, such as time or attention, entirely to a particular activity, cause, or person

dialect (dī′ə lĕkt) – a local form of a language that differs from the standard or literary form of the language

dictator (dĭk′tā tər) – a ruler who has complete and absolute authority; a tyrant

dike (dīk) – a bank of earth for controlling the waters of the sea or a river

disciple (dĭ sī′pəl) – a follower or supporter of another's teachings

disembark (dĭs ĕm bärk′) – to go ashore from a ship, plane, or other vehicle

displace (dĭs plās′) – to take the place of, or to move from the usual place

distant (dĭs′tənt) – remote or far away in space or time

distinct (dĭ stĭngkt′) – clearly separate or different in kind from others

district (dĭs′trĭkt) – a division of an area for political or administrative purposes

disturbance (dĭ stûr′bəns) – an upsetting of the peaceful or settled condition of something

domesticate (də mĕs′tĭ kāt′) – to train animals or plants to live in a human environment and be of use to humans

dusk (dŭsk) – the period just before darkness when the sun is below the horizon but there is still some light in the sky

earthly (ûrth′lē) – referring to the earth and human life on Earth

ease (ēz) – absence of painful effort or discomfort

edible (ĕd′ə bəl) – fit to be eaten; food

editorial (ĕd′ĭ tôr′ē əl) – a newspaper, magazine, radio, or television statement that expresses the opinion of the editor, publisher, station, or network

elaborate (ĭ lăb′ər ĭt) – with many parts or details; complicated

elegant (ĕl′ĭ gənt) – tasteful, graceful, and beautiful in appearance or style

emerge (ĭ mûrj′) – to come up or out from; to come into view

employ (ĕm ploi′) – to put to use or put to work

enforce (ĕn fôrs′) – to compel or force obedience to

enlighten (ĕn līt′n) – to inform or give knowledge to

ensure (ĕn sho͝or′) – to make sure or certain

entry (ĕn′trē) – an item written or entered in a diary, list, or other record

ethnic (ĕth′nĭk) – of or relating to a group of people who share a common national, linguistic, religious, racial, or cultural heritage

exaggerate (ĭg zăj′ə rāt′) – to make something seem larger or better, or smaller or worse, than it really is

execute (ĕk′sĭ kyo͞ot) – to carry out an order or put a plan into effect

experience (ĭk spîr′ē əns) – skill or knowledge gained from participation in activities or events

exploit (ĕk′sploit) – to take the fullest possible advantage of

ă pat / ā pay / âr care / ä father / ĕ pet / ē bee / ĭ pit / ī pie / îr pier / ŏ pot / ō toe / ô paw / oi noise / o͝o took / o͞o boot / ou out / ŭ cut /

express (ĭk **sprĕs′**) – to show or make known; to communicate

extinct (ĭk **stĭngkt′**) – no longer existing or living

extract (ĭk **străkt′**) – to take or pull out by force or effort, or by chemical or mechanical means

F

facility (fə **sĭl′**ĭ tē) – something built to provide a particular service or function, such as a laboratory or hospital

fatality (fā **tăl′**ĭ tē) – a death resulting from an accident or a disaster

fatigue (fə **tēg′**) – tiredness resulting from hard work or effort

fault (fôlt) – a break or dislocation of layers of rock, caused by movement of Earth's crust

feature (**fē′**chər) – a distinctive or noticible characteristic of something

fellow (**fĕl′**ō) – being of the same kind, group, occupation, or otherwise united

floe (flō) – a sheet of floating ice

flourish (**flûr′**ĭsh) – to grow well or do well; to be successful

fluent (**flo͞o′**ənt) – able to express oneself smoothly and easily

former (**fôr′**mər) – of an earlier period of time; in the past

frigid (**frĭj′**ĭd) – extremely cold

fundamental (fŭn′də **mĕn′**tl) – being a very important or essential part of; a foundation

fungi (**fŭn′**jī) – plants, including mushrooms and molds, that have no leaves, flowers, or green coloring and that grow on both dead or living matter

G

galley (**găl′**ē) – the kitchen on a ship or aircraft

generally (**jĕn′**ər ə lē) – usually or most often

glazed (glāzd) – coated with glass or another glossy surface

globalization (glō′bə lĭ **zā′**shən) – the process of becoming worldwide in scope or application

grime (grīm) – ground-in dirt or soot

H

haggle (**hăg′**əl) – to argue over the price or terms of something

horizontal (hôr′ĭ-**zŏn′**tl) – parallel to the horizon or skyline

I

identify (ī **dĕn′**tə fī′) – to associate oneself closely with a person or group

identity (ī **dĕn′**tĭ tē) – the set of characteristics by which something is clearly recognizable or known

immense (ĭ **mĕns′**) – extremely large; huge

impact (**ĭm′**păkt) – the influence or effect of something new, such as an idea

imperial (ĭm **pîr′**ē əl) – of or relating to an empire, emperor, or empress

indebted (ĭn **dĕt′**ĭd) – having moral, social, or financial obligations to another; owing

industry (**ĭn′**də strē) – the commercial or large scale manufacture or production of goods

infinite (**ĭn′**fə nĭt) – having no limit or boundaries; endless

influence (**ĭn′**flo͞o əns) – the power to affect a person, thing, or course of events

fungi

infinite

ûr firm / hw which / th thin / *th* this / zh vision /
ə about, item, edible, gallop, circus

irrigation

mechanize

inherit (ĭn hĕr′ĭt) – to receive something from an ancestor by legal succession or will

innocent (ĭn′ə sənt) – free of all evil or wrongdoing

inscription (ĭn skrĭp′shən) – words or letters that are written, printed, carved, or engraved on a surface

instance (ĭn′stəns) – a case, occurrence, or example of something

interview (ĭn′tər vyo͞o) – a formal meeting or conversation with a person to obtain comments and information

irrigation (ĭr′ĭ gāt′shən) – a supply of water for land by means of ditches, pipes, or streams

jostle (jŏs′əl) – to push and shove roughly, especially in a crowd

justice (jŭs′tĭs) – honorable and fair treatment

keel (kēl) – the main structure, running lengthwise along the base of a ship, to which the ship's framework is attached

labor (lā′bər) – to work hard; to make a great effort

linguistic (lĭng gwĭs′tĭk) – relating to language and the structure of language

logical (lŏj′ĭ kəl) – in accordance with what seems reasonable or natural

magistrate (măj′ĭ strāt) – a minor judge or civil officer who administers the law

magnitude (măg′nĭ to͞od) – the measure of amount of energy released by an earthquake, as indicated on the Richter Scale

manner (măn′ər) – a person's way of acting or behaving

mechanize (mĕk′ə nīz) – to equip with machines or to use machines for

military (mĭl′ĭ tĕr′ē) – of or relating to soldiers or the armed forces

moral (môr′əl) – concerned with the goodness and badness of human action or character

mournful (môrn′fəl) – sorrowful; showing great sadness or grief

murmur (mûr′mər) – softly spoken words or a low, soft sound

myth (mĭth) – a traditional story or legend, typically ancient, containing ideas or beliefs about the natural world, gods, heroes, and customs

narrative (năr′ə tĭv) – a spoken or written story or account of something

neglect (nĭ glĕkt′) – failure to do, pay attention to, or take care of properly

nobles (nō′bəlz) – those belonging to the upper class of a country by birth or rank

nomad (nō′măd) – a member of a group of people who have no fixed home and roam from place to place seeking food, water, and pasture

observe (əb zûrv′) – to see or notice; to watch carefully

ă pat / ā pay / âr care / ä father / ĕ pet / ē bee / ĭ pit / ī pie / îr pier / ŏ pot / ō toe / ô paw / oi noise / o͝o took / o͞o boot / ou out / ŭ cut /

opportunity (ŏp′ər **to͞o′**nĭ tē) – a time or occasion that is favorable for a particular purpose

organism (ôr′gə nĭz′əm) – an individual form of life, such as an animal, plant, bacterium, or fungus

originate (ə rĭj′ə **nāt′**) – to come into being; to start

P

pale (pāl) – faint, not bright or brilliant

parka (pär′kə) – a hooded jacket, often made of fur, for use in cold weather

partake (pär **tāk′**) – to participate in or to take a part of, as food

peal (pēl) – the loud ringing of a bell

penetrate (**pĕn′**ĭ trāt) – to pierce or make a way into

perceive (pər **sēv′**) – to understand or become aware of

philosophy (fĭ **lŏs′**ə fē) – the study of principles of reality and human nature and conduct

photosynthesis (fō′tō **sĭn′**thĭ sĭs) – the process by which green plants use energy from sunlight to convert carbon dioxide (from the air) and water into carbohydrates, usually releasing oxygen

physical (**fĭz′**ĭ kəl) – of or related to nature or material things

pillar (**pĭl′**ər) – a slender, upright structure or column used for support or ornamentation

plod (plŏd) – to move or walk heavily and slowly

plumage (**plo͞o′**mĭj) – the covering of feathers on a bird

populous (**pŏp′**yə ləs) – containing many people or inhabitants

portray (pôr **trā′**) – to describe in words or make a picture of

possessions (pə **zĕsh′**ən) – things owned, including wealth, property, or goods

preserve (prĭ **zûrv′**) – to protect and keep in unchanged condition for future use or enjoyment

privilege (**prĭv′**ə lĭj) – a special advantage or benefit enjoyed by a particular person or persons

proclaim (prō **klām′**) – to announce officially and publicly

promote (prə **mōt′**) – to contribute to or advance the progress or growth of

prone (prōn) – having a tendency toward; likely to happen

proof (pro͞of) – successful in resisting or withstanding something, as in *waterproof*

prosper (**prŏs′**pər) – to be successful; to thrive

puncture (**pŭngk′**chər) – a small hole made by something sharp and pointed

Q

quarrel (**kwôr′**əl) – an angry dispute or disagreement

quote (kwōt) – to repeat or copy the words of another

R

rank (răngk) – an official position

recover (rĭ **kŭv′**ər) – to return to or regain a normal condition

refine (rĭ **fīn′**) – to remove impurities or defects from

refugee (rĕf yo͞o-**jē′**) – a person who has left his home and seeks shelter elsewhere, as from war or natural disaster

regal (**rē′**gəl) – like or relating to a king or queen

reign (rān) – a period of royal rule or rule by a dominating power

plumage

relay

ûr firm / hw which / th thin / *th* this / zh vision /
ə about, item, edible, gallop, circus

reservoir

ripple

relatively (rĕl′ə tĭv lē) – considered in comparison to something else

relay (rē′lā) – an act of passing something along from one person or group to another

reliable (rĭ lī′ə bəl) – dependable or trustworthy in quality or performance

relief (rĭ lēf′) – ease gotten by a reduction or removal of pain, anxiety, or a burden

remains (rĭ mānz′) – ancient ruins, fossils, or other objects that have survived from earlier times

remote (rĭ mōt′) – far away or hidden away

republic (rĭ pŭb′lĭk) – a country in which the supreme power is held by the people or their elected officials

reservoir (rĕz′ər vwär) – a natural or man-made pond or lake used for storing water

respire (rĭ spīr′) – to breathe in and out; to go through the process by which an organism without lungs exchanges gases such as oxygen with its environment

restore (rĭ stôr′) – to bring back to a former, normal, or original condition

reveal (rĭ vēl′) – to make known; to uncover and allow to be seen or known

revere (rĭ vîr′) – to feel deep respect for or devotion to

revitalize (rē vīt′l īz′) – to give new life or vigor to

rhythm (rĭ*th*′əm) – a regular pattern formed by a series of sounds of differing duration and stress

ripple (rĭp′əl) – to move like a small wave or series of waves

sacrifice (săk′rə fīs) – the killing of an animal or person as an offering to win the favor of a god

scholar (skŏl′ər) – a person with great learning in a particular subject

section (sĕk′shən) – a part, portion, or piece of something

sense (sĕns) – to become aware of or detect something

sigh (sī) – a long, deep breath given out, as in sadness, relief, or tiredness

site (sīt) – the place where an activity takes place (or took place), or where a town or building stands (or stood)

slump (slŭmp) – to drop or sink heavily; to collapse

smudge (smŭj) – dense smoke that protects crops against frost or insects

soot (so͝ot) – the black powdery substance that comes from the smoke of burning coal, oil, or wood

species (spē′shēz) – a basic category of biological classification composed of related organisms that resemble one another and are able to breed among themselves

specify (spĕs′ə fī) – to state instructions, conditions, or details clearly and definitely

stall (stôl) – to stop suddenly due to loss of power

standardize (stăn′dər dīz) – to make something be like, or agree with, an accepted model or example

station (stā′shən) – the place where a person is assigned to be; a post

ă pat / ā pay / âr care / ä father / ĕ pet / ē bee / ĭ pit / ī pie / îr pier / ŏ pot / ō toe / ô paw / oi noise / o͝o took / o͞o boot / ou out / ŭ cut /

stationary (stā′shə nĕr′ē) – not moving; immoveable

stock (stŏk) – a group or quantity of closely related organisms in a breed or species

strait (strāt) – a narrow stretch of water connecting two larger bodies of water

strategy (străt′ə jē) – a plan of action for achieving something

structure (strŭk′chər) – something that is built or constructed, such as a building or a bridge

subsequent (sŭb′sĭ kwĕnt) – coming after or following in time or order

suspend (sə spĕnd′) – to hang or to keep from falling or sinking

suspicious (sə spĭsh′əs) – having doubt or mistrust about something

symbol (sĭm′bəl) – something that is used for, or regarded as, representing something else

T

talcum (tăl′kəm) – a soft, smooth powder made of the mineral talc, used to keep things dry or moving smoothly

tectonic (tĕk tŏn′ĭk) – relating to the movement or deformation of Earth's crust

temporary (tĕm′pə rĕr′ē) – lasting, or meant to last, for only a limited time; not permanent

term (tûrm) – a word or phrase having a particular meaning

terrain (tə rān′) – the surface features of a stretch of land

threaten (thrĕt′n) – to warn of or express an intention of doing something undesirable

thrust (thrŭst) – a strong forward force or push

torture (tôr′chər) – the inflicting of severe and extreme physical or mental pain

traitor (trā′tər) – a person who is disloyal to, or betrays, his country

translate (trăns′lāt) – to express in another language

transmit (trăns mĭt′) – to send or pass from one person, place, or thing to another

tremor (trĕm′ər) – a slight shaking or trembling movement

tribute (trĭb′yo͞ot) – a payment from one country or ruler to another more powerful one

tsunami (tso͞o nä′mē) – an unusually large ocean wave caused by an underwater earthquake or volcanic eruption

U

underlying (ŭn′dər-lī′ĭng) – being the foundation or basis of; lying beneath

unique (yo͞o nēk′) – being one of a kind or very unusual

unravel (ŭn răv′əl) – to undo or untangle something, such as the threads of fabric

unusual (ŭn yo͞o′zho͞o əl) – not common or ordinary; rare

V

vast (văst) – very great in area, amount, or size

vein (vān) – a narrow strip of a different color or material in substances such as rock, wood, or cheese

vertical (vûr′tĭ kəl) – upright or at right angles to the horizon

suspend

vein

ûr firm / hw which / th thin / *th* this / zh vision /
ə about, item, edible, gallop, circus

Acknowledgments

A Song for Ba by Paul Yee, illustrated by Jan Peng Wang. Text copyright © 2004 by Paul Yee. Illustrations copyright © 2004 by Jan Peng Wang. Reprinted by permission of House of Anasi Press.

Finding Miracles by Julia Alvarez. Text copyright © 2004 by Julia Alvarez. Reprinted by permission of Susan Bergholz Literary Services.

The Code Talkers Speak by Kenji Kawano. Copyright © 1990 by Kenji Kawano. Reprinted by permission of Cooper Square Publishing, a division of Rowman & Littlefield Publishing Group.

"Final Curve" from *The Collected Poems of Langston Hughes* by Langston Hughes, edited by Arnold Rampersad,with David Roessei, Associate Editor. Copyright © 1994 by the Estate of Langston Hughes. Reprinted by permission of Alfred A. Knopf, a division of Random House, Inc.

"Celebration" by Alonzo Lopez. Copyright © 1972 by the Institute of American Indian Arts. Reprinted by permission of Random House.

"The Drum" by Nikki Giovanni. Copyright © 1971, 1985 by Nikki Giovanni. Reprinted by permission of Farrar, Straus & Giroux LLC.

"Digging for China" by Richard Wilbur from *A Green Place:Modern Poems* compiled by William Jay Smith. Copyright © 1956 by Richard Wilbur. Reprinted by permission of Houghton Mifflin Harcourt Publishing Company.

"There Isn't Time!" by Eleanor Farjeon, illustrated by Peter Bailey, from *The Oxford Book of Children's Poetry*, edited by Michael Harrison and Christopher Stuart-Clark. Copyright © by Eleanor Farjeon. Illustrations copyright © 2007 by Peter Bailey. Reprinted by permission of David Hingham Associates Limited.

"To Dark Eyes Dreaming" by Zilpha Keatley Snyder. Copyright © 1969 by Zilpha Keatley Snyder. Reprinted by permission of the author.

The Honorable Prison by Lyll Becerra de Jenkins. Copyright © 1988 by Lyll Becerra de Jenkins. Reprinted by permission of Penguin Group (USA) Inc.

Coast to Coast with Alice by Patricia Rush Hyatt. Copyright © 1995 by Carolrhoda Books, Inc. Reprinted by permission of Carolrhoda Books, a division of Lerner Publishing Group, Inc. All rights reserved. No part of this excerpt may be used or reproduced in any manner whatsoever without the prior written permission of Lerner Publishing Group, Inc.

The Lamp, the Ice, and a Boat Called Fish by Jacqueline Briggs Martin, illustrated by Beth Krommes. Text copyright © 2001 by Jaqueline Briggs Martin. Illustrations and illustrator's note copyright © 2001 by Beth Krommes. Reprinted by permission of Houghton Mifflin Harcourt Publishing Company.

Reflections of a Black Cowboy by Robert H. Miller. Text copyright © 1991 by Robert H. Miller. Reprinted by permission of the publisher, Just Us Books, Inc.

"A Red Palm" by Gary Soto. Copyright © 1990 by Gary Soto. Reprinted by permission of Chronicle Books LLC.

Esperanza Rising by Pam Muñoz Ryan. Copyright © 2000 by Pam Muñoz Ryan. Reprinted by permission of Scholastic Press, a division of Scholastic Inc.

"Skyscraper" from *We the People* by Bobbi Katz. Text copyright © 1998, 2000 by Bobbi Katz. Reprinted by permission of HarperCollins Children's Books, a division of HarperCollins Publishers, Inc.

English-Language Arts Content Standards for California Public Schools reproduced by permission, California Department of Education, CDE Press, 1430 N. Street, Suite 3207, Sacramento, CA 95814

Photo Credits

iv (falling book) © EyeWire. **iv** (red book) © Comstock. **iv-v** (clouds) © Don Farrall, LightWorks Studio/PhotoDisc. **iv-v** (desert) © Jack Hollingsworth/PhotoDisc. **v** (buttefly) © CMCD, Inc./PhotoDisc. **v** (elephant) © CMCD, Inc./PhotoDisc. **v** (fish bowl) © CMCD, Inc./PhotoDisc. **v** (frog) © CMCD, Inc./PhotoDisc. **v** (in window left) © PhotoLink/PhotoDisc. **v** (in window right) © Jeremy Woodhouse/PhotoDisc. **v** (lizard) © Stockdisk. **v** (monarch butterfly) © Siede Preis/PhotoDisc. **v** (open book) © PhotoDisc. **v** (scallop shell) © Siede Preis/PhotoDisc. **v** (shuttle) © Stockbyte. **v** (stack books) © Siede Preis/PhotoDisc. **v** (starfish) © Siede Preis/PhotoDisc. **v** (window frame) © Ryan McVay/PhotoDisc. **vi** (Ankh) © CMCD, Inc./PhotoDisc. **vi** (codetalkers) © Corbis. **vi** (dog) © Shutterstock. **vi** (drum) © Artville. **vi** (kimono) © Victoria & Albert Museum, London/Art Resource, NY. **vi** (letters) © Comstock. **vi** (movie camera) © Comstock. **vi** (rhino) © Cybermedia/PhotoDisc. **vi** (stringed instrument) © Stapleton Collection/Corbis. **vi** (television) © CMCD, Inc./PhotoDisc. **vii** (compass) © CMCD, Inc./PhotoDisc. **vii** (field workers Library of Congress. **vii** (first aid kit) © Corbis. **vii** (frame) © Image Farm. **vii** (handprint) © Shutterstock. **vii** (horses) © Edmond Van Hoorick/PhotoDisc. **vii** (kite) © Shutterstock. **vii** (rocks) © Shutterstock. **vii** (seal) © Charles & Josette Lenars/Corbis. **vii** (suitcase) © Stockdisk. **viii** (tl) © Digital Stock. **viii** (tr) © Gianni Dagli Orti/Corbis. **viii** (cr) © Artville. **viii** (crab) © AP Photo/California Department of Fish and Game. **viii** (bl) © CMCD, Inc./PhotoDisc. **viii** (br) © Michael Prince/Corbis. **viii** (nest) © CMCD, Inc./PhotoDisc. **ix** (tl) © Chris

A Crumley/Alamy. **ix** (cr) © Dallas and John Heaton/Free Agents Limited/Corbis. **ix** (b) © Stapleton Collection/ Corbis. **x** (t) © Lloyd Cluff/Corbis. **x** (cr) © Bettmann/ Corbis. **x** (bl) © Ed Freeman/Stone/Getty/Images. **x** (br) © C Squared Studios/PhotoDisc. **xi** (tr) © Getty Images. **xi** (figs) © Artville. **xi** (cr) Library of Congress. **xi** (bl) © Jean-Yves Ruszniewski/TempSport/Corbis. **xi** (bc) © Burstein Collection/Corbis. **2-3** © Digital Stock. **4** (c) © C. Borland/ PhotoLink/PhotoDisc. **4** (b) © Scenics of America/ PhotoLink/PhotoDisc. **5** (tl) © C Squared Studios/ PhotoDisc. **5** (c) © Artville. **5** (b) © Getty Images. **5** (pick) © Comstock. **8-9** (t) © AP Photo/Sergey Ponomarev. **8-9** (b) © HMCo. **9** (t) © HMCo. **10** © Prehistoric/The Bridgeman Art Library/Getty Images. **11** © Cybermedia/ PhotoDisc. **12-3** (t) © Prehistoric/The Bridgeman Art Library/Getty Images. **12-3** (b) © Don Farrall, LightWorks Studio/PhotoDisc. **14** (t) © Sisse Brimberg/National Geographic/Getty Images. **14-5** © Cybermedia/PhotoDisc. **18-9** (t) © HMCo. **18-21** (plane) © C Squared Studios/ PhotoDisc. **19** (tr) © Stockdisk. **19** (c) © Hans Weisenhoffer/PhotoDisc. **19** (b) © Gianni Dagli Orti/ Corbis. **20** (cl) © Dean Conger/Corbis. **20** (bl) © Shutterstock. **20** (bc) © Siede Preis/PhotoDisc. **21** (t) © Roger Wood/Corbis. **21** (cr) © CMCD, Inc./PhotoDisc. **22** (bl) © Shutterstock. **22** (bc) © Artville. **22** (br) © Stockdisk. **23** © Bettmann/Corbis. **24** (tl) © Artville. **24** (cl) © CMCD, Inc./PhotoDisc. **24** (c) © Stapleton Collection/Corbis. **24-5** (t) © Shutterstock. **26** (t) © Don Farrall, LightWorks Studio/PhotoDisc. **26** (cr) © HMCo. **26** (b) © Bill Curtsinger/National Geographic Image Collection. **27** (t) © PhotoDisc. **27** (cr) © Digital Stock. **28-9** © Michael Freeman/Corbis. **36-7** © Michael Prince/ Corbis. **38** (t) © Alamy. **38** (b) © AP Photo/California Department of Fish and Game. **39** (t) © Corbis. **39** (c) © Getty Images. **39** (b) © CMCD, Inc./PhotoDisc. **42** © Brand X Pictures. **43** © Aerial Archives/Alamy. **44** © Corbis. **45** © Comstock. **47** © Norbert Wu/Minden Pictures. **48-9** © AP Photo/California Department of Fish and Game. **48-9** (b) © Siede Preis/PhotoDisc. **52** (t) © Dave Thompson /LifeFile/PhotoDisc. **52** (cr) © HMCo. **53** © Matthieu Paley/Corbis. **53** (cr) © Artville. **54** (t) © AP Photo/Dolores Ochoa. **54** (b) © HMCo. **55** © Getty Images. **56** © Corbis. **57** (c) © CMCD, Inc./PhotoDisc. **57** (b) © Brand X Pictures. **58** © David Fleetham/Taxi/Getty Images. **59** © S. Alden/PhotoLink/PhotoDisc. **60** © Robert Glusic/PhotoDisc. **61** © Peter Johnson/Corbis. **62** © CMCD, Inc./PhotoDisc. **63** © Rick & Nora Bowers/Alamy. **70-1** © Chris A Crumley/Alamy. **72** (mask left) © CMCD, Inc./PhotoDisc. **72** (mask center) © CMCD, Inc./PhotoDisc. **72** (mask right) © CMCD, Inc./PhotoDisc. **72** (b) © Classic PIO Images. **73** (t) © Artville. **73** (c) © Dennis Cox/Alamy. **73** (b) © R. Morley/PhotoLink/PhotoDisc. **76** © Artville. **82-3** © Artville. **83** (cr) © Getty Images. **92** (l) © Ron Sachs/CNP/Corbis. **93** © Jan Butchofsky-Houser/Corbis. **94** © Corbis. **96-7** © Corbis. **98-9** © Bettmann/Corbis. **106-7** © Dallas and John Heaton/Free Agents Limited/Corbis. **108** (c) © Artville. **108** (b) © C Squared Studios/PhotoDisc. **109** (t) © Cartesia/PhotoDisc Imaging. **109** (c) © Stockdisk. **109** (b) © CMCD, Inc./PhotoDisc. **112** © Cartesia/ PhotoDisc Imaging. **112-3** (bkgd) © PhotoDisc. **112-3** (map) © HMCo. **114** © PhotoDisc. **116** © akg-images/ Gérard Degeorge. **117** © Charles & Josette Lenars/Corbis. **120** © akg-images. **121** © akg-images. **122** © National Museum of Karachi, Karachi, Pakistan,/The Bridgeman Art Library International. **123** (bl) © The Bridgeman Art Library International. **124** © Lowell Georgia/Corbis. **126-7** © Redlink/Corbis. **127** (br) © Chuck Yuen. **128** © Stapleton Collection/Corbis. **129** © Victoria & Albert Museum, London/Art Resource, NY. **130** © Comstock. **131** (t) © Werner Forman/Corbis. **131** (b) © Artville. **132** (tl) © Shutterstock. **132** (cl) © Image Ideas. **132** (b) © National Geographic Image Collection. **133** (t) © Brand X Pictures. **133** (b) © Visual Arts Library (London)/Alamy. **140-1** © Lloyd Cluff/Corbis. **142** (c) © Getty Images. **142** (b) © PhotoDisc. **143** (t) © PhotoDisc. **143** (c) © Getty Images. **143** (b) © Stocktrek/PhotoDisc. **146** © Cartesia/PhotoDisc Imaging. **147** (b) © HMCo. **148** (t) © HMCo. **149** (c) © Corbis. **149** (bl) © Comstock. **149** (bottles) © Comstock. **150** (l) © HMCo. **150** (r) © HMCo. **154** © Jim Sugar/ Corbis. **155** © Bettmann/Corbis. **156** © Ted Streshinsky/ Corbis. **157** (t) © Corbis. **157** (b) © Underwood & Underwood/Corbis. **158-9** © Bettmann/Corbis. **160** © Liu Guoqiang/Xinhua Press/Corbis. **161** © José Jácome/epa/ Corbis. **162** © DIGITAL GLOBE/HANDOUT/epa/Corbis. **163** © Shutterstock. **164** © Corbis. **165** (c) © CMCD, Inc./ PhotoDisc. **165** (ladder) © C Squared Studios/PhotoDisc. **166** (bl) © Comstock. **166** (br) © Comstock. **166-7** © Siede Preis/PhotoDisc. **167** (bl) © PhotoDisc. **174-5** © Ed Freeman/Stone/Getty/Images. **176** (c) © Hans Weisenhoffer/ PhotoDisc. **176** (b) © Jack Hollingsworth/PhotoDisc. **177** (t) © Hans Weisenhoffer/PhotoDisc. **177** (c) © Image Farm. **177** (b) © Stockbyte. **180** (t) © CMCD, Inc./PhotoDisc. **180** (cl) © Cartesia/PhotoDisc Imaging. **180** (b) © Comstock. **180-1** (bkgd) © Albert J. Copley/PhotoDisc. **183** © AP Photo. **184** (tl) © CMCD, Inc./PhotoDisc. **184** (pad) © CMCD, Inc./PhotoDisc. **184** (r) © CMCD, Inc./PhotoDisc. **185** (t) © AP Photo. **185** (cr) © Comstock. **186** (bl) © Comstock. **186** (br) © Luis Acosta/AFP/Getty Images. **187** (b) © C Squared Studios/PhotoDisc. **188** © Comstock. **189** (image) © AP Photo/Fernando Llano. **189** (tv set) © CMCD, Inc./PhotoDisc. **192** (cow) © CMCD, Inc./ PhotoDisc. **192** (tl) © J. Luke/PhotoLink/PhotoDisc. **193** © Car Culture/Corbis. **193** (br) © Artville. **194** (c) © Robert Glusic/PhotoDisc. **194** (bl) © CMCD, Inc./PhotoDisc. **194** (rope) © Brand X Pictures. **195** (farm) © Scenics of America/PhotoLink/PhotoDisc. **195** (frame) © Image Farm.

196 (telegrams) © Comstock. 196 (fields) © PhotoLink/PhotoDisc. 196 (frame) © Shutterstock. 196 (bl) © Comstock. 197 (frame) © Ryan McVay/PhotoDisc. 197 (horses) © Shutterstock. 210-1 © Art Kowalsky/Alamy. 212 (t) © PhotoDisc. 212 b) © Comstock. 213 (t) © Getty Images. 213 (c) © CMCD, Inc./PhotoDisc. 213 (b) © CMCD, Inc./PhotoDisc. 216 (cr) © HMCo. 216 (t) © Digital Stock. 216 (b) © HMCo. 216-7 (bkgd) © Brand X Pictures. 218 (tr) © Getty Images. 218 (cl) © EyeWire. 218 (bl) © CMCD, Inc./PhotoDisc. 219 (t) © HMCo. 219 (cr) © akg-images/Bildarchiv Steffens. 219 (bl) © Scala/Art Resource, NY. 220 (cl) © EyeWire. 220 (bl) © CMCD, Inc./PhotoDisc. 221 © Scala/Art Resource, NY. 222-3 © Scala/Art Resource, NY. 226 (letter T) © Brand X Pictures. 226-9 bkgd © Bruce Heinemann/PhotoDisc. 227 © Erich Lessing/Art Resource, NY. 227 (letter B) © Brand X Pictures. 228 © Scala/Art Resource, NY. 228 (letter S) © Brand X Pictures. 229 (letter P) © Brand X Pictures. 230 (bl) © Artville. 230 (br) © Artville. 231 © North Wind Picture Archvies. 232 © Scala/Art Resource, NY. 233 © Getty Images. 234 © akg-images/Bildarchiv Steffens. 235 © AP Photo/Italian Culture Ministry. 236 © Dennis Hallinan/Alamy. 238 © akg-images/Werner Forman. 239 (t) © HMCo. 239 (b) © Brand X Pictures. 246-7 © Jean-Yves Ruszniewski/TempSport/Corbis. 248 (t) © C Squared Studios/PhotoDisc. 248 (b) © Shutterstock. 249 (t) Library of Congress. 249 (c) © Edmond Van Hoorick/PhotoDisc. 249 (b) © Comstock. 252 (t) © CMCD, Inc./PhotoDisc. 252 (b) © Stockbyte. 253 © Corbis. 254 © Burstein Collection/Corbis. 255 © Burstein Collection/Corbis. 256-7 © Burstein Collection/Corbis. 258 (cr) © Burstein Collection/Corbis. 258-9 (hand) © Shutterstock. 259 (hand) © Shutterstock. 262 © Larry Brownstein/PhotoDisc. 263 Library of Congress. 263 (frame) © Image Farm. 264 © Iconotec. 265 Library of Congress. 266 (cb) © C Squared Studios/PhotoDisc. 266 (br) © Photospin. 267 © Iconotec. 268 © North Wind Picture Archives. 269 © Edmond Van Hoorick/PhotoDisc. 270 © North Wind Picture Archives. 271 © Curtis Richter/Alamy. 272 © Comstock. 273 © North Wind Picture Archives. 280 (t) © Shutterstock. 280 (b) © Corbis. 281 (t) © Artville. 281 (b) © Shutterstock. 282 (t) © PhotoLink/PhotoDisc. 282 (b) © Steve Cole/PhotoDisc. 283 (t) © Corbis. 283 (b) © Albert J. Copley/PhotoDisc. 284 (t) © PhotoLink/PhotoDisc. 284 (b) © EyeWire Collection/PhotoDisc. 285 (t) © Corbis. 285 (b) © Steve Cole/PhotoDisc. 286 (t) © Scenics of America/PhotoLink/PhotoDisc. 286 (b) © Don Farrall, LightWorks Studio/PhotoDisc. 287 (t) © R. Morley/PhotoLink/PhotoDisc. 287 (b) © PhotoLink/PhotoDisc.

Illustration Credits

Illustrations by Escletxa: 16-7, 50-1, 84-5, 118-9, 152-3, 190-1, 224-5, 260-1.

California English–Language Arts Content Standards

READING

1.0 Word Analysis, Fluency, and Systematic Vocabulary Development

Word Recognition

1.1 Read aloud narrative and expository text fluently and accurately and with appropriate pacing, intonation, and expression.

Vocabulary and Concept Development

1.2 Identify and interpret figurative language and words with multiple meanings.

1.3 Recognize the origins and meanings of frequently used foreign words in English and use these words accurately in speaking and writing.

1.4 Monitor expository text for unknown words or words with novel meanings by using word, sentence, and paragraph clues to determine meaning.

1.5 Understand and explain "shades of meaning" in related words (e.g., *softly* and *quietly*).

2.0 Reading Comprehension (Focus on Informational Materials)

Structural Features of Informational Materials

2.1 Identify the structural features of popular media (e.g., newspapers, magazines, online information) and use the features to obtain information.

2.2 Analyze text that uses the compare-and-contrast organizational pattern.

Comprehension and Analysis of Grade-Level-Appropriate Text

2.3 Connect and clarify main ideas by identifying their relationships to other sources and related topics.

2.4 Clarify an understanding of texts by creating outlines, logical notes, summaries, or reports.

2.5 Follow multiple-step instructions for preparing applications (e.g., for a public library card, bank savings account, sports club, league membership).

Expository Critique

2.6 Determine the adequacy and appropriateness of the evidence for an author's conclusions.

2.7 Make reasonable assertions about a text through accurate, supporting citations.

2.8 Note instances of unsupported inferences, fallacious reasoning, persuasion, and propaganda in text.

3.0 Literary Response and Analysis

Structural Features of Literature

3.1 Identify the forms of fiction and describe the major characteristics of each form.

Narrative Analysis of Grade-Level-Appropriate Text

3.2 Analyze the effect of the qualities of the character (e.g., courage or cowardice, ambition or laziness) on the plot and the resolution of the conflict.

3.3 Analyze the influence of setting on the problem and its resolution.

3.4 Define how tone or meaning is conveyed in poetry through word choice, figurative language, sentence structure, line length, punctuation, rhythm, repetition, and rhyme.

3.5 Identify the speaker and recognize the difference between first- and third-person narration (e.g., autobiography compared with biography).

3.6 Identify and analyze features of themes conveyed through characters, actions, and images.

3.7 Explain the effects of common literary devices (e.g., symbolism, imagery, metaphor) in a variety of fictional and nonfictional texts.

WRITING

1.0 Writing Strategies

Organization and Focus

1.1 Choose the form of writing (e.g., personal letter, letter to the editor, review, poem, report, narrative) that best suits the intended purpose.

1.2 Create multiple-paragraph expository compositions:

a. Engage the interest of the reader and state a clear purpose.

b. Develop the topic with supporting details and precise verbs, nouns, and adjectives to paint a visual image in the mind of the reader.

c. Conclude with a detailed summary linked to the purpose of the composition.

1.3 Use a variety of effective and coherent organizational patterns, including comparison and contrast; organization by categories; and arrangement by spatial order, order of importance, or climactic order.

Research and Technology

1.4 Use organizational features of electronic text (e.g., bulletin boards, databases, keyword searches, e-mail addresses) to locate information.

1.5 Compose documents with appropriate formatting by using word-processing skills and principles of design (e.g., margins, tabs, spacing, columns, page orientation).

Evaluation and Revision

1.6 Revise writing to improve the organization and consistency of ideas within and between paragraphs.

2.0 Writing Applications (Genres and Their Characteristics)

Using the writing strategies outlined in Writing Standard 1.0, students:

2.1 Write narratives:

a. Establish and develop a plot and setting and present a point of view that is appropriate to the stories.

b. Include sensory details and concrete language to develop plot and character.

c. Use a range of narrative devices (e.g., dialogue, suspense).

2.2 Write expository compositions (e.g., description, explanation, comparison and contrast, problem and solution):

a. State the thesis or purpose.

b. Explain the situation.

c. Follow an organizational pattern appropriate to the type of composition.

d. Offer persuasive evidence to validate arguments and conclusions as needed.

2.3 Write research reports:

a. Pose relevant questions with a scope narrow enough to be thoroughly covered.

b. Support the main idea or ideas with facts, details, examples, and explanations from multiple authoritative sources (e.g., speakers, periodicals, online information searches).

c. Include a bibliography.

2.4 Write responses to literature:

a. Develop an interpretation exhibiting careful reading, understanding, and insight.

b. Organize the interpretation around several clear ideas, premises, or images.

c. Develop and justify the interpretation through sustained use of examples and textual evidence.

2.5 Write persuasive compositions:

a. State a clear position on a proposition or proposal.

b. Support the position with organized and relevant evidence.

c. Anticipate and address reader concerns and counterarguments.

Written and Oral English Language Conventions

1.0 Written and Oral English Language Conventions

Sentence Structure

1.1 Use simple, compound, and compound-complex sentences; use effective coordination and subordination of ideas to express complete thoughts.

Grammar

1.2 Identify and properly use indefinite pronouns and present perfect, past perfect, and future perfect verb tenses; ensure that verbs agree with compound subjects.

Punctuation

1.3 Use colons after the salutation in business letters, semicolons to connect independent clauses, and commas when linking two clauses with a conjunction in compound sentences.

Capitalization

1.4 Use correct capitalization.

Spelling

1.5 Spell frequently misspelled words correctly (e.g., *their, they're, there*).

Listening and Speaking

1.0 Listening and Speaking Strategies

Comprehension

1.1 Relate the speaker's verbal communication (e.g., word choice, pitch, feeling, tone) to the nonverbal message (e.g., posture, gesture).

1.2 Identify the tone, mood, and emotion conveyed in the oral communication.

1.3 Restate and execute multiple-step oral instructions and directions.

Organization and Delivery of Oral Communication

1.4 Select a focus, an organizational structure, and a point of view, matching the purpose, message, occasion, and vocal modulation to the audience.

1.5 Emphasize salient points to assist the listener in following the main ideas and concepts.

1.6 Support opinions with detailed evidence and with visual or media displays that use appropriate technology.

1.7 Use effective rate, volume, pitch, and tone and align nonverbal elements to sustain audience interest and attention.

Analysis and Evaluation of Oral and Media Communications

1.8 Analyze the use of rhetorical devices (e.g., cadence, repetitive patterns, use of onomatopoeia) for intent and effect.

1.9 Identify persuasive and propaganda techniques used in television and identify false and misleading information.

2.0 Speaking Applications (Genres and Their Characteristics)

Using the speaking strategies outlined in Listening and Speaking Standard 1.0, students:

2.1 Deliver narrative presentations:

a. Establish a context, plot, and point of view.

b. Include sensory details and concrete language to develop the plot and character.

c. Use a range of narrative devices (e.g., dialogue, tension, or suspense).

2.2 Deliver informative presentations:

a. Pose relevant questions sufficiently limited in scope to be completely and thoroughly answered.

b. Develop the topic with facts, details, examples, and explanations from multiple authoritative sources (e.g., speakers, periodicals, online information).

2.3 Deliver oral responses to literature:

a. Develop an interpretation exhibiting careful reading, understanding, and insight.

b. Organize the selected interpretation around several clear ideas, premises, or images.

c. Develop and justify the selected interpretation through sustained use of examples and textual evidence.

2.4 Deliver persuasive presentations:

a. Provide a clear statement of the position.

b. Include relevant evidence.

c. Offer a logical sequence of information.

d. Engage the listener and foster acceptance of the proposition or proposal.

2.5 Deliver presentations on problems and solutions:

a. Theorize on the causes and effects of each problem and establish connections between the defined problem and at least one solution.

b. Offer persuasive evidence to validate the definition of the problem and the proposed solutions.

PORTALS

PORTALS